The SAP S/4HANA Handbook for EPC Projects

An End-to-End Solution for the Engineering, Construction and Operations (EC&O) Industry

Sohail Ahmed

The SAP S/4HANA Handbook for EPC Projects: An End-to-End Solution for the Engineering, Construction and Operations (EC&O) Industry

Sohail Ahmed
Karachi, Pakistan

ISBN-13 (pbk): 979-8-8688-1465-5   ISBN-13 (electronic): 979-8-8688-1466-2
https://doi.org/10.1007/979-8-8688-1466-2

Managing Director, Apress Media LLC: Welmoed Spahr
Acquisitions Editor: James Robinson-Prior
Desk Editor: Divya Modi
Editorial Project Manager: Gryffin Winkler
Copy Editor: April L Rondeau Martinez

Cover designed by eStudioCalamar

Cover image designed by rawpixel.com on freepik.com

Distributed to the book trade worldwide by Springer Science+Business Media New York, 1 New York Plaza, New York, NY 10004. Phone 1-800-SPRINGER, fax (201) 348-4505, e-mail orders-ny@springer-sbm.com, or visit www.springeronline.com. Apress Media, LLC is a Delaware LLC and the sole member (owner) is Springer Science + Business Media Finance Inc (SSBM Finance Inc). SSBM Finance Inc is a **Delaware** corporation.

For information on translations, please e-mail booktranslations@springernature.com; for reprint, paperback, or audio rights, please e-mail bookpermissions@springernature.com.

Apress titles may be purchased in bulk for academic, corporate, or promotional use. eBook versions and licenses are also available for most titles. For more information, reference our Print and eBook Bulk Sales web page at http://www.apress.com/bulk-sales.

Any source code or other supplementary material referenced by the author in this book is available to readers on GitHub. For more detailed information, please visit https://www.apress.com/gp/services/source-code.

If disposing of this product, please recycle the paper

To the dedicated professionals in the engineering, construction, and operations industry, whose commitment to innovation and excellence continues to shape the world's future.

Table of Contents

About the Author

Sohail Ahmed is a seasoned program manager and SAP solution architect with over 30 years of diverse experience in the SAP, engineering, construction, IT infrastructure, and utility industries. He has successfully led and delivered IT, SAP, and construction projects and programs across North America and the MENA. Currently, he specializes in helping organizations establish Enterprise Project Management Offices (EPMOs) and provides training for corporate and academic sectors.

He holds a master's degree in engineering management and a bachelor's in mechanical engineering, along with interdisciplinary certifications in IT, SAP, project management, quality management, finance, and manufacturing management.

About the Technical Reviewer

Miguel Figueiredo is a passionate software professional with more than 30 years of experience in technical solution architecture. He has a degree in information systems and an MBA from Mackenzie University, as well as an international MBA in business administration from FIA Business School in partnership with Vanderbilt University.

Miguel gained his experience delivering business intelligence solutions for a number of Fortune 500 companies and multiple global corporations. As the SAP HANA Services Center of Excellence leader, he was responsible for the evangelization and best-practice adoption of data management and business intelligence in his region.

Currently, Miguel advises companies on maximizing value realization in their digital transformation journeys and moving to cloud initiatives. Miguel is dedicated to supporting his family and encouraging the development of good habits for health of body and mind.

Acknowledgments

All praise is due to Allah, the Most Merciful, the Source of all knowledge and wisdom. Without His guidance and blessings, this work would not have been possible.

"Exalted are You; we have no knowledge except what You have taught us. Indeed, it is You who is the Knowing, the Wise." (Qur'an 2:32)

I extend my deepest gratitude to my parents, whose prayers have shaped me into the person I am today. My heartfelt appreciation also goes to my wife, whose patience and belief in me kept me focused and determined throughout this journey.

I would also like to express my sincere thanks to Jawwad Akhtar for his support and encouragement in taking the step toward becoming an author. I am also deeply grateful to Mohid Javed for his invaluable technical support throughout this work. My gratitude extends to the publishing team for their support in bringing this work to life.

Finally, I appreciate everyone who has been part of this journey, directly or indirectly. May this work serve as a small contribution to the field, benefiting those who seek knowledge and growth.

Introduction

In the engineering, construction, and operations (EC&O) industry, managing large-scale projects efficiently is critical to success. The complexity of engineering, procurement, and construction (EPC) projects demands an integrated approach that aligns planning, execution, and financial management. With the evolution of digital technologies, enterprise resource planning (ERP) systems, particularly SAP S/4HANA, have emerged as key enablers of efficiency, transparency, and control in EC&O project management.

This book stands out by offering a unique approach, thoroughly covering project management from the contractor's perspective—an area often overlooked—while primarily focusing on the project owner's viewpoint. Throughout this book, we follow a case study of PrimeCon—an EPC contractor's bidding and execution of RefineX, a refinery upgrade project—to demonstrate SAP S/4HANA's capabilities in real-world scenarios.

Who This Book Is For

This book is intended for the following:

- Project Managers & Engineers: To gain insights into how SAP S/4HANA supports project planning, scheduling, resource management, and budget control.

- SAP Consultants & Solution Architects: To understand how SAP S/4HANA's capabilities can be implemented in real-world EC&O projects.

- Business Executives & Decision-Makers: To evaluate the strategic benefits of digital transformation in project management using SAP solutions.

Structure of the Book

Each chapter presents step-by-step guidance, best practices, and insights to help readers successfully implement SAP's project management solutions.

Chapter 1: Introduction

This chapter provides an overview of project management in the EC&O industry, covering EPC project processes, contract types, and production strategies. It highlights challenges in IT adoption, particularly ERP systems, and the role of SAP S/4HANA in addressing these issues.

Chapter 2: SAP S/4HANA—An Enterprise Solution

This chapter explores SAP S/4HANA's role as the next-generation ERP solution enhanced by SAP Business Technology Platform (BTP). This chapter covers various deployment models to accommodate evolving business needs.

Chapter 3: Enterprise Portfolio and Project Management

This chapter details the integration of SAP S/4HANA's Enterprise Portfolio and Project Management (EPPM) solutions for EC&O projects. It covers SAP S/4HANA Project System, SAP Commercial Project Management (CPM), and SAP Project and Portfolio Management (PPM), offering different implementation scenarios, from both project owner and contractor perspectives.

Chapter 4: Bidding and Estimation

Following PrimeCon's bid for the RefineX refinery project, this chapter outlines the bidding and estimation process using SAP S/4HANA and SAP CPM. It covers inquiry creation, proposal development, cost and revenue planning, and bid-to-execution integration.

Chapter 5: Planning and Scheduling

This chapter explains the concept of project planning levels (from overview to execution) and project structuring within SAP S/4HANA using work breakdown structures (WBS) and project networks. It includes scheduling techniques, critical path analysis, and optimization using SAP Project System.

Chapter 6: Scope Management

Focusing on scope definition and control, this chapter details WBS development for engineering, procurement, and construction projects. It highlights SAP PS Project Builder's role in coordination, performance evaluation, and scope change management.

Chapter 7: Engineer-to-Order (ETO) Planning

This chapter explores how SAP S/4HANA supports integrated planning for engineering, procurement, fabrication, and construction. Following the RefineX project, it demonstrates engineering plan development and document control, including SAP-Tekla integration for material takeoff (MTO) extraction. It also covers the use of network variants for execution scenarios and WBS bill of material (BOM) features for procurement alignment with project plan.

Chapter 8: Resource Management

This chapter continues with the RefineX project to explore internal and external resource planning for manpower, machinery, and subcontractor management in SAP PS, including Primavera P6 integration via SAP BTP. It also explores equipment planning, maintenance strategies, and subcontractor service management to optimize project execution.

Chapter 9: Handling Project Materials

This chapter covers material classification, procurement, and inventory management in EPC projects using SAP S/4HANA. Advanced requirement and inventory optimization features, such as project-oriented procurement, expediting, nesting, and material traceability, are discussed, along with long-term contracts and scheduling agreements.

Chapter 10: Quality Management

Focusing on SAP S/4HANA Quality Management, this chapter details quality planning, material and service inspections, defect tracking, nonconformance handling, audit processes, and quality analytics in EPC projects.

Chapter 11: Cost Management

This chapter explores project costing, budgeting, revenue planning, and financial tracking using SAP S/4HANA. It covers cost planning, budget allocation, and cost control methods and highlights SAP Cloud Analytics (SAC) integration for financial planning with various versioning techniques.

Chapter 12: Risk and Change Management

This chapter explores SAP S/4HANA and SAP CPM's capabilities in risk and issue management, and change control. It also discusses the use of change requests, claim management, and engineering change management features for efficient tracking of design and material changes.

Chapter 13: Project Monitoring and Control

This chapter explores SAP S/4HANA's real-time progress tracking, various measurement methods for percentage of completion calculation, earned value analysis, predictive analytics using SAC, and BTP integration for workflow automation and scenario-based planning.

Chapter 14: Financial Performance

This chapter explores period-end reporting, financial closure, cost allocation, and various billing methods in EPC projects. It also covers revenue recognition using different International Financial Reporting Standards (IFRS 15) compliant methods applicable for different contract types.

Chapter 15: Performance Analysis

This chapter introduces SAP Project Information System, Fiori applications, and Core Data Services (CDS) views for financial and schedule tracking. It highlights SAC integration for advanced reporting, forecasting, and scenario planning. Now, let's get started.

CHAPTER 1

Introduction

The engineering, construction, and operations (EC&O) industry deals with complex engineering, procurement, and construction processes to deliver large-scale infrastructure and heavy manufacturing projects.

1.1. Introduction to the EC&O Industry

The EC&O industry integrates different disciplines of engineering, such as civil, mechanical, piping, process, and electrical engineering. The main component of the EC&O industry is infrastructure projects. They include the design and construction of refineries, dams, bridges, and power plants.

These projects require meticulous planning, strategic procurement, detailed designing, complex construction processes, and strict project discipline to deliver desired results.

1.1.1. Importance of the EC&O Industry

The construction industry alone contributes[1] about 6% of global gross domestic product (GDP), according to the World Bank report. It does not only create infrastructure projects but also stimulates the world's economy by supporting other industries, such as cement, steel, shipping, and so forth.

---

[1] https://www.mckinsey.com/capabilities/operations/our-insights/infrastructure-productivity

© Sohail Ahmed 2025
S. Ahmed, *The SAP S/4HANA Handbook for EPC Projects*,
https://doi.org/10.1007/979-8-8688-1466-2_1

As reported by McKinsey, the world invests USD 2.5 trillion annually in the transportation, power, water, and telecom systems on which businesses and human populations depend. This investment in infrastructure is projected to reach USD 3.3 trillion by the year 2030.

1.1.2. The Way Forward

To capitalize on the available opportunities, EC&O organizations must optimize their practices and adopt groundbreaking solutions. With innovative technology and industry best practices, EC&O companies can enhance project performance, reduce project cost, and improve risk management.

1.2. Industry Challenges

The EC&O industry has traditionally relied heavily on manual and paper-based processes, so overcoming resistance to change remains a key challenge in adopting digital transformation. McKinsey Global Institute identified that only 13% of construction firms have fully embraced digital tools.

Challenges in IT adoption for the EC&O industry primarily arise from the complex and dynamic nature of its revenue-generating projects. High levels of risk associated with engineering requirements, ongoing regulatory changes, unexpected geographical conditions, and technological advancements make project outcomes vulnerable to changes in scope, timeline, and budget.

This section will discuss the biggest challenges the EC&O industry is facing in the adoption of information technology.

1.2.1. Unique Project Requirements

The biggest challenge in adopting IT solutions is the uniqueness of projects. Each project has distinct resource needs, product specifications, and industry regulations, while IT solutions need a stable process flow to be established. The absence of standard processes makes it more difficult to implement a single, universal IT solution. These unique requirements often require customizing IT solutions to ensure that they are aligned precisely with project-specific requirements and also follow industry standards.

1.2.2. Complexity of Processes

The other major cause of resistance toward a major digital transformation arises from the complex nature of engineering, procurement, and construction (EPC) projects due to their unique project requirements and the frequent changes made to plans, supply chain fluctuations, and hazardous environments.

1.2.3. Harsh Project Environment

The EC&O industry is characterized by working in remote and temporary facilities. The flow of information depends largely on those individuals who are working in harsh and IT-unfriendly conditions and have limited or no incentive to record information digitally. For these reasons, a single and reliable source of truth is largely absent, thus causing obstacles in the information flow.

1.2.4. Lack Of Standardization

Unlike in manufacturing, where businesses can rely on detailed industry-wide standards and practices, the EC&O industry faces unique regulatory and project-specific standards. This data incompatibility and lack of

3

standardization affects information sharing and collaboration for project organizations. Moreover, project timelines and complacency with bespoke legacy systems often restrict the standard process to be implemented.

1.2.5. Heterogeneous it Landscape

Engineering and construction projects demand multiple stakeholders to collaborate for project delivery. However, this becomes challenging since project stakeholders often use different IT systems and different data formats for communication. This presents a challenge, requiring an ecosystem of flexible IT solutions that can provide interoperability and seamless integration among heterogeneous IT systems.

1.3. Opportunities and Benefits

The EC&O industry has a history of developing project management practices. It pioneered the program evaluation and review technique (PERT) and critical path methods (CPM)—key concepts of project scheduling that originated in the construction sector during the 1950s for managing large-scale infrastructure projects. Later on, software tools enabled more precise scheduling, resource allocation, and risk mitigation strategies.

While the industry has built a strong foundation in core design, engineering, building management, and planning software, it has shown to be slower, compared to other industries, in adopting business process automation tools.

The EC&O industry can gain significantly from the adoption of IT solutions and overcome its challenges by adopting SAP S/4HANA enterprise solutions as an integrated enterprise solution. This section explores how SAP S/4HANA can address these challenges and provide practical solutions for them.

1.3.1. Streamlined Project Management

From sales to procurement to financial control and from real-time progress tracking to issuing change requests, SAP S/4HANA brings together all financial, logistics, and project management functions in a single platform. SAP S/4HANA helps organizations adopt a single central hub from which to spot and fix any issues; all project planning, execution, and controlling can be performed from a single view.

1.3.2. Project Analytics

SAP S/4HANA offers project analytics and provides real-time updates that enhance communication across departments. Every stakeholder stays on the same page and gets a clear picture of the project's status as the embedded business warehouse processes the data from various sources into a single source. SAP cloud-based platforms enable real-time sharing of information among different departments to enhance the effectiveness of communication channels and to bring transparency to the project status.

1.3.3. Collaboration Platform

SAP solutions utilize a central communication hub for all project stakeholders. These platforms provide planning and requisitioning of human resources, material and services, and equipment; and the secure sharing of documents.

1.3.4. Automated Workflows

Automated workflows handle routine tasks like approvals and task assignments. Whether these workflows are used directly or are enhanced with simple no-code or low-code tools, they are designed to reduce manual work and improve business efficiency.

1.3.5. Mobility

SAP S/4HANA's user experience keeps the users connected to project details and with team members. The project team members can execute transactions regardless of their physical presence. With role-based access, from internal teams to external partners, all stakeholders stay informed and engaged.

1.3.6. Interoperability

SAP S/4HANA offers bi-directional and real-time data integration with commonly used project and portfolio management (PPM), building information modeling (BIM), and computer-aided design (CAD) software.

1.3.7. Enhanced Control

SAP S/4HANA provides risk and issue management tools for risk managers to proactively identify and mitigate potential issues. Whether it's scope creeping, budget adjustments, design changes, or schedule updates, SAP S/4HANA provides features to track and monitor all changes.

1.3.8. Access Control

In SAP S/4HANA, multi-level access control mapped with business roles, organizational units, and transactions offers strong control of data accessibility. By using these features, you ensure only authorized users can access the system and perform transactions based on approved user roles and authorization.

1.4. Project Management Overview

This section provides a general overview of the fundamental concepts of project management. It aims to provide a refresher of only those key concepts that are relevant to the topic of this book. It assumes that the readers will refer to project management material.

1.4.1. Definitions

The detailed concepts of project management defined in this section will later be elaborated on in the context of SAP S/4HANA's application in the EC&O industry.

i.   Product

A *product* is defined as an artifact that is quantifiable and can either be used as an end-item itself or as a component item.

ii. Project

A temporary endeavor undertaken to create a unique product, service, or result within a defined timeframe, budget, and quality standards. These projects can range in size and complexity. Therefore, projects require special skills and tools to manage.

iii. Program

A *program* is a collection of related projects that are managed in a coordinated manner to achieve a common goal or strategic objective not achievable by managing them individually.

iv.   Portfolio

A *portfolio* is defined as a collection of projects or programs and other work that are grouped together to facilitate effective management of that work to meet strategic business objectives.

1.4.2. Management Processes

Organizations require different approaches to manage projects and programs. This section gives an overview of different approaches, each focusing on specific layers of management to achieve the overall business objectives.

Project Management

Project management is defined as the application of knowledge, skills, tools, and techniques to manage project activities to meet project requirements. In simpler terms, it is the application of planning and organizing to execute the work.

Program Management

Program management is the process of overseeing a group of interdependent projects with a common objective. It requires coordinating resources, managing cross-project interdependencies, and aligning the outcomes of the overall program objectives.

Portfolio Management

Portfolio management is the strategic management of an organization's investment portfolio to achieve business objectives. Portfolio management includes the selection, prioritization, and management and controlling of projects and programs. The main focus of PPM is the optimization of resources, balancing portfolio risks, and aligning investments with strategy.

Product Lifecycle Management

The integration of people, data, processes, and business systems to create, maintain, and develop a product or a service throughout its lifecycle is *product lifecycle management.*

While all of these processes are closely related, product lifecycle management (PLM) is a product-centric approach that places it outside the scope of this book. Program management, albeit beneficial in interrelated projects, is also not the focus here.

Similarly, this book will briefly discuss portfolio management, but our main emphasis in this book will be on the exploration of SAP solutions for EPC project management.

1.5. Project Management Best Practices

Industry best practices serve as a foundation for effective project management. This section will explore key concepts from the Project Management Institute (PMI) in the *PMBOK Guide* 6th edition.

1.5.1. Triple Constraints of Project

Projects may appear to be similar, but they are all subject to an interconnected set of constraints defined as the "Triple Constraint" or the "Iron Triangle." These core constraints are shown in Table 1-1.

Table 1-1. *Triple Constraint*

TIME	The timeframe allocated for project completion
SCOPE	The work required to complete the project
COST	The financial resources required to complete the project

1.5.2. Project Management Knowledge Areas

PMBOK offers a valuable framework known as project management knowledge areas, which represent the collection of processes and best practices critical for effective project management. Knowledge areas are the building blocks that are combined strategically to create a successful project delivery strategy.

There are ten PMI knowledge areas. Four are core knowledge areas (scope, schedule, resource, cost), five are support knowledge areas, and one is integration management.

Project Scope Management

Project scope management includes the processes of breaking down the work to ensure that the project tasks include all the work required to complete the project and that no extra work is included in it. This includes defining project structure and development of work breakdown structure (WBS).

Project Schedule Management

Project schedule management includes the processes required to manage the duration of the project and ensures timely completion of the project. Alignment of project activities, preparation of project schedule, defining of task dependencies, and so on are covered under this knowledge area.

Project Cost Management

Project cost management includes the processes involved in the estimation, planning, budgeting, allocation, and controlling of cost items directly or indirectly. This knowledge area ensures that projects are completed within the approved budget.

Project Resource Management

Project resource management includes the processes of identification, planning, recruitment/acquiring, and mobilization/demobilization of labor and equipment needed for the successful completion of the project.

Project Quality Management

Project quality management includes the processes for defining the policy, specifications, and standards that would develop the acceptance criteria of a product or a service. This knowledge area includes inspection, quality control, management of non-conformance, and project quality audit.

Project Stakeholder Management

Project stakeholder management includes the processes of identifying the people, groups, or organizations that are part of the project delivery or that could impact or be impacted by the outcome of a project. This knowledge area involves management of project partners, local authorities, and the key members of the community.

Project Communications Management

Project communications management includes the processes that ensure the timely collection, storage and retrieval, and disbursement of project-related information to project stakeholders. This involves periodic project meetings, development of key performance indicators, maintaining central project data repository, and publication of project reports.

Project Risk Management

Project risk management includes the processes of risk identification, risk analysis, risk monitoring, and risk response planning.

Project Procurement Management

Project procurement management includes the processes of planning, requisitioning, sourcing, contracting, and acquiring necessary materials and services necessary for project execution.

Project Integration Management

Project integration management includes the processes and activities that integrate and coordinate various aspects of the project. For example, it involves the development of project plans and coordination among designers, procurement, site teams, and subcontractors.

It is important to note that a specific project may require additional knowledge area(s). For example, EPC projects may require environment, health, and safety (EHS) or financial management (not cost management), not covered by PMI.

1.5.3. Process Groups

How project management knowledge areas translate processes into action within a project lifecycle is defined by PMBOK® as project management process groups (earlier called the IPECC® model). This model is a logical grouping of project management processes to achieve specific project objectives.

The IPECC model defines five process groups into which all project management processes are grouped: Initiating, Planning, Executing, Monitoring and Controlling, and Closing.

These process groups provide a logical sequence to tasks within a particular knowledge area, segregate planning from execution and controlling, and define a clear initiation and closeout of every phase and stage of the project.

Later in the book, process groups and knowledge areas will be covered in the context of EPC project lifecycle management using SAP S/4HANA.

1.6. EC&O Industry Framework

Project management in the EC&O industry is particularly complex due to the involvement of stakeholders and the need for meticulous planning and coordination. This section provides an overview of project management practices within this industry. Understanding these complexities will make professionals appreciate the need for an enterprise solution for large-scale projects.

1.6.1. Stakeholders

EC&O projects involve a network of stakeholders working as project partners. It is important to discuss here the role of each partner to fully understand how project responsibilities and segregation of duties impact the working model of a project.

This section defines key partners and their roles in the EC&O industry.

Project Owner

The owner, also called the project owner or the customer, is the one that funds and commissions the project. This entity defines project objectives, approves project budget, and specifies the requirements that drive the design and subsequent construction scope. Project owners work closely with consultants, contractors, and regulators to ensure that the project meets expected results.

13

Primary Contractor

The primary contractor is tasked with the actual delivery of the project based on the plans and specifications provided by the owner or their nominated consulting engineers or architects. Depending on the project delivery model, the contractor could be tasked with construction only or with engineering, procurement, and project management.

The contractor manages project tasks, coordinates with subcontractors, procures materials, and ensures that the project is completed on time and within budget.

Subcontractor

Subcontractors are specialized firms or individuals hired by the primary contractor to perform specific tasks or provide specialized services within a larger construction project. They bring specialized skills and expertise in areas such as electrical work, plumbing, rigging, or structural steelwork. Subcontractors are responsible for executing defined portions of the project and must coordinate their activities with the primary contractor and other subcontractors to ensure seamless integration.

Consulting Engineer

The consulting engineer, or consultant, is a specialist role hired as either a firm or an individual by the owner of the project to provide expert advice and technical solutions across various engineering disciplines, and also to approve project specifications. The consultant is responsible for conducting detailed analyses, preparing engineering designs, and overseeing the construction process to ensure compliance with technical specifications and regulatory standards of quality, health, and safety. In some cases, architects, in addition to consultants, are hired by the owners for expert advice and design.

Regulators

Regulators enforce building codes, safety standards, and other regulatory requirements. They review project plans, issue permits, and conduct inspections throughout the construction process to ensure that the work complies with legal and safety standards. Regulators help maintain the integrity and safety of the construction process.

While other stakeholders—such as financial institutions, suppliers, and design and construction teams—are important, this book focuses on key stakeholders and roles essential for IT-enabled EPC project management. The primary focus is on the owner–contractor model, with a single EPC contractor managing engineering, procurement, and construction, supported by subcontractors.

1.6.2. Delivery Models

This section will discuss various project delivery models, including their risks and benefits.

Each delivery model offers unique characteristics that can best suit different project requirements. Understanding these models is essential for selecting the most effective solution. Let's look at the primary models.

Engineering, Procurement, and Construction (EPC)

The EPC model is one of the most comprehensive and widely used delivery models in the EC&O industry when the scope of work involves design and engineering, procurement, fabrication, construction, and erection activities.

In this model, a single contract is issued to a primary contractor, known as the EPC or prime contractor, who oversees the entire project lifecycle. It is a common practice by prime contractors to subcontract part of the scope to other contractors.

One of the key advantages of the EPC model is its ability to centralize responsibility. The EPC contractor assumes the project risks associated with engineering complexities, material handling, and scope changes during fabrication and erection. This shift of responsibility from the owner to the EPC contractor simplifies contract management. The enhanced coordination among stakeholders ensures that all project components are seamlessly integrated and managed effectively. Due to this integrated approach, this model is particularly effective for large-scale projects and ensures that all project components are coordinated and managed efficiently and seamlessly.

Engineering, Procurement, Construction, and Commissioning (EPCC)

The EPCC model extends the EPC approach to include commissioning, ensuring that all systems and components are made operational by the EPC contractor before the project is handed over to the owner. While this adds an additional phase to the contract, it is generally considered an extension of the EPC model to minimize post-construction issues and improve operational readiness.

Engineering, Procurement, and Construction Management (EPC/M)

The EPC/M model is another variation of the EPC project delivery model where the EPC/M contractor manages engineering, procurement, and construction management but does not necessarily perform the construction work directly. This model offers flexibility in managing subcontractors but adds complexity in coordination and project management.

Design-Bid-Build (DBB)

The design-bid-build (DBB) model is a traditional model in which the architect or the consulting engineer designs the project and solicit bids for construction. While EPC is a turnkey model with a single contract issued to the EPC contractor for all phases of the project, the DBB model separates the design and construction contracts.

Integrated Project Delivery (IPD)

The IPD model is a contractually complex model but fosters collaboration among all key stakeholders, including the owner, consultant, and contractor. All stakeholders are engaged from the project's inception, with shared risk and reward.

While various other project delivery models, such as design-build (DB), construction management at risk (CMAR), and construction management multi-prime (CMMP), are also employed in the EC&O industry, this book will focus on the EPC (engineering, procurement, and construction) delivery model and its variations.

1.6.3. Contracts

In this section, we will discuss various contract types commonly applicable in the EC&O industry. To meet specific project requirements and to effectively manage the roles, costs, and risks of a project, each of the following contract types offers a different benefit.

Fixed-Price Contract

A fixed-price contract, also known as a lump-sum or turnkey contract, is the most commonly used contract type in the EC&O industry. The EPC delivery models are mostly based on lump-sum contracts. This contract type, however, also applies to the following:

- Supply only or supply and erection projects where there is only one price for the entire contract.

- Partial deliveries may be made for the effective progress of the project, but there is only one revenue item.

- Project billing is based on project progress or pre-defied milestones.

Under turnkey contracts, the project owner agrees to pay the prime contractor a predetermined fixed price for completing the project. The contractor, based on certain scope and specification agreements, assumes the risk of cost overrun due to changes in market condition, price escalation, or supply chain disruption.

Time and Materials (T&M) Contract

Time and materials contracts, also called time and expenses contracts, can be considered as the opposite of a fixed-price contract. This contract defines that the payment to the contractor is based on the actual time and materials used by the contractor to complete the project. This type of contract is used when the scope of work is unclear, product specifications are not final, or the design is subject to change during the project. This type of contract provides flexibility to the prime contractor in managing project requirements but increases the financial risk of the owner.

Unit Price Contract

In a unit-price contract, the project owner pays the prime contractor based on the quantity of specific units of work performed. For example, the contract may be the fabrication and erection in tons of steel structure at a unit price. These unit prices are agreed upon in the contract, and the contractor is paid based on the quantity of work executed.

1.6.4. Production Strategies

EPC projects require tailored production strategies to meet customer-specific requirements. *Production* in this context refers to the manufacturing of products or parts required for the construction phase, such as the prefabrication of steel structure for modular equipment—for example, heat exchangers, modular buildings, etc.

There are three commonly used production planning strategies that differ in their approach to project execution: make-to-stock (MTS), make-to-order (MTO), and engineer-to-order (ETO).

Make-to-Stock Strategy

Make-to-stock (MTS) is a planning strategy where products are manufactured and stocked in anticipation of customer demand. This planning strategy is suitable for standardized products with stable demand patterns that are not widely applicable in the EC&O industry.

However, MTS strategy has very limited application in EPC projects. For example, in the production of standardized piping spools or electrical switchgears, the MTS strategy could be employed if the demand forecast is predictable. This requires that the project organization has a history of repeated product demand, and the product is required for installation without any change in the specifications.

Make-to-Order Strategy

Make-to-order (MTO) is a planning strategy where products are manufactured or assembled based on an individual customer order. This approach allows some level of changes in specifications based on the customer's needs, but the high-level design remains the same.

19

MTO offers a balance between efficiency and customization within EPC projects. It reduces stock level compared to MTS and lead times compared to ETO. For example, an EPC contractor may offer pre-fabricated boilers or modular heat exchangers for its customer rather than manufacturing this equipment from design onward.

Engineer-to-Order Strategy

Engineer-to-order (ETO) is a production planning strategy where a product is engineered and produced entirely based on customer-specific requirements after an order has been received.

The product design and production sequencing require complete customization, making ETO the predominant strategy for turnkey projects in EC&O industries for EPC projects. Customer requirements play a significant role in defining product specifications, operational sequences, bill of materials, machine setup times, and labor and equipment composition.

This book will focus exclusively on ETO production planning strategies within the broader framework fabrication process during EPC project execution.

1.7. EPC Project Management Lifecycle

Every successful project, regardless of industry, adheres to a well-defined lifecycle. This lifecycle provides a project roadmap, from initial concept to final completion.

The IPECC model discussed earlier serves as the foundation for defining the roadmap of successful EPC projects too. This section breaks down each process group into processes, highlighting key activities performed during a typical EPC project lifecycle.

1.7.1. Initiation

The Initiation process group focuses on elaborating on the "Why" of the project. These processes result in the authorization of a new project. Following are the key tasks of the Initiation phase.

Project Feasibility

Studies are conducted by the project owner to determine if the project is technically and financially viable.

Front End Engineering Design (FEED)

A consultant or architect conducts initial engineering studies to establish the basic technical concept and assess economic viability.

Bidding & Estimation

Qualified contractors submit proposals outlining their approach to engineering, procurement, and construction, along with cost estimates.

Project Award

The owner selects and awards the project to a contractor based on technical expertise, experience, and competitive pricing.

1.7.2. Planning

The Planning process group focuses on elaborating on the "How" of the project. Following are the key tasks of planning phase.

Initial Planning

The contractor's planning team collaborates with the owner and potential subcontractors to create a comprehensive project plan following the initial design and estimates.

Project Communication

Clear protocols for communication among all project stakeholders are established. Project reporting and measurable key performance indicators (KPIs) are defined to track progress and performance metrices.

Basic Engineering & Design

The overall technical concept from FEED is refined and converted into design documents.

Procurement Planning

Necessary materials, consumables, tools, and equipment are identified based on the engineering plan, and a detailed procurement plan is devised to distinguish short-term and long-term procurement strategies.

Subcontracting

Subcontractors are hired for specialized tasks. Partial or complete scope of services (manufacturing, fabrication, erection, inspection, etc.) may be outsourced to third-party subcontract(s) by the main contractor.

Construction Planning

A defined methodology outlining how the project is built, including workforce planning, fabrication and construction sequencing, rigging, and mobilization planning, is planned.

Site Establishment & Mobilization

The construction site is established by mobilizing equipment, personnel, and temporary facilities as per the construction plan.

1.7.3. Execution

The Execution process group focuses on carrying out the project plan. Following are the key tasks of the Execution phase.

Detailed Design & Engineering

The contractor's engineering team translates project requirements into detailed technical specifications and drawings to guide procurement and construction activities.

Procurement Execution

From the initiation of the purchase requisition till the time of goods receipts the team is involved in contracting, subcontracting, sourcing, and vendor management.

Inventory Management

The contractor ensures timely availability and controlled distribution of material for project execution. This involves tracking, monitoring, and controlling the stock of materials and equipment on site to ensure there's enough for ongoing construction activities and to avoid overstocking or shortages.

Construction Execution

The construction team translates design into real-world objects. This team executes construction activities across multiple disciplines (civil, process, mechanical, piping, electrical, etc.). Construction tasks generally include manufacturing, fabrication, and erection, but for simplicity, pre-commissioning and commissioning are sometimes also covered under this definition.

1.7.4. Monitoring And Control

The Monitoring and Controlling process group ensures the project stays on track and meets its objectives. Following are the key tasks of this phase.

Performance Monitoring

Progress is continuously monitored and controlled to manage deviations from the plan. The planning and controlling teams oversee schedule, progress, and budget variance; submission of delivery documents; record labor and equipment efficiencies; and prepare progress reports.

Risk and Issue Management

Risks and issues are monitored and recorded throughout the project. With every new risk identified, the response plans are implemented and uncontrolled risks are managed as issues. Earlier, during planning, risk management methodology is established to identify risks and develop response strategies.

QHSE Control

Quality, health, safety, and environmental (QHSE) control measures are implemented by the quality control (QC) and health, safety, and environmental (HSE) teams to ensure compliance with QHSE standards. This includes inspections, testing, and documentation to verify that construction activities comply with approved plans and specifications.

Change and Claim Management

Claims may arise during the project due to unforeseen circumstances. Whether there are changes in scope, extension of timelines, or disagreement during project execution, all such claims are continuously recorded, along with their impacts on project time, budget, or specifications. Variation claims are settled between the contractor and the owner.

Project Billing

EPC projects are usually billed periodically based on pre-defined milestone completion or a certain progress percentage being achieved. Billing is initiated after quantities are approved.

1.7.5. Closeout

The Closeout process group formally concludes the project and ensures all activities are completed. Following are the key tasks of closeout phase.

Provisional Completion

All project deliverables and facility access are handed over to the owner by the contractor. A provisional certificate of completion is awarded to the contractor acknowledging the significant completion of the project.

Project Dossier

The final dossier is formally handed over to the owner after the consultant's approval. This is a comprehensive document package that serves as a permanent record of the entire project and typically includes all contractual and project management documents, such as As-Built drawings, QHSE documents, test reports, inspection records, change orders, and so forth.

Punchlist

A punchlist is a document to list minor incomplete items or to rectify work identified by the owner or consultant during final inspection, where the rectification is not urgently required. The owner provides the list to the prime contractor, who is responsible for closing these open items before final project acceptance.

Final Completion

Final completion is the certificate awarded by the owner to the prime contractor confirming that the final project deliverables have been handed over to the owner and the project meets all contractual requirements and specifications.

Warranty Period

A warranty period is typically included in the EPC contract. This period guarantees the quality and performance of the constructed facility for a specified timeframe after completion. During the warranty period, the contractor is responsible for rectifying any defects or malfunctions identified in the facility.

1.8. Conclusion

In this chapter we have gained insight into the details of what makes EC&O a complex industry and how unique project requirements have made EC&O a challenging industry in which to implement IT solutions. The EC&O industry can overcome its challenges and improve its project delivery by adopting SAP S/4HANA. This chapter also provided insights into EPC project management practices. In the next chapter, we will explore how an ERP solution such as SAP S/4HANA can address these challenges and improve EPC project delivery.

CHAPTER 2

SAP S/4HANA: An Enterprise Solution

The concept of enterprise resource planning (ERP) is not new to any organization. ERP systems are considered the backbone of business processes these days. The evolving digital landscape, however, demands a more innovative approach. This is where most ERP systems fall short.

Traditional ERP systems have matured in providing operational efficiency, but they often struggle to deliver real-time insights or predict trends.

To overcome this shortcoming, SAP has offered a new ERP, SAP S/4HANA, as its next-generation enterprise management solution. It offers a complete suite of applications designed to streamline complex business processes and deliver real-time insights.

2.1. Core Components of S/4HANA

To realize the full potential of SAP S/4HANA, a deeper understanding of its underlying technology is essential. This section is dedicated to the core components of SAP S/4HANA that empower the platform.

© Sohail Ahmed 2025
S. Ahmed, *The SAP S/4HANA Handbook for EPC Projects*,
https://doi.org/10.1007/979-8-8688-1466-2_2

2.1.1. In-Memory Database

Traditional databases rely heavily on disk storage, which can introduce latency in data retrieval and processing. In contrast, SAP S/4HANA's in-memory database architecture stores and processes data directly in the system's main memory (RAM). This innovative approach enables rapid access to data, allowing for complex calculations and analyses to be performed with remarkable speed. SAP S/4HANA's near-instantaneous response time significantly enhances the user experience.

Consequently, any dependency on separate data warehouses for generating analytical reports is greatly diminished. For instance, executing large financial reports in SAP S/4HANA is notably faster than doing so in traditional database systems.

2.1.2. Modern Interface

In addition to the traditional interface, SAP S/4HANA has provided thousands of applications on the *Fiori* user interface.

The Fiori interface is built on SAPUI5 user interface, which provides a role-based, user-friendly experience across all devices. This results in higher user productivity and improved solution adoption for EC&O professionals who mostly work in the remote fields or are on the go.

By using the following three types of mobile-friendly Fiori applications, teams can stay connected and informed.

Transactional

Transactional applications support business transactions. This is similar to transaction codes in traditional GUI; for example, "create purchase requisitions" or "purchase order processing."

Analytical

Analytical applications are designed for data-driven decision-making. Real-time analytics provide insights through visualizations and key performance indicators (KPIs); for example, "monitor purchase contract items" and "my budget alerts."

Fact Sheet

Fact sheet applications offer quick access to key information in a simplified format; for example, "employee fact sheet" and "customer master fact sheet."

2.1.3. Embedded Analytics

SAP defines *embedded analytics* as an integrated analytics solution based on S/4HANA core data services as part of the S/4HANA data model. It enables real-time operational reporting by using SAP Fiori as the front-end user interface.

S/4HANA embedded analytics makes decision-making seamless and faster. Project managers benefit from these insights for critical functions such as predictive maintenance and cash flow forecasting. For instance, real-time analytics of on-site inventory levels enable the logistics team to make quick adjustments to delivery plans or transportation routes.

2.2. Deployment Models

SAP S/4HANA can be deployed in many ways to fit different organizations' IT environments. This section provides an overview of these options.

2.2.1. On-Premise Deployment

This is the traditional approach. It involves the installation of SAP S/4HANA on the SAP customer's own servers. It provides maximum control over the IT landscape but requires significant upfront investment and ongoing maintenance costs. Following are its key characteristics:

- SAP customers maintain full control over their IT infrastructure. SAP allows tailored configurations and customization.

- Deployment requires significant upfront investment in hardware and software licensing.

- Recurring maintenance cost in hardware and software fee is applicable.

- Regular maintenance and updates are the responsibility of SAP customer to ensure system performance and security, while scalability and security are also a challenge.

2.2.2. GROW with SAP

SAP S/4HANA Public Cloud is a ready-to-run cloud ERP that delivers the latest industry best practices and continuous innovation. Public Cloud deployments offer flexible infrastructure, rapid deployment, scalability, and reduced IT overhead GROW with SAP, is the SAP public cloud offering that delivers a fully managed S/4HANA Cloud environment, providing rapid deployment and reduced IT overhead. This model addresses unique customer scenarios by delivering the benefits of cloud infrastructure while maintaining control over specific business processes.

- SAP customers have less direct control over the underlying infrastructure. SAP allows cloud extensions only.

- Quarterly subscription-based or pay-as-you-go payment models are typically applicable.

- Lower upfront costs. The investment often includes software licensing, hardware maintenance, and upgrades.

- High scalability is offered. IT resources are based on changing business requirements. Cloud security measures and compliance certifications are covered under cloud license.

2.2.3. RISE with SAP

RISE with SAP is a comprehensive private cloud offering that accelerates digital transformation by combining software, services, and support. It enables organizations to deploy SAP S/4HANA on their preferred cloud provider (AWS, Azure, or Google Cloud) with preconfigured industry best practices and offers managed services.

This option is suitable for organizations with specific data residency or security requirements. It offers a dedicated cloud environment while still benefiting from cloud-based services. This model addresses unique customer scenarios by delivering the benefits of cloud infrastructure while maintaining control over specific business processes.

2.2.4. Hybrid Deployment

A hybrid cloud approach combines on-premise and cloud infrastructures. This is useful if the SAP customer wants to gradually move to the cloud or needs to integrate with other cloud products. It requires careful planning due to its complexity and dual maintenance.

2.2.5. Tailored Data Center Integration (TDI)

This option allows organizations to leverage existing hardware infrastructure for their SAP HANA deployment, offering flexibility and cost savings while maintaining control over the IT environment.

2.3. S/4HANA Digital Core

The S/4HANA enterprise suite encompasses all the main aspects of a traditional ERP system, including business process modeling, data processing, and system integration, while exceeding traditional ERP capabilities by incorporating advanced technologies, such as advanced analytics, artificial intelligence, and process automation. This is where the concept of a digital core emerges. A digital core, as shown in Figure 2-1, integrates operational and analytical data into a single platform that uncovers data patterns for advanced analytics.

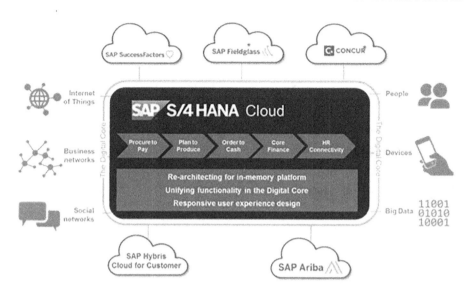

Figure 2-1. *SAP S/4HANA enterprise solution*

This section provides a comprehensive introduction of the SAP S/4HANA digital core in the context of its capabilities as a project management system, and also demonstrates how SAP Project System, as the core module for the EC&O industry, integrates with other SAP modules to create a comprehensive end-to-end project management solution.

2.3.1. Project System

SAP S/4HANA Project System (PS) effectively manages the project lifecycle by integrating with core SAP S/4HANA modules. Its greatest strength is its flexible project structuring. Unlike other SAP modules that rely on fixed organization structures, Project System is designed to manage the dynamic and cascading nature of projects.

Its comprehensive planning and enterprise-wide monitoring and controlling of cost, revenue, resources, and analytics raise it to the level, where it stands unparalleled among other project management systems (PMS).

While Oracle's Primavera P6 and Microsoft Project are generally considered de facto PMS solutions as standalone project management, Project System's strength lies in its integrated project execution approach. Similarly, the S/4HANA PPM solution too offers project management capabilities, but SAP S/4HANA PS is often superior due to its strong integration with core SAP modules. This integration prevents departmental silos, reduces manual effort, and removes data inconsistencies.

Project Structuring

PS provides a work breakdown structure (WBS), breaking down projects into manageable components. This hierarchical structure is integrated with SAP CPM and SAP PPM.

Project Planning

Network planning further extends the WBS by defining tasks, timelines, and task dependencies among activities. PS functions such as budgeting, cost estimation, resource planning, and revenue planning and recognition are supported through its strong integration capabilities with other SAP S/4HANA modules.

Project Execution

PS offers project status management for controlling project budget and resources, real-time visibility by monitoring project progress against the project plan, and the ability to control deviations from project scope and timeline.

PS stands out for managing complex projects by offering end-to-end visibility and control. Its integration with SAP core modules ensures data consistency, reduces manual effort, and provides a holistic project overview.

2.3.2. S/4HANA Integration with Project System

This section explores the key integrations between PS and other foundational modules crucial for effective project execution and oversight.

Finance (FI)

Finance (FI) is the backbone of financial transactions for record-to-report processes. It records revenue, expenses, assets, and liabilities. For projects, FI tracks project-related financial data, including cost allocation, revenue recognition, final cost and revenue settlement, and asset transfer. It provides the foundation for financial analysis, reporting, and decision-making.

Controlling (CO)

Controlling (CO) supports management accounting with its strong integration with PS for cost planning, control, and analysis. CO enables integration with cost centers, cost element accounting, internal order management, and profitability analysis, helping to monitor project performance, identify cost variances, and make informed decisions.

Sales and Distribution (SD)

PS and Sales and Distribution (SD) integration encompasses order-to-cash processes, including sales order creation, delivery, billing, and revenue recognition. SD plays a crucial role in managing customer inquiries, generating quotes, and processing sales orders for project-specific deliverables.

Materials Management (MM)

Materials Management (MM) and SAP Ariba encompass the source-to-pay business process cycle. MM optimizes procurement and inventory management, requisition of materials and services through purchase requisitions, creation of purchase orders and contracts, and production of goods receipts. MM-Services focuses on service procurement, service delivery confirmation, and subcontracting. MM-Inventory Management controls goods movement, inventory control, availability of project stock, and consumption through integration with PS.

Production Planning (PP)

Production Planning (PP) is crucial for production planning and execution, covering demand planning, material requirements planning, production scheduling, and capacity planning. PP integrates with PS for scheduling production plans, issuing production orders for project-based production, and establishing cost allocation to projects. It also integrates with MM and QM to ensure seamless production processes.

Quality Management (QM)

Quality Management (QM) ensures product and service quality through quality planning, inspection, and control. QM ensures project deliverables meet quality standards through inspection, testing, and quality notifications. The QM module supports quality planning, inspection execution, and the management of quality-related issues within the project lifecycle.

Audit Management

SAP S/4HANA also supports quality audits for project evaluation and quality assurance initiatives to prevent defects. Although SAP Audit Management is not directly integrated with SAP PS, it offers a strong platform to support project governance through audit planning, creating questionnaires, and audit execution.

Document Management System (DMS)

Document Management System (DMS) is a cross-application component within S/4HANA that centralizes documentation for easy access and control. This component allows users to attach business documents—such as Microsoft Office files, scanned images, videos, and so forth—through its integration with S/4HANA objects, such as project work breakdown elements, tasks, purchase orders, maintenance orders, and so on. DMS enables authorized document creation and change; status control; workflow management for document approval; document version control; and search and retrieval. In addition to S/4HANA components, DMS offers direct integration with computed aided design (CAD) systems to view drawings and save CAD files.

SAP Content Server manages the seamless storage and retrieval of documents. Whenever the user checks in the original document associated with the DMS, the files are stored in a central repository. Based on business requirements, there can be multiple content servers installed.

SAP also offers different options for DMS. In addition to S/4HANA DMS—a built-in component—a cloud-based stand-alone SAP DMS solution on the SAP Business Technology Platform (BTP) platform is also available. It is a complete document management solution for an organization and can be integrated with S/4HANA to provide integration similar to that of S/4HANA DMS. This product can be used to integrate with the HANA database offered by SAP BTP for content management.

Engineering Change Management (ECM)

DMS integration with Engineering Change Management (ECM) offers document and bill of material change control, change trails, and revisions in technical documentation. ECM also supports the management of engineering changes impacting project scope and deliverables.

Plant Maintenance (PM)

Plant Maintenance (PM), integrated with Equipment and Tools Management (ETM), manages the complete asset management lifecycle. The integration of Project Systems (PS) with Plant Maintenance (PM) simplifies the management of project-related assets and tools and equipment maintenance.

Maintenance plans of technical objects, such as equipment and facilities, are coordinated with the overall project plan so as to avoid untimely maintenance interventions. SAP also supports the transfer of maintenance costs, fuel costs, and asset depreciation costs from maintenance to project cost objects.

Equipment and Tools Management (ETM)

While traditionally a module in SAP ERP Central Component (ECC) and available in the earlier S/4HANA versions, its functionalities are now primarily offered through specialized partner solutions integrated with SAP S/4HANA. Conceptually, ETM offers a comprehensive suite of functionalities to manage equipment throughout its lifecycle. The module effectively handles equipment master data creation and maintenance, ensuring accurate records for all assets. It covers equipment planning and optimization, requisition-based resource allocation, and deployment strategies. ETM efficiently tracks equipment movements, status changes, and maintenance needs. The module also facilitates equipment disposal processes and provides insightful reporting on equipment utilization, costs, and performance metrics.

Human Capital Management (HCM)

Human Capital Management (HCM) manages the recruit-to-retire lifecycle of an employee through its strong integration with SAP SuccessFactors (SF). HCM is also integrated with PS for human resource planning, time management, and cost allocation of project teams to respective scope items.

The system supports the assignment of personnel and positions to the project structure, and allocates planned and actual personnel costs to projects. The Cross-Application Time Sheets (CATS) solution records employee attendance and working hours for project-related activities, ensuring accurate labor cost allocation.

In conclusion, SAP digital core provides the most effective and innovative features for managing projects effectively.

2.4. Business Technology Platform (BTP)

To further enhance the value of SAP S/4HANA and to keep the digital core clean of any extensions and customizations, SAP has provided a platform known as Business Technology Platform (BTP).

BTP provides a comprehensive set of tools and services that enables businesses to innovate, integrate, and transform their operations in the digital age.

2.4.1. Application Development

SAP BTP empowers developers to create, deploy, and manage applications efficiently. It offers various development tools and services to support different programming languages and development approaches. Additionally, SAP BTP provides support for low-code/no-code development, enabling business users to create applications without extensive coding knowledge.

2.4.2. SAP Build Process Automation

SAP BTP offers robust automation capabilities to streamline business processes and enhance efficiency. SAP Build Process Automation empowers organizations to design, execute, and monitor complex business workflows with ease.

Workflows

A workflow represents a sequence of connected activities or tasks designed to achieve a specific outcome. By leveraging intuitive drag-and-drop tools, both business users and IT professionals can create automated processes without extensive coding knowledge.

Robotics Process Automation

SAP Build Process Automation accelerates automation by providing pre-built connectors and Robotics Process Automation (RPA) bots for seamless integration with SAP and non-SAP systems. It helps organizations automate repetitive tasks and streamline business processes to improve productivity, reduce errors, and enhance overall operational performance.

2.4.3. Integration Suite

SAP BTP offers SAP Integration Suite, an integration platform-as-a-service (iPaaS) that enables seamless communication and data exchange between different systems, applications, and data sources.

SAP Integration Suite facilitates connectivity across on-premise and cloud environments, as well as with external partners and customers. It includes pre-built integrations managed by SAP, AI-assisted development, and integration optimization.

2.4.4. Data And Analytics

SAP BTP data and analytics solutions help organizations integrate, manage, and analyze data from various sources (SAP and non-SAP) in a multi-cloud environment. It provides tools for data warehousing, business intelligence, and AI-powered analytics to help users gain insights, optimize planning, and make informed decisions. There are four main components of SAP BTP Data and Analytics platform, as follows:

1. **SAP Datasphere**

   SAP Datasphere simplifies the data landscape
   by providing access to all data across hybrid and
   cloud environments. It transforms various types of
   data into a unified, understandable format. This
   harmonization creates a business semantic model,
   making it easier to analyze and use diverse data sets
   together.

2. **SAP HANA Cloud**

   SAP HANA Cloud is a multi-model database
   management system that empowers the architects of
   the future to build and deploy the next generation of
   intelligent data applications at scale. It goes beyond
   transactional apps and empowers developers to
   build applications that utilize generative AI, and also
   shifts developer focus from administrative tasks to
   innovative creation.

3. **SAP Analytics Cloud**

   SAP Analytics Cloud (SAC) is a complete solution for
   analytics and planning that is designed to unlock the
   full potential of valuable data sources. SAC offers two
   key areas of functionality: analytics and planning.
   SAC Analytics possesses complete business
   intelligence (BI) capabilities and delivers industry-
   specific analytics with pre-built business content.

   SAC Planning transforms enterprise planning and
   enables collaborative planning by unifying financial,
   supply chain, and operational planning within a
   single solution.

4. **SAP Master Data Governance**

    SAP Master Data Governance (MDG) provides a
    unified, trusted view of business data, enabling
    organizations to work more efficiently and make
    better decisions. The SAP MDG application
    consolidates master data and manages it centrally
    using a master data management layer. It supports
    master data stewardship and quality through
    monitoring, root-cause analysis, and remediation.
    Businesses can gain a unified view of master data
    across domains through consolidation, central
    governance, and replication. Accelerate time-to-
    value with prebuilt data models, business rules,
    workflows, roles, and industry-specific content.

2.5. SAP Line Of Business Solutions

SAP offers a wide range of cloud-based solutions designed to enhance
various business areas beyond the SAP S/4HANA digital core. These
solutions address specifics of a particular line of business, such as sales,
supply chain, talent management, expense management, as well as needs
in procurement, human resources, and customer experience, providing
specialized tools and integrations that complement the S/4HANA digital
core. This section explores four key SAP line of business solutions—Ariba,
SuccessFactors, C/4HANA, and Concur—detailing their roles and
integration with SAP Project System (PS) and other SAP modules.

2.5.1. SAP Ariba

Ariba is a cloud-based procurement platform that streamlines detailed
sourcing and contract management processes.

Although SAP Ariba is not directly integrated with SAP Project System, it can be seamlessly integrated with SAP MM to enhance procure-to-pay business scenarios with the inclusion of sourcing, contracting, and supplier lifecycle management processes. By making vendors part of the organization's workflow portal, this integration of purchasing documents offers real-time workflow and document status visibility to both customers and vendors.

2.5.2. SAP SuccessFactors

SuccessFactors has become increasingly important in the HR domain because of its strong talent management and workforce analytics capabilities.

The emphasis in this book is on the process integration between SAP Project System (PS) and SAP Human Capital Management (HCM), including CATS. By focusing on this core integration, this book provides a comprehensive understanding of how to optimize human resource management within EPC projects.

2.5.3. SAP C/4HANA

Formerly known as SAP C/4HANA, SAP now offers its Customer Experience (SAP CX) portfolio as a cloud-based solution designed for end-to-end customer experience, encompassing sales, service, marketing, commerce, and customer data management. It integrates with the S/4HANA SD module and offers powerful tools for end-to-end customer engagement and relationship management.

2.5.4. SAP Concur

SAP Concur offers a suite of travel and expense management solutions designed to streamline and automate business travel and expense reporting. EPC projects require frequent travelling and mostly out-of-office work. SAP Concur enhances operational efficiency by providing a self-service model of booking travel and other expenses. On remote projects, it ensures transparency, audit compliance, and visibility into project-related costs.

    i.   Concur Expense manages and automates expense tracking and reimbursement processes.

   ii.   Concur Invoice automates invoice management with reduced processing time and errors.

  iii.   Concur Travel provides a comprehensive platform for booking and managing business travel.

  iv.   Concur Request provides workflow for initiating and approving requests before they occur.

These line-of-business products are significant but fall outside the scope of this book. The focus here is specifically on the EPC project management lifecycle, concentrating on processes directly related to project management within the context of SAP S/4HANA.

2.6. Conclusion

The SAP S/4HANA, unlike any other ERP system or even its predecessors, is not just a platform that integrates different business modules. It offers more than a traditional ERP system through its in-memory HANA database, embedded analytics, and real-time predictive capabilities.

The flexibility of deployment and the licensing options allow organizations to choose the setup that best fits their business needs. Additionally, SAP Business Technology Platform (BTP) offers the clean core concept that extends its capabilities in application development, automation, and innovation and agility.

CHAPTER 3

Enterprise Portfolio and Project Management

Having built our understanding of SAP S/4HANA as an enterprise solution, we will now focus on its application within the EC&O industry. This chapter focuses on the management of portfolios, initiatives, proposals, and projects through the SAP S/4HANA Enterprise Portfolio and Project Management (EPPM) solution.

3.1. S/4HANA Products for EPPM

The SAP S/4HANA EPPM offers an integrated approach that uses the following three products to create a comprehensive solution.

For project management, these products are designed to work as stand-alone options too, but for a complete EPPM solution an integrated approach with different possible combinations must be adopted, as follows:

1. SAP S/4HANA Portfolio and Project Management (PPM)

2. SAP Commercial Project Management (CPM)

3. SAP S/4HANA Project System (PS) module

© Sohail Ahmed 2025
S. Ahmed, *The SAP S/4HANA Handbook for EPC Projects*,
https://doi.org/10.1007/979-8-8688-1466-2_3

These SAP products can be used for managing capital investment, innovation, operational, and commercial projects. The focus of this book is on commercial projects, particularly in the EC&O industry.

3.1.1. Commercial Projects

Commercial projects in general terms are revenue-generating projects. It is important to first understand how commercial projects are defined and structured in SAP S/4HANA.

A commercial project combines multiple business objects from different source systems into a single integrated object. It provides a central reference for all the activities that relate to different roles in a project setup.

3.1.2. Implementation Approach for the EC&O Industry

The preceding definition of *commercial project* is applicable to all three SAP products; therefore, SAP Commercial Project Management (CPM) should not be considered as the one for managing commercial projects.

In the next sections, we will introduce each of the products followed by three approaches toward EPPM. At the end of this chapter, the recommended approach for managing commercial projects that best suits the EC&O industry will be discussed.

3.2. Portfolio Management

SAP S/4HANA EPPM empowers organizations in strategic and operational portfolio management, allowing them to oversee multiple investment portfolios, such as product innovation, capital projects, and IT initiatives.

A portfolio in SAP PPM is a collection of portfolios, buckets, items, and initiatives that represent an organization's strategic goals and objectives.

3.2.1. Portfolio Structure

A portfolio structure in SAP S/4HANA PPM serves as a centralized repository for managing and tracking projects, programs, and other strategic initiatives.

Portfolio

A portfolio is the highest-level object in a portfolio structure.

Portfolio Bucket

A portfolio bucket, or a bucket, is a container within a portfolio used to categorize and group portfolio items based on specific criteria. A bucket always belongs to a portfolio to provide hierarchical strategic, financial, and capacity planning and analysis within a portfolio.

Organizations can develop portfolio structure hierarchically from an organizational or a functional viewpoint, as shown in Figure 3-1.

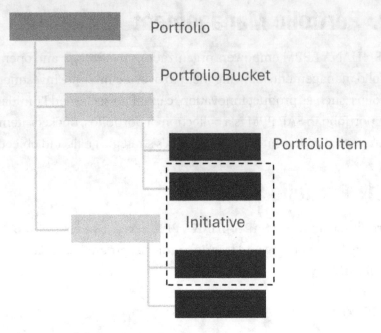

Figure 3-1. *Portfolio structure*

Portfolio Item

A portfolio item, or an item, is the representation of an individual project within a portfolio. An item contains details of the proposal of a project, an individual project, or an initiative of a project or services within the organization. defining their goals, resources, timelines, and budget.

Decision Points

Decision points are checkpoints, milestones, and quality gates that subdivide portfolio items and initiatives into phases, such as selection of consultant, approval of front-end engineering designs, and awarding of project to the EPC contractor.

Initiative

Initiative is a group of related portfolio items that share a common goal or objective, providing a way to manage and track a set of projects as a cohesive unit. Initiatives can span multiple portfolio buckets, allowing for flexibility in grouping projects based on strategic objectives.

3.2.2. Financial Planning

SAP S/4HANA PPM financial planning is a critical component for successful portfolio and project management. As shown in Figure 3-2, it involves budgeting, forecasting, and controlling project costs to ensure they align with organizational financial objectives. SAP PPM also facilitates the evaluation of financial details from linked projects to provide a comprehensive overview.

Figure 3-2. *S/4HANA PPM financial planning*

3.2.3. Resource and Capacity Planning

SAP S/4HANA PPM efficiently tracks and prioritizes resource requests
from various project management systems, reconciling availability data
from HCM and financial systems, as shown in Figure 3-3.

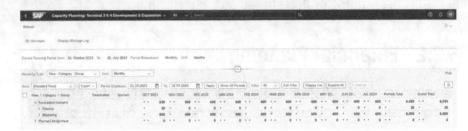

Figure 3-3. *PPM capacity planning*

Resource planning aligns project needs with overall portfolio capacity,
enabling a comparative analysis of strategic and operational resource
allocation. Role definitions specify required resources; their tasks,
timelines, and skillsets; and whether they are internal or external.

3.3. SAP S/4HANA Project Management

SAP Project Management, a component of SAP PPM, focuses on
operational project execution and the delivery of individual projects. A
project is directly linked with the item of a portfolio. If an organization
intends to plan resources for a portfolio item or requires further division
of a portfolio item, the portfolio structure from S/4HANA Portfolio
Management is extended to S/4HANA Project Management.

3.3.1. Project Management Structure

In this section, we will discuss the project management structure within SAP S/4HANA PPM. As shown in Figure 3-4, SAP PPM projects can be structured using phases, checklists, and tasks, with project definitions serving as an overall framework linked with the portfolio item.

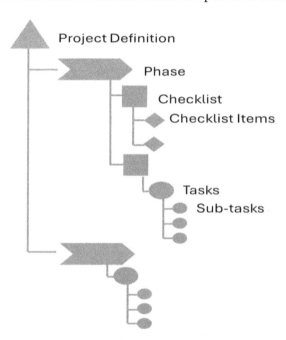

Figure 3-4. *PPM project structure*

Project Definition

The project definition is the highest-level element in the project hierarchy within SAP S/4HANA Project Management. It contains the general data for a project, including the name and identification of the project, planned start and finish dates, assignment to an organizational unit of the company, and the project's start and finish times. Additionally, the project definition encompasses budget controls, project types, and authorization settings, all of which are defined at this level to guide and manage the overall project structure.

Phase

Phases define the second level of the project hierarchy. A phase divides the project into manageable segments, where each phase represents a distinct stage of the project lifecycle.

Phases are sections of a project that are completed within specific timeframes. Execution of a phase begins with phase release and ends with an approval process. However, depending upon the planning approach and system configuration, phases may overlap or be restricted to start only after the preceding phase is completed. This provides the concept of quality gates or decision gates between phases. Quality gates are defined to ensure that the criteria to move to the next phase have been met.

Checklist

A checklist is a structured list of items that need to be completed within a project or an individual phase. It is the third hierarchy level of a project. Each checklist is assigned to a phase and contains multiple checklist items. The basic data for a checklist include the name, description, priority, roles, and status to govern the execution and monitoring of tasks.

Checklist Items

Checklist items are the specific tasks or aspects that make up a checklist. The checklist items help track important aspects of a phase. Checklist items can be flagged as mandatory or as requiring approval in order to manage and control the phase execution. This means that a specific item must be completed before a phase can be approved or considered complete.

Tasks

Tasks are the fundamental process steps in a project that define specific units of work and identify the assigned resources required to deliver the project. They are structured at various levels. Tasks can be assigned to the project definition, to a phase, and to a checklist level.

Phase-level tasks are the fundamental elements of determining the project timeline as their duration and dependencies must be assessed within the network of tasks. Checklist-level tasks represent individual activities within a checklist used to monitor the steps required to control phase-specific requirements. Tasks in phases and checklist items can be further subdivided into subtasks.

Subtasks

Subtasks are the components of tasks that break down a task into more manageable parts. Subtasks inherit the behavior of tasks to provide additional levels of planning and control.

3.3.2. Project Management Functions

S/4HANA Project Management is most suited for managing companywide internal projects and initiatives related to IT, professional services, product development, and research and development. Organizations can keep track of project schedule, resource utilization, and budget.

Resource Management

S/4HANA Project Management facilitates the identification and assignment of internal resources. Resource managers can define roles, such as site managers, discipline engineers, and commodity specialists. After the project roles are defined, resource managers can evaluate possible project team candidates based on their availability, location, and qualifications and assign resources based on these comparisons. The organization can decide to create business partners manually in SAP S/4HANA Portfolio and Project Management or use SAP S/4HANA HCM HR master data.

Cost Management

S/4HANA Project Management also enables detailed cost planning, tracking, and analysis against planned budgets. Integration with S/4HANA Controlling and Project System modules for accurate cost allocation and revenue calculation based on project milestones is also supported. Through its integration with S/4HANA Cross Application Time Sheets posting of actual hours by project resources can also be enabled.

3.4. Commercial Project Management (CPM)

SAP Commercial Project Management (CPM) covers project management areas that are not traditionally available in SAP. These core areas are risk, issue, and change management; project cost; quantity; and revenue planning at the bid stage, forecasting, and project dashboards. The following are the three main components of SAP CPM.

3.4.1. Project Workspace

Project Workspace is the role-based core application of CPM for project management, control, procurement, and so on. CPM Project Workspace, as shown in Figure 3-5, provides a consolidated view of project-related information from various SAP modules and provides real-time insights into project performance through its built-in analytics and reporting capabilities.

Figure 3-5. *Commercial Project Management Project Workspace*

In addition to the overview of projects, Project Workspace also provides specific views such as the following:

- **Commercial View:** Provides access to sales-related information, displaying data on sales, billing, invoices, and revenue recognition. The view updates automatically based on the selected document within the sales and billing module.

- **Procurement View:** Offers access to procurement-related information, displaying data on purchase requisitions, purchase orders, service entry sheets, and open invoices. Users can view, edit, or change purchase orders depending on access.

- **Team View:** Provides a graphical overview of teams, sub-teams, responsibility assignments, and project team hierarchy. Users can assign team members (employees, vendors, and customers) to project roles at different levels.

- **Document Management:** Centralized storage and access to project-related documents. Users can view, attach, or change attachments via the Documents tab.

3.4.2. Financial Plan

The Financial Planning solution in CPM offers a unified platform for financial planning, forecasting, and controlling, ensuring accurate financial visibility for informed decision-making. It provides comprehensive tools for detailed cost and revenue estimates and facilitates the creation of detailed bids.

User can create detailed structure that support calculation of Bill of Quantities (BOQ), derive estimated costs and revenues, build assumptions and creation of bid versions for scenario planning.

SAP CPM provides a seamlessly integration with SAP PPM and SAP S/4HANA, therefore, when changes occur, the system updates cost estimates, revises revenue projections, projects profitability, and calculates the overall cost impact.

3.4.3. Project Issue and Change Management

The Project Issue and Change Management module allows users to record and track project issues and allows issues to convert to change requests if they affect project timeline, scope, or budget.

This application integrates seamlessly with purchase orders, project structures, sales order with document management capabilities and cost and revenue planning. It helps in recording, tracking, planning, and monitoring the progress of issues and change requests reported during project execution.

Risk management features allow users to identify, analyze, and respond to risks with details of risk impact and probability within the project. It also provides analysis of risks and opportunities such as risk heat matrix.

3.4.4. CPM Project Structure

CPM offers a flexible architecture adaptable for Cost and Revenue planning. It provides the following two option to create structure for Financial Plans:

Commercial Project Structure

In this option SAP CPM offers the integration with SAP S/4HANA Project System. This type of structure known as Commercial Project creates a project structure where CPM hierarchy is seamlessly linked with SAP S/4HANA Work Breakdown Structure, SD Sales Order line items, or SAP PPM project structures.

This structure is inflexible as it replicates the project structure from SAP S/4HANA modules. However, this mirroring is beneficial for organizations seeking strict compliance throughout the project lifecycle.

Bid Structure

The second option allows users to create project structures using SAP CPM structural elements. This flexibility allows users to benefit CPM in creating bid structures. The bid structure fits unique bid requirements during bid preparation and evaluation, which may be different from the execution project structures.

The bid structure is adaptable to any hierarchy particularly required for bid preparation. Multiple bid structuring is possible to evaluate different scenarios for informed decision making. Creation of master data is also independent of installed base ERP system. This option provides fast and easy bid preparation process as it does not rely on any ERP data. The bid structure can be mapped to the Commercial Project Structure at a later stage.

Master Data Integration

Apart from project structures, SAP CPM can also be linked with S/4HANA to retrieve master data objects and valuations. Organizations can utilize pre-defined and established master data objects of SAP S/4HANA digital core. In addition, Reference project from the CPM database to copy plan data from a reference structure into a bid structure.

3.5. SAP Enterprise Project Connection

SAP Project System is an excellent tool for project planning and controlling due to its strong integration with other core business functions on the S/4HANA platform, while S/4HANA Project Management shows its strength for internal project because of its seamless integration with portfolio management.

However, both tools can show limitations when complex projects with thousands of activities demand detailed scheduling, frequent resource planning, leveling, and frequent updates. It also makes operational reporting a challenge when multiple stakeholders with diverse needs are onboarded on the same project.

SAP offers SAP Enterprise Project Connection (EPC) to bridge this gap by seamlessly integrating SAP Project System and S/4HANA Portfolio Project Management with Oracle's Primavera P6 Enterprise Project Portfolio Management (Primavera P6). Using SAP EPC, project data from SAP to Primavera P6 can be synchronized consistently and reliably in real-time without putting manual efforts.

While EPC has reached its end of mainstream maintenance and is no longer strategically supported by SAP for new integrations, the need for robust SAP-Primavera integration remains. A dedicated section in Chapter 8 further discusses the integration of Primavera P6 with SAP.

SAP S/4HANA provides third-party add-ons and pre-built connectors with standardized interfaces that enable bidirectional synchronization of critical project data, including project structure, activities, resources, and progress.

3.6. S/4HANA EPPM Implementation Scenarios

We have discussed the difference between portfolio and project management and have also understood how different functionalities are offered in SAP using different solutions are products. We will now understand the three main approaches that organizations may adopt in order to utilize SAP to integrate portfolio and project management.

3.6.1. Portfolio And Project Management in SAP PPM

In this approach, as depicted in Figure 3-6, organizations utilize SAP PPM for both portfolio and project management.

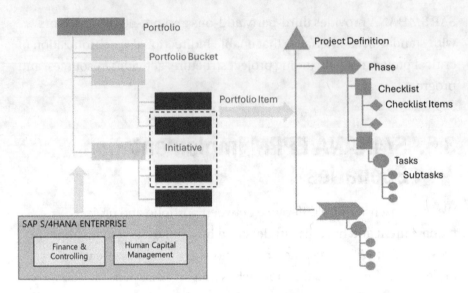

Figure 3-6. *Implementation Scenario: Portfolio and Project Management in SAP PPM*

This solution is best suited for capital expenditure projects focusing mainly on budgeting and capacity planning with some insights on the operational project management is also required.

The primary focus is on the prioritization and management of multiple portfolio items for departments or functions. The Project Management component of SAP PPM can easily manage the project execution requirements, which are relatively straightforward, without complex planning or reporting needs. S/4HANA FI, CO, and CATS are directly integrated with SAP PPM Portfolio Management component of actual cost allocations and timesheets for actual resource consumption.

3.6.2. SAP PPM and SAP S/4HANA Integration

This approach, depicted in Figure 3-7, combines strategic portfolio oversight in SAP PPM with detailed project execution managed within SAP S/4HANA's Project System (PS) and integrated modules.

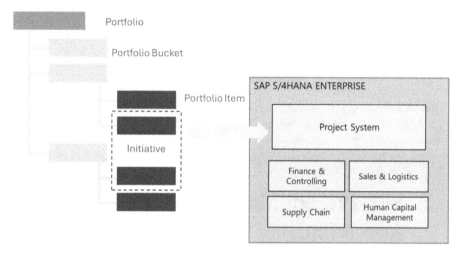

Figure 3-7. *Implementation Scenario: Portfolio Management in SAP PPM and Project Management in S/4HANA*

It is suitable for organizations with complex projects requiring specialized management capabilities and leveraging internal processes for procurement, resource allocation, and labor-intensive tasks.

3.6.3. SAP PPM Integration with External Tools

This approach combines strategic portfolio oversight in SAP PPM with project execution managed in external tools. Suitable for organizations with significant investments in third-party project management software or highly specialized project needs, this scenario, as shown in Figure 3-8, offers flexibility but requires robust data integration and potential custom development.

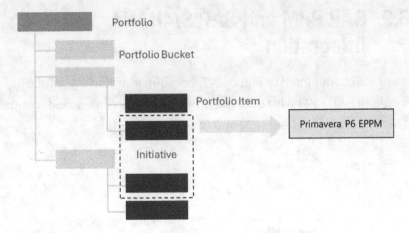

Figure 3-8. *Implementation Scenario: SAP PPM integration with External Project Management Tools*

3.7. EPC Project Management Approach

An integrated approach combining Commercial Project Management (SAP CPM), SAP S/4HANA Project System, and Primavera P6 is often optimal for organizations executing turnkey EPC projects.

To illustrate this approach, consider the case of Global Oil Company (GOC), a multinational energy company, planning a major expansion of one of its refineries to increase its production capacity.

3.7.1. RefineX Project- Use Case

GOC, the owner, initiated the "RefineX Project" for the design and construction of new units and upgrading existing facilities. GOC engaged PrimeCon, a leading EPC contractor, as the primary implementation partner. The initial scope of the RefineX project includes the extension of a tank farm and the addition of new process skids and equipment.

Under a turnkey contract, PrimeCon is responsible for the complete engineering, procurement, and construction of the items, as well as project management scope.

Before the RefineX project, both GOC and PrimeCon relied on different non-integrated IT systems, creating a diversified landscape that posed significant challenges for both organizations. Therefore, both organizations decided to adopt SAP S/4HANA Enterprise Project and Portfolio Management (EPPM) solutions. In the later chapters, we will explore how SAP S/4HANA facilitated the successful delivery of the RefineX project.

3.7.2. Owner's Perspective

GOC, as the project owner, implements SAP S/4HANA PPM to strategically manage its project portfolio. By aligning projects with business objectives and optimizing resource allocation, GOC can make informed decisions and track project performance against strategic goals.

SAP S/4HANA PPM provides project owners with a platform to define, monitor, and control these projects as capital investments or operational initiatives by creating portfolio items and projects.

While SAP EPC can offer deeper integration with Primavera, its implementation may not be necessary for projects awarded under turnkey contracts, where owners focus primarily on overall budget and progress monitoring. SAP S/4HANA PPM alone often provides sufficient visibility into these aspects. However, for projects involving complex scheduling, resource allocation, or real-time collaboration, SAP EPC can deliver significant benefits. It is particularly useful for managing multiple interconnected workstreams and leveraging advanced scheduling and resource management techniques.

Organizations already using other SAP modules may also find SAP EPC valuable for achieving seamless integration. Ultimately, the decision to implement SAP EPC should be based on evaluating the organization's specific reporting needs and the level of involvement of their project management office (PMO).

The book will not discuss the owner's perspective. It assumes that GOC used SAP S/4HANA PPM during the process of awarding the RefineX project under a turnkey contract to PrimeCon.

3.7.3. Contractor's Perspective

PrimeCon, as the primary contractor, chose a combination of SAP and external tools to execute EPC projects.

To successfully win and execute the RefineX project, PrimeCon utilizes SAP CPM for bid planning and estimation, SAP S/4HANA Enterprise suite with SAP Project System (PS) as its digital core for operative project planning and execution, and Primavera P6 for detailed project scheduling, resource allocation, levelling, and construction management tasks. Primavera P6 is integrated with S/4HANA Project System using SAP Enterprise Project Connection. This arrangement is shown in Figure 3-9.

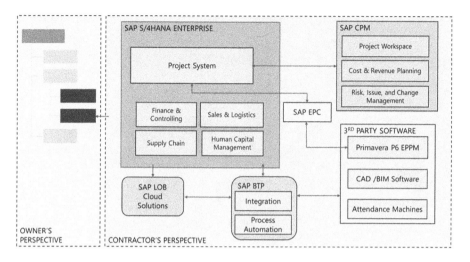

Figure 3-9. *EPC projects: contract's perspective of S/4HANA*

The focus of this book will be on the perspective of the prime contractor, PrimeCon, and how it leverages SAP solutions throughout the project lifecycle. By examining how PrimeCon manages detailed planning and scheduling, project execution, and financials, readers will gain an in-depth understanding of how SAP S/4HANA can be used to deliver complex projects successfully.

3.8. Conclusion

This chapter has introduced the complex landscape of portfolio and project management within the EC&O industry, and how SAP S/4HANA offers a comprehensive suite of tools to address these challenges. In subsequent chapters we will dive deep into the process of optimizing EPC project management using SAP S/4HANA.

CHAPTER 4

Bidding and Estimation

This chapter covers PrimeCon's initial steps of bidding for projects. It describes the following processes for the bidding and proposal development for the RefineX project, for its customer Global Oil Company (GOC):

Customer Information ➤ Project Inquiry ➤ Estimation ➤ Proposal Development ➤ Proposal Submission ➤ Award of Project

4.1. Inquiry

Inquiries mark the start of the sales process. It focuses on the identification of customer needs and the evaluation of a project's scope. This phase sets the foundation for sales activities such as quotations, orders, and execution.

4.1.1. Customer Information

In the pre-sales phase, the sales team actively explores the market for potential projects. The sales team gathers information about forthcoming projects and expresses their interest to the project owners or customers.

© Sohail Ahmed 2025
S. Ahmed, *The SAP S/4HANA Handbook for EPC Projects*,
https://doi.org/10.1007/979-8-8688-1466-2_4

Customer Master

Once the sales team identifies a promising engineering, procurement, and construction (EPC) project opportunity with GOC for one of their refineries, its sales engineer records GOC's essential details in the SAP S/4HANA Sales and Distribution system. In the future, this information is used for creating sales documents and invoices, and tracking payments.

The sales engineer maintains the *Business Partner (BP)* object in the system and assigns the Customer role. The following information is maintained in the system:

- Customer number: A system-generated or external unique identifier for the customer in SAP

- Name and address: Customer's legal name and contact address(es)

- Industry and category: Classification of the customer based on industry and business type

- Payment terms: Defines the payment methods and delivery terms for transactions with the customer

- Sales area and tax jurisdiction: Assigns the customer to a specific sales organization and tax jurisdiction for accurate reporting

- Customer segmentation: Customers can also be classified based on industry, size, and other relevant criteria to enable targeted marketing and sales efforts

- Customer hierarchy: If the organization has multiple sales organizations or subsidiaries, the customer hierarchy can also be maintained accordingly

If an organization has also deployed SAP C/4HANA, then C/4HANA becomes the primary solution for maintaining customer data. C/4HANA works as the central repository for maintaining customer information, and with the help of integration with SAP S/4HANA Sales and Distribution (SD), the customer data is also extended to SAP as a business partner or a customer.

Customer Approval

After customer information is entered in the system, a formal workflow for the approval of customer information is initiated.

Since PrimeCon is a large organization with multiple business areas dealing in different types of projects, it needs a resilient data governance and approval process for customer data management. Therefore, PrimeCon has also acquired licenses for the SAP Master Data Governance (MDG) module.

By implementing SAP MDG, PrimeCon has garnered the following benefits:

1. Central data governance occurs through data stewards.

2. Data duplication is no longer a concern.

3. Complex search criteria and taxonomy can be defined.

4. Rules are defined for master data creation and approval.

5. Change requests can be initiated from the MDG customer governance tab.

6. No conflict of interest. Duties are segregated based on roles and access control.

4.1.2. Inquiry Management

After maintaining customer information in the system, the sales team creates a customer inquiry document. Inquiry serves as the foundation for capturing essential proposal details.

In SAP S/4HANA, executing transaction code VA11 generates a unique inquiry number in SAP S/4HANA.

Inquiry Synopsis

Proposal details are generally captured in a document called an inquiry synopsis. The inquiry synopsis is a short summary of the proposed project covering all the important aspects required for bidding.

Once an invitation to bid (ITB) is received from the customer, the sales engineer studies the ITB and prepares the inquiry synopsis. It captures the essential project details required to prepare a successful bid. Some of the important fields that must be maintained in the inquiry synopsis are as follows:

1. Project details: Type of project, location, capacity, scale

2. Brief description of the project

3. High-level scope of work

4. Technical requirements: Design specifications, expected functionalities

5. Resource capacity requirements

6. Important project milestone dates

7. Commercial inquiries: Expected budget, payment terms, etc.

8. Additional notes for proposal teams

If the organization is also using SAP C/4HANA Sale Cloud, then the sales team will create a customer lead or an opportunity (depending on the qualification criteria) in C/4HANA. The process for inquiry creation will then start through the transfer of information from C/4HANA to SAP SD for the creation of the inquiry document.

Inquiry Status

The sales team can use inquiry document status management in S/4HANA. This feature allows users to track the status of each inquiry passing through different stages, such as "New," "In Progress," "Approved," or "Closed."

4.1.3. Inquiry Documentation

After creating the inquiry document in S/4HANA SD, the sales engineer uploads the documents received with the ITB. For this, the sales engineer uses the SAP Document Management System (DMS) module.

Invitation to Bid (ITB)

For an EPC project, the following documents are usually received with an invitation to bid (ITB):

- Technical specifications: Detailed descriptions of the project's technical requirements and standards, including project-specific standards that must be followed during execution

- Front end engineering and design and tender drawings: Initial design and drawings provided to outline the scope and requirements of the project

- Bill of quantities: A document that specifies the required material. This is particularly important if the supply of material is separately mentioned in the contract.

- Contractual terms and conditions: Outlining the legal framework for the project, including payment terms, warranties, and risk allocation.

73

To handle high document volume, transaction load, and access from multiple locations, PrimeCon has deployed a central repository using SAP S/4HANA Content Server.

Document Management

PrimeCon has also configured a specific document type "INQ" in S/4HANA DMS to organize and control all inquiry-related documents.

This document type serves a dual purpose:

1. It categorizes documents based on their characteristics and controls access by defining authorization by document type.

2. Defines approval workflow based on the organization's Limit of Authority.

The sales engineer created a unique document information record (DIR) using document type INQ in S/4HANA DMS. The ITB and synopsis documents are attached with the DIR and checked in so the system can link the DIR and the associated documents. After completing the check-in step, the sales engineer saves it in a centralized repository.

4.1.4. Bid Decision

After finishing the inquiry documentation, the next step for the sales engineer is to submit the synopsis to the senior management for approval to bid.

The approval process is triggered by changing the status of the document. After going through approval steps defined by company policy, the inquiry synopsis reaches PrimeCon's head of sales. During the review, S/4HANA analytical applications provide insight into the capacity availability, cash flow, and historical project costs to make informed decisions about the proposal's feasibility.

After comprehensive analysis, the head of sales approves the inquiry and authorizes the sales team to bid for the project.

4.2. Bidding for Project

After the successful bid approval, the sales team hands over the inquiry documentation to the estimation team. This handover is done in S/4HANA by updating the inquiry status and triggering the workflow. This process, as depicted in Figure 4-1, marks the conclusion of the pre-sales process and starts the proposal development process.

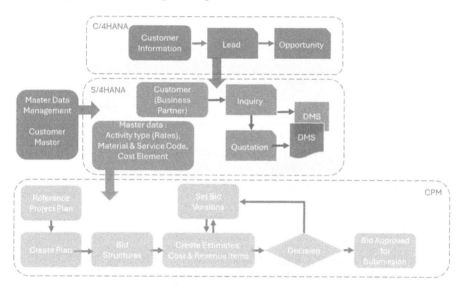

Figure 4-1. *Bidding for projects*

An estimation engineer is tasked to prepare a comprehensive proposal in response to the inquiry shared by the sales team. The knowledge base for the proposal is derived from the ITB and any subsequent revisions. S/4HANA DMS version control guarantees that the estimation engineer receives the latest version of inquiry documents.

4.2.1. Bid Structure

PrimeCon adds SAP CPM to its IT landscape and utilizes its Financial Planning component for bid preparation.

4.2.2. Bid Estimation

For bid preparation, the estimation team creates the financial plan in SAP CPM, as shown in Figure 4-2.

Figure 4-2. *CPM financial plan*

Bid Structure

After setting up the plan, a bid structure is created to break down the plan into manageable components, as shown in Figure 4-3.

Plan Structure	Plan Item Description	Object Type	
∨ Construction Bid Project	Construction Bid Project	CMP	
▲ Engineering	Engineering	WBS	∨
▲ Procurement	Procurement	WBS	∨
▲ Subcontracting	Subcontracting	WBS	∨
▲ Site Management	Site Management	WBS	∨
▲ Construction	Construction	WBS	∨
▲ Project Management	Project Management	WBS	∨

Figure 4-3. *CPM bid structure*

PrimeCon decides to use S/4HANA integration with CPM solely for master data while opting for the CPM bid structure during the bidding stage. This approach ensures the reliability and compliance of master data from S/4HANA while utilizing the flexibility of SAP CPM's structuring to expedite the bidding process.

Detailed Estimation

Within each bid structure, CPM provides planning workbooks to plan and determine the cost and revenue of a project.

Planning workbooks provide a structured framework for estimating project costs and revenues aligned with project hierarchies. The planning area offers fields and objects, like resource type, resource, quantity, cost, price, and grouping structures. These elements categorize and value required resources. Users can customize resource characteristics or link to S/4HANA master data. Additionally, characteristics like billable, non-billable, or overhead can be assigned for reporting purposes.

The estimation engineer can create cost and revenue items to generate work estimates as well as to calculate quantities of resources required to deliver the work, such as skilled and non-skilled labor; details of materials, services, tools, and equipment; and general expenses.

For high-level bid estimates, when not all quantities are available for bid preparation, the scope of work is achieved by focusing primarily on planning the work. SAP CPM provides two views: an input view and an output view.

For example, the ITB for the RefineX project outlines the excavation activity at a very high level, specifying only that 12,000 cubic meters of excavation are in the scope. The engineer estimates that this task should be completed within four days to meet project milestones. The resource required to perform this task is a standard midsize excavator with the capacity to excavate 1500 cubic meters of earth in a ten-hour shift.

Using SAP CPM, the estimation engineer inputs the information as shown in Table 4-1.

Table 4-1. *Engineer Inputs*

Field Name	Description	Example
Activity	Level of project hierarchy where the quantity, cost, and resource are entered for estimation.	Excavation
Resource Type	A category of resources used in the project, such as Activity, Expense, Human, Material, etc.	Machine
Resource	Specific resource to be used	Excavator Type A
Quantity	The planned amount of work to be performed for this activity. System will use key figures to maintain this value.	12,000 cubic meters
Productivity	An indicative rate at which the corresponding resource or resource type is estimated to perform; proposed by the system.	1,500 cubic meter/day
Unit Cost Rate	For each resource, you can either manually enter a cost rate or use valuation to propose a rate based on the valuation strategy for the plan scenario.	$200/cubic meter
Input Cost	Total cost for the scope of work of an activity. Multiply quantity by unit cost rate.	$2,400,000
Unit Price	Price per unit for the scope of work.	$250/cubic meter

For more precise estimates, the estimate engineer requires specific master data. Integration between CPM Financial Planning and S/4HANA provides access to critical master data, like material master, service master, activity types, cost elements, and so forth. These data elements are incorporated into CPM plans for accurate quantity, cost, and revenue planning. Additionally, indirect costs—such as project management and site establishment—are allocated using cost elements from SAP S/4HANA Controlling (CO).

Bid Evaluation

As the bidding process evolves, the estimation team finds the need to adjust bid structures due to changes in scope or specification. They require flexibility in the bid structure, which can be adjusted to accommodate these changes.

CPM provides the required flexibility to create multiple bid structures within a plan without the hierarchy restrictions required for execution. It provides users with different what-if scenarios and allows them to compare various scenarios and select the most viable option.

The financial plan further allows the creation of multiple plan versions and allows status management for regular tracking of the bidding progress.

The estimation engineer, after receiving internal feedback, creates multiple bid structures and updates cost and/or revenue items in the estimates and saves them as different versions, as shown in Figure 4-4.

Figure 4-4. *Estimates*

Bid Approval

After finalizing and approving the bid from the head of estimation, the status of the financial plan is set as "Approved." This status shows that the bid is ready for submission to the customer and is handed over to the sales team.

4.3. Quotation

The sales team creates the quotation document in the S/4HANA SD module with reference to the inquiry document created earlier for the RefineX project. After finalizing and approving the bid internally, the bid is prepared for submission to the customer.

4.4. Award of Contract

The innovative bid strategy, which included the strategic use of SAP CPM and S/4HANA for bid preparation, resulted in the successful acquisition of the contract by PrimeCon.

The RefineX project is awarded as a turnkey engineering, procurement, and construction project with a fixed cost contract, with any additional work beyond the defined scope of work or design specifications to be claimable as a variation order.

4.5. Transfer Plan Data

After the project is created in SAP S/4HANA Project System (PS), the PrimeCon estimation engineer is asked by the planning team to transfer the planned data from the bid plan in CPM to the execution structure (or operative project, as it is called in S/4HANA PS). The process of creating the operative project will be discussed in the next chapter.

The approved version of the bid plan becomes the baseline for transferring the bid structure to S/4HANA for execution.

4.6. Sales Order Creation

For EPC projects, S/4HANA SD integration with PS is straightforward. The sales engineer creates a sales order for a bid plan for the RefineX project in the S/4HANA SD module. The sales order must be created with reference to the corresponding quotation number to maintain the document trail that started in the inquiry document.

After the execution structure is ready, the sales order line item is updated by linking with the work breakdown structure (WBS) code marked as "Billing Element." This integration, discussed further in section 11.8, "Revenue Planning," allows revenue-related information to flow between SD and PS.

This book focuses on EPC projects; however, other contracts are also applicable in the EC&O industry. To address these scenarios, the following SD and PS integrations are applicable.

4.6.1. Supply Projects

There can be multiple WBS elements (WBSE) marked as "Billing Elements," but for EPC projects, the sales order is created with a single line item using item category E, and only the root WBSE is marked as "Revenue Element." This link between SD line item and Project WBS is required to create the billing plan for the project.

4.6.2. Assembly Processing

For make-to-order (MTO) and make-to-stock (MTS) scenarios, assembly processing enables the automatic creation of a project when a sales order or quotation is processed. This is especially useful when using configurable materials to align production and sales with specific customer requirements.

4.6.3. Time and Material

In time and material projects, DIP (dynamic item processors) profiles'
functionality is configured. DIP profiles integrate PS and SD for resource-
related billing. Customers are billed based on the actual amount of
resources consumed within the project in a defined period, regardless of
the progress.

4.7. Handover to PMO

All the necessary documents prepared during the bid preparation process
are updated using DMS. The sales engineer initiates the handover of
project documents by assigning new version numbers to each document
as they are handed over. The S/4AHANA DMS version-control feature
tracks these changes, and the most recent version is shown as the default.

　　Once the project documents from the sales team are handed over to
the project management office (PMO), the documents are thoroughly
reviewed and confirmed for completeness. To initiate the project, the head
of the PMO nominates a project manager for the project. In the following
chapter, we will look at in detail the project structuring and project scope
management processes using SAP S/4HANA.

CHAPTER 5

Planning and Scheduling

Project planning is a fundamental process in project management. It is essential for coordinating the various activities required to complete a project successfully. This chapter deals with the critical processes and methodologies essential for structuring, sequencing, and timing project activities within the SAP S/4HANA.

5.1. Planning Levels

Project planning involves breaking down the project into smaller tasks.

The level approach of structuring provides a clear overview of how each object contributes to the overall project. The planning is conducted in various levels, where each lower level increases the granularity of the plan.

Planning levels are commonly described as: Level 1, Level 2, Level 3, and Level 4 planning. Project Management Institute's (PMI) or other project management standards do not explicitly define these levels, but each level increases the granularity of project planning. In this book, the planning levels are defined as follows.

© Sohail Ahmed 2025
S. Ahmed, *The SAP S/4HANA Handbook for EPC Projects*,
https://doi.org/10.1007/979-8-8688-1466-2_5

5.1.1. Level 1: Project Overview

A Level 1 plan is the highest-level overview of the project. It defines project phases (engineering, procurement, etc.) and key milestones within each phase (completion of basic design, completion of delivery at site, etc.).

5.1.2. Level 2: Deliverable Overview

A Level 2 plan breaks down the project into key deliverables, subdeliverables (basic design, long-lead procurement, erection of pumps, etc.), and sections where work packages are assigned.

5.1.3. Level 3: Detailed Plan

A Level 3 plan, also known as a detailed plan or activity plan, provides the activity-level details of each work package. It offers a comprehensive account of each activity to be performed, duration, resources and assignments, and dependencies on other activities. The outcome of the detailed plan provides the logic for how the project will be executed, including predecessors and successors, and the overall duration of the project. It also helps the project management team derive procurement, resource, subcontracting, and cost and revenue plans.

The planning process identifies tasks for each work package that represent more granular aspects of the project. Scheduling is another essential component of project management. It involves calculating the start and finish dates for each task and aligning them with dependencies on other tasks. By setting up a project timeline, project managers can determine the overall project duration, the time required for each deliverable, and potential constraints and bottlenecks.

5.1.4. Level 4: Execution Plan

A Level 4 plan provides the detailed operational-level control of the project. Subtasks are defined at this level to help monitor and control the day-to-day execution of projects. It provides individual task assignments, detailed resource scheduling, task dependencies, and operational control measures.

5.2. Project Structure

During the bidding and estimation phase of a project, the project is planned at a high level. Even for project estimates where the estimation levels are detailed, the idea is not to encompass the execution details. The bid-level details serve as the baseline for the project's scope, time, effort, and cost. However, as the project progresses, more-detailed planning and a tight integration with finance, HR, sales and logistics, and supply chain is needed.

Project Builder is an S/4HANA PS platform used to create and maintain different objects with which to plan and control the projects. The following are the key components.

5.2.1. Project Definition

The project definition is the framework where all the objects related to a project are defined. A project can only have one project definition, which serves as the foundational blueprint for a project. When initially created, it inherits all configurations from the project profile.

The project definition is not capable of directly handling any planning or actual data. Instead, it functions as the project's "header" that provides overarching parameters copied from the system configuration under the project profile.

Project Profile

The project profile defines the overall characteristics and attributes of the project. The profiles for network, scheduling, and budgeting are configured for the project profile, as shown in Figure 5-1. The lower-level project structures, with the option to adjust data manually, automatically inherit the key organizational and profile data from the project definition.

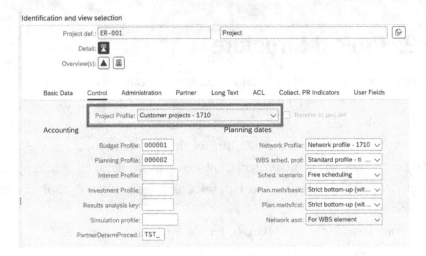

Figure 5-1. *Project profile*

Project Coding

Project coding is necessary to create a unique project identifier with which to track projects within an organization.

The following coding mask is configured by the organization to decide how the project numbers and hierarchy are structured.

XX.NNNN

The preceding project ID is composed of two segments:

1. Project Key (**XX**): This is a double-digit alphanumeric code that is mostly used by an organization to define types of projects executed by or within the organization.

2. Project Number (**NNNN**): This is a unique identification of the project within the S/4HANA system.

5.2.2. Work Breakdown Structure

A work breakdown structure (WBS) is a hierarchical decomposition of a project's scope into smaller, more manageable deliverables. It is hierarchical and deliverable oriented. The hierarchy is broken down into WBS elements (WBSE).

Operative WBS

A WBSE is a component within the WBS hierarchy that represents a specific scope of work that allows detailed planning and actual data gathering. The WBS element represents a specific project deliverable. In S/4HANA, a WBSE serves as the main hub through which to connect the project with other SAP module objects.

WBS Characteristics

SAP Project System relies heavily on the WBS to connect the project with other SAP modules.

During project execution, whether the planned and actual costs and revenue are allowed to be transferred to a particular WBSE is controlled by operative indicators set as a Planning Element, Account Assignment Element, or Billing Element, as shown in Figure 5-2.

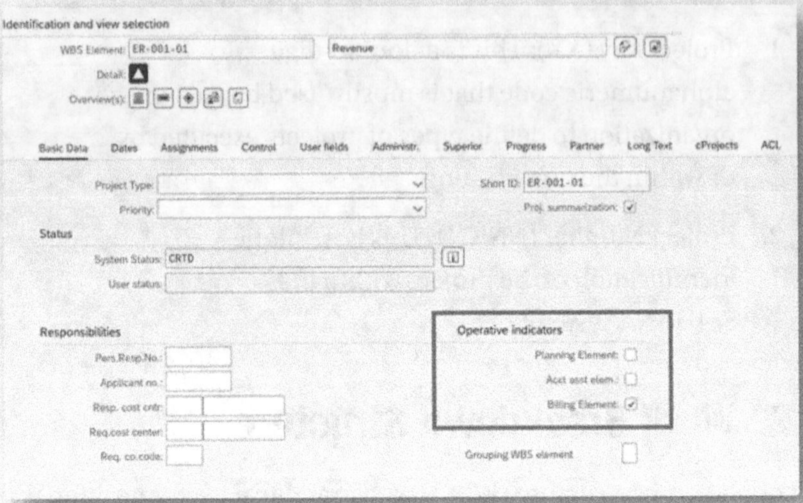

Figure 5-2. *Operative indicators*

WBS Levels

The typical work breakdown structure is organized into multiple levels, as shown in Table 5-1. Each level represents a different level of detail and granularity.

Table 5-1. *Work Breakdown Structure*

WBS Levels	Functions
Root WBS	Level 1, or the root WBSE, is the highest level and represents the root of the project's scope. It copies the characteristics from the project definition. The root WBSE is also marked as "Revenue Element" to allow the system to integrate with the sales order line item. This integration between SD and PS modules is required for project billing through SD and revenue recognition. In some cases, where multiple performance obligations exist in a contract, multiple Level 1 WBS elements may be created to comply with IFRS revenue recognition requirements.
Second-level WBS	The Level 2 WBS provides further breakdown of the project scope. The structure at this level depends on the project type and should encompass all necessary elements to define the project scope comprehensively. This level is most critical as it covers every aspect of the project. In EPC projects, a typical Level 2 WBS covers project phases.
WBS Level 3 and Below	The lower levels of the WBS represent more-detailed elements of the project scope. The WBS elements at these levels vary based on the specific scope and deliverables of the project, enabling better planning, resource allocation, and progress tracking. The levels below each Level 2 WBSE provide further details of each phase and allow the planning team to cover all deliverables. S/4HANA does not limit the number of WBSEs in a project, but the coding mask does limit the creation of levels. Therefore, it is important to finalize WBS levels with this limitation in mind.

Standard WBS

A standard work breakdown structure serves as a template for creating operative work breakdown structures. It comprises individual WBS elements that define a standard project to ensure consistency. Multiple standard WBS instances can be defined in the system for different project types.

5.2.3. Network

A network serves the purpose of a work package in the project hierarchy. It logically connects the tasks required to deliver the scope of the project. The planned and actual dates and cost from the network activities are aggregated and rolled up to the WBS element where the activity is assigned.

WBS and network orders can be used as independent objects in SAP PS in certain scenarios; for example, the scenario of assembly processing does not require as detailed a structure as is found in a WBS, and so only a network is assigned with the sales order. Meanwhile, if the organization is only interested in rough-cut cost and date planning there is no need for networks.

As depicted in Figure 5-3, a typical EPC project, due to its complex nature, requires a combination of WBS instances, networks, and its components to provide a comprehensive solution. This section provides a detailed explanation of the role of networks and their various components in the overall project management process.

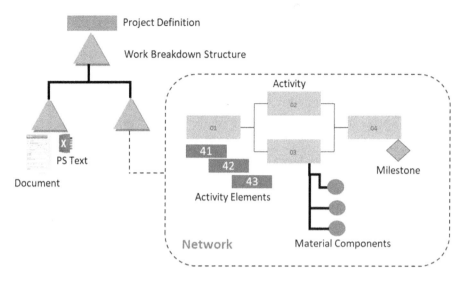

Figure 5-3. *Project structure in SAP PS*

Network Order

A network represents the process flow in a logical sequence of tasks or activities to define relationships, durations, and resources, and forms the basis for project planning and scheduling. Similar to production, maintenance, quality, or inspection orders, a network is also a type of work order, therefore is called a network order in the SAP system.

Network Header

A network consists of a network header and activities. The network header defines the attributes and characteristics of the activities associated with a particular network order through the network profile.

Network Profile

A network profile contains default values and parameters for controlling the processing of networks. In EPC projects, network profiles are typically used to define parameters for scheduling, access control, behavior of activities and components assigned to activities, and graphical settings.

Activity-Assigned Network

SAP allows networks to be configured as header-assigned networks or activity-assigned networks. In activity-assigned networks, activities of the same network can be assigned to different WBS elements regardless of the network header's assignment. There can be multiple networks (each grouped under a network header) in a project. In an activity-assigned network, the planned, committed, and actual costs can be analyzed at the activity level.

Standard Network

Operative networks can be derived from standard network templates. Standard networks are like standard work packages, with a pre-defined set of activities, activity relationships, and standard durations. A repository of such work packages can be saved in the system as standard networks for future use. Using standard networks independently or in combination with a standard WBS saves time and increases the consistency of business processes.

5.2.4. Subnetwork

A *subnetwork* is similar to a network in functionality but differs in its assignment. Unlike networks, which can be assigned to a WBS or a sales order, subnetworks can be assigned only to a network header or a network activity.

Multiple subnetworks can be assigned to an activity. Frequent use of subnetworks can make a project plan complex. Therefore, this functionality should be used when a work package cannot be managed through activity elements or assignment of production or maintenance orders.

5.2.5. Network Activities

An activity in project management is the lowest level of the project work breakdown structure that defines the process of a work package. In EPC projects, networks activities (or simply activities) are the components of a work package that define the type of work to be executed in order to complete the deliverable.

Activities form the basis for defining the schedule, resources, and cost of a project. SAP Project System defines the following categories of network activities.

Internally Processed Activities

Internal activities represent the work performed by internal resources. As the name suggests, this activity category is used to plan and execute work using internal human resources, usually skilled labor or machines owned by an organization. Internal resources are planned using work centers, while the unit rates are defined using activity types in a SAP Controlling (CO) module. For example, if drafting, welding, or fabrication is done by an internal PrimeCon draftsman, welder, or cutting machine, respectively, then "internal activity" will be used in Project Builder.

This type of activity is also used for assigning material components. This step is useful for triggering material requirements planning (MRP), initiating a purchase requisition, or creating material reservations.

Externally Processed Activities

This activity category is used to procure external services or material without the need to define a material or a service master in the system. Its use in EPC projects should be limited due to weak procurement control.

Service Activities

This activity category is used to acquire external services. Unlike the internally processed, this activity category is particularly useful in EPC projects where multiple activities of this type are integrated with an MM module. It allows users to create a detailed multi-level service bill of material using a service master and service entry sheet. It also allows the user to benefit from the standard service bill of material that can be utilized for recurring use.

General Costs Activities

This activity type is used to plan and for the actual cost posting of general costs that do not require external procurement or internal resources. The cost is planned using cost elements from the CO module.

5.2.6. Activity Element

Activity elements represent subactivities within a network. Except for service activities, they share the same categories as activities: internally processed, externally processed, and general cost.

They are similar to activities in functionality, with some limitations. For example, they can only be assigned to an activity. The system, however, provides the flexibility of assigning any type of activity element to any type of network activity within the same network. The planned dates cannot be planned on an activity element. Instead, they are calculated with respect to the start or finish dates of the corresponding activity. The user can only enter an offset to specify lead or lag time from the activity dates.

5.2.7. Material Component

Material components are the PS objects where materials are planned and specified in the project structure. Material components can only be assigned to network activities. When a material component is entered, its cost is determined by the system and planned at the activity level.

5.2.8. Milestone

In project management terms, a milestone is a significant event or achievement marking the completion of a phase or project. Milestones can be assigned to either WBSEs or network activities. In Project System, milestones have the following features.

Billing Milestone

This milestone function, when selected, creates a link between the sales order in the S/4HANA SD module, and the milestones in the Project System (PS) module resulting the billing milestones to appear in the SD sales order billing plan.

For the RefineX project, the planning engineer creates a milestone "Basic Design Completion" with a weight of 10% to reflect the payment percentage from the contract. This milestone is assigned to the relevant network activity within the "Basic Design" network. Once the activity is completed and confirmed in the system, this milestone is triggered. This process unlocks the corresponding billing process. The milestone's actual dates are automatically copied to the billing plan, triggering the start of the billing process for that specific scope of work.

Progress Milestones

SAP PS provides different progress measurement methods for tracking project progress. One of these methods is milestone progress, which is used to measure progress based on milestone completion. These milestones are used for reporting the progress of milestones in the Milestone Trend Analysis report.

Automatic Actions from Milestones

In addition to progress measurement and triggering billing, a milestone performs the following functions:

- It is used as a trigger for the auto-creation of a new network by copying from a standard network with predefined activities and attributes.

- It includes a new subnetwork from standard.

- It activates SAP standard or customer-defined workflow tasks.

- It defines standard milestones to automatically create new milestones.

The planning engineer applies some of these functions to the RefineX project and defines a milestone "Basic Design – Skid Pump B" in the "Basic Design" network. After the work is completed, the system automatically creates a new network, named Detailed Design, based on a standard network .

Similarly, a milestone is defined to trigger the workflow for delivery, so that once the assembly network is completed, the milestone is triggered and the project delivery team is informed to be prepared.

5.2.9. PS Text

In addition to integrating Project Builder with SAP Document Management System (DMS) for comprehensive document management across S/4HANA, Project Builder offers features for associating various texts with WBSEs and activities for simpler purposes.

PS Texts include plain text entries or attachments in formats like Microsoft Word and Excel that are effective for documenting requirements or instructions for a particular project deliverable.

In the RefineX project, the planning engineer utilizes PS Text to document specific installation instructions for the "Pipe Installation" activity within the construction phase. This text includes references to installation process, safety guidelines, and pipe alignment specifications to be considered during the installation.

Additionally, the planning engineer attached a Microsoft Excel sheet containing a checklist for quality inspections. This documentation ensures that all relevant details are readily available to the site team for efficient communication and adherence to project standards.

5.3. Project Scheduling

Project scheduling within SAP Project System (PS) is a structured process that integrates project planning, resource management, and time management into a cohesive timeline. The scheduling process in SAP PS begins with defining the project structure and activities, and then proceeds to establish the logical sequence, assign durations, and calculate key dates that guide project execution.

After the scope is structured, the user moves on to define work packages as networks and activities. This process is done in close collaboration with teams in engineering, procurement, production, and construction management.

5.3.1. Basic Scheduling Elements

In S/4HANA Project System, Project Builder supports Level 1 and Level 2 of the project through work breakdown structure, while Level 3 uses network activities and Level 4 uses activity elements.

Activity Definition

In larger EPC projects, separate networks are developed for each work package. Number ranges are configured for networks to generate internal network numbers that are unique in the entire system. Activities carry unique identifiers inherited from the network header. The system also supports copying the WBSE code to which the network is assigned as the network ID.

Each activity in a network has four digits prefixed by a unique network number. For example, for 1000011-0002, the first set of seven digits identifies the network ID and second set of four digits identifies the activity number. Network and activity descriptions can be entered separately to identify the name of the work package and the tasks within.

Assigning Durations

Once the activities are defined within the networks, the next step involves assigning durations to each activity. The duration may be a product of the estimating process or may be developed through consensus among the project team planners. These durations enable the system to calculate start and finish dates for each activity.

Set Basic Dates

In SAP Project System, basic dates represent the planned start and finish dates for a project or its elements, such as work breakdown structure (WBS) elements, networks, or activities. These dates are entered or calculated by the system as planned dates during activity planning to establish the initial timeline of the project.

Forecast Dates

SAP Project System uses Forecast Dates as baseline dates. These dates remain unchanged, providing a fixed reference point to compare the current schedule against the original plan and evaluate project performance. For multiple baseline versions, SAP PS provides the functionality of creating project versions.

5.3.2. Scheduling Procedure

During project updates, Basic Dates are updated to reflect the changes in the schedule. For EPC projects, it is recommended to use Network-determined dates rather than WBS-determined dates. Network-determined dates account for the entire network of activities, calculating dates based on the earliest possible start and the latest permissible finish while considering all dependencies and constraints. This method is particularly suited for complex EPC projects with interconnected networks.

Activity Dependencies

SAP PS supports various types of activity dependencies that define how activities are interrelated. These include Finish-to-Start (FS), Start-to-Start (SS), Finish-to-Finish (FF), and Start-to-Finish (SF) relationships. These dependencies determine the sequence of activities to identify the Critical Path of the project and to help the planning team evaluate which activities are critical for keeping the project close to the agreed timeline.

Key Dates Calculations

Once activity logic and dependencies are established, SAP PS calculates the key start and finish dates of the project. Early Start and Early Finish Dates represent the earliest possible times an activity can commence and conclude, determined by network logic and constraints. Conversely,

Late Start and Late Finish Dates specify the latest times an activity can start and finish without affecting subsequent activities (Free Float) or the overall project schedule (Total Float).

Defining all the above scheduling parameters and dependencies, the start and finish dates of each activity and the overall project is calculated to get a project schedule.

Saving the Baseline

Once the schedule is generated, setting a baseline is critical for all stakeholders. The baseline schedule locks the planned schedule as a reference point for all agreements. It creates a snapshot of the planned schedule which serves as a benchmark for monitoring and controlling actual progress.

5.3.3. Advanced Scheduling Scenarios

Factory and Holiday Calendars

During system configuration, setting up different Factory and Holiday Calendars is essential to accurately define the working and non-working days for the project. These calendars ensure that the schedule accounts for holidays and weekends. Multiple Factory Calendars can be configured, and it's recommended to include all applicable combinations, such as 5-day, 6-day, and 7-day calendars, to accommodate the working schedules of different teams. The duration entered in activities will then be interpreted as working times. For more extensive planning, such as in services or turnaround projects, working hours and shifts can also be defined.

Scheduling Parameter

Scheduling profile in SAP PS should be configured to use Strictly Bottom-Up Scheduling scenario as default. In this method of scheduling the activities are scheduled at the lowest level first and then aggregated to respective WBS Elements at the higher levels until the project dates are updated. This approach is particularly important for complex EPC projects, where precise scheduling of individual activities is essential before consolidating them into the overall project schedule.

SAP PS also supports both Forward and Backward Scheduling. In Forward Scheduling the start date of Project Definition is entered, and the system calculates the finish date by progressing forward. In contrast, Backward Scheduling starts with entering the end date and calculates the start date by working backward. Setting Forward Scheduling as default calculates the project finish date and the overall duration by only entering the start date of the project.

Constraints

Schedules often depend on activities managed by others, such as owners or subcontractors. Various constraints control the timing of these activities. For example, delays in design specifications from the customer or equipment delivery from the vendor can significantly impact the project timeline. The system allows for setting constraints like Start No Earlier Than and Finish No Later Than to override the logic and manage when the activity can begin or must be completed.

Schedule Analysis

Gantt charts, Network Charts, and Milestone Trend Analysis are the different views in the Project System that allow the project team to visualize the project.

Gantt chart is the most common visual tools used by project managers to track progress and understand task relationships. Gantt charts, as shown in Figure 5-4 provides visualization of tasks as horizontal bars on a timeline. The project team can easily analyze activity durations, dependencies, start and finish dates, and how the impact is rolled up from activities to WBS to the project definition. By making appropriate settings, SAP PS shows the Critical Path of the project.

Figure 5-4. *Project Gantt Chart*

The Critical Path Method is used to identify the longest sequence of dependent activities that determine the project's minimum completion time. It helps in focusing on tasks that directly impact the project duration and managing potential delays.

After successful execution of scheduling transaction, the schedule identifies the events and activities that are particularly important to the project. These activities are called Critical Activities, and the logical network of these activities is called the Critical Path.

5.4. Conclusion

This chapter highlighted the comprehensive capabilities within SAP S/4HANA for dynamic and precise project planning and scheduling. By mastering the concepts of planning levels, project structure components, and various scheduling procedures, organizations can gain in depth visibility and control over their projects. Building upon this foundation, the next chapter will guide you through the most critical processes of defining and controlling the project scope.

CHAPTER 6

Scope Management

Scope management is a critical process in engineering, procurement, and construction (EPC) projects. It involves defining, controlling, and managing the scope of the project for successful delivery within the defined boundaries of work. With the help of effective scope management, the project management team can avoid scope creep, cost overruns, and schedule delays.

6.1. Scope Statement

A scope statement defines the boundaries and specified objectives of a project. It outlines what is included and what is excluded in the scope of work.

6.2. WBS Development

After the contract is awarded, PrimeCon's project management office conducts scope clarification meetings with various internal and external stakeholders. The objective of these meetings is to clearly identify the deliverables and to determine out-of-scope items.

After receiving formal approval in the form of a letter of intent or a purchase order from the customer, Global Oil Company (GOC), the sales engineer hands over the bid data to the PMO using the DMS.

© Sohail Ahmed 2025
S. Ahmed, *The SAP S/4HANA Handbook for EPC Projects*,
https://doi.org/10.1007/979-8-8688-1466-2_6

The project management office at PrimeCon assigns a planning engineer the task of defining the scope and developing the execution structure—known as the work breakdown structure (WBS). The planning engineer uses a standard EPC project template to copy the first two levels to the operative project and decides to create the lower levels of the WBS using Project Builder features. A typical project work breakdown structure in SAP Project Builder is shown in Figure 6-1.

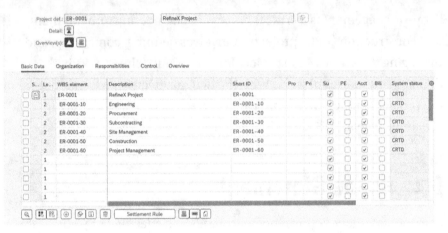

Figure 6-1. *EPC project WBS*

For the RefineX project, the scope encompasses the design, supply, fabrication, and construction of a tank farm and equipment area, including the associated civil works. The WBS would include the following information:

Tank Farm

Design, supply, fabrication, and erection of three vertical steel tanks, including insulation; installation of all associated components, piping, and internal systems.

Equipment Area

Design, supply, and setup of prefabricated skids for the installation of two pumps and one compressor. This includes procurement, delivery, erection, testing, and commissioning of equipment and associated piping, instrumentation, and electrical systems.

Civil Works

Design, supply of material, and construction activities. It includes excavation and backfilling for foundations, concrete work, paving, and drainage work for equipment and tanks.

The scope statement clearly identifies that all engineering, procurement, delivery, prefabrication, erection, and civil works are included in the scope of work.

This section will show how comprehensive scope management through the creation of a hierarchical work breakdown structure using Project Builder can accurately define and structure project deliverables.

6.3. Engineering Scope

The engineering WBS outlines the engineering scope of work. At Level 3, it may be structured into different disciplines, phases, or areas associated with construction. A typical engineering scope structure is depicted in Figure 6-2.

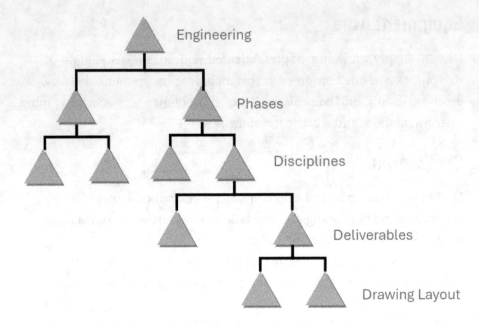

Figure 6-2. *Engineering WBS*

6.3.1. Phases of Engineering

Phases of engineering define the sequential stages in which individual engineering disciplines will work to ensure a technically viable and compliant solution is designed.

Basic Design

This phase involves high-level conceptual design. It includes development of foundational documents.

Detailed Engineering

This phase further refines and expands the deliverables from the basic design and provides the necessary detail for procurement, fabrication, and erection activities.

6.3.2. Engineering Disciplines

Engineering disciplines are the specialized branches of engineering that focus on the design, analysis, and implementation of a system. Each discipline is focused on the functionality, safety, economy, and efficiency of the design with a goal to optimize the whole solution.

Process Engineering

Process engineering focuses on the design, optimization, and implementation of processes for creating products such as petrochemicals.

Structural and Civil Engineering

Structural and civil engineering covers the design and construction of buildings and infrastructure. Structural engineering focuses on the analysis and design of structural elements to ensure the safety and stability of buildings and infrastructure, while civil engineering deals with the planning, design, construction, and operations of infrastructure facilities, including roads and water supply systems.

Mechanical, Electrical, and Plumbing (MEP)

MEP engineering encompasses the design and integration of mechanical, electrical, and plumbing systems within buildings. It ensures that these systems work seamlessly to provide essential services.

Piping Engineering

Piping involves the design and layout of pipes and related components to transport fluids within industrial facilities. It includes material selection, routing, and support to ensure safe and efficient fluid flow.

6.3.3. Engineering Deliverables

Engineering deliverables are technical documents, including drawings, specifications, and reports, that serve as a blueprint for the manufacturing, construction, procurement, and operational phases of a project.

Basic Engineering Deliverables

These are the preliminary outputs of the engineering phase and provide foundational information about the design, such as design calculations, preliminary general arrangement (GA) drawings, process flow diagrams (PFD), and preliminary structural plans.

Detailed Engineering Deliverables

These are comprehensive drawings and documents produced during the advanced stages of the engineering phase. These documents include fabrication, assembly, and construction methods; shopfloor, assembly, and isometric drawings; piping and instrumentation diagrams (P&IDs), and so on.

6.3.4. Engineering WBS Design

The engineering WBSE may be divided into two phases at Level 3, and then each phase will define deliverables. This approach is simple and offers a clear representation of project scope identification within the phase. For an engineering project this may be a good structure; however, for an EPC project, this structure does not address the complexity where the procurement, shipping, and site planning also play a significant role and impact the flow of work for the engineering teams.

The engineering WBS for an EPC project should consider not only the scoping and scheduling of design and engineering deliverables, but also how each engineering deliverable is aligned with the material planning, fabrication sequence, and construction site layout.

With the preceding consideration, the planning engineer of the RefineX project works closely with the engineering coordinator to define the engineering WBS. After the collaboration is completed, the planning engineer defines the engineering scope of work in Project Builder using WBS. Figure 6-3 shows a glimpse of this scoping exercise.

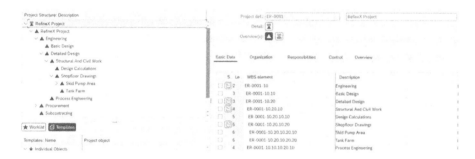

Figure 6-3. *Scoping excercise*

The last level is optional, but it is effective to further break down the deliverables to match the engineering scope with the fabrication and construction scope.

At this level, the scope is divided to match with the specific sections of the construction plan, such as zones (such as Tanks Zone, Equipment Zone, etc.), areas (Utility Area, Warehouse, etc.), buildings, floors, and so on. Construction scope will be discussed later in section 6.7.

Due to incomplete design details at the initial planning stage, the planning engineer creates a WBS up to Level 4, Discipline level. As engineering work progresses and design details emerge, the WBS is refined to include the lower-level *deliverables*. The last WBS level, where applicable, includes Drawing Layouts, incorporating specific deliverables and site layout considerations.

At the initial stage of a project, complete details are often unavailable due to the need for a detailed design and full scope definition. Consequently, the planning engineer creates a high-level WBS. Initially, the WBS includes elements up to Level 4, representing the disciplines, but as the engineering tasks progress and more details are received from the engineering team, additional WBS elements are developed at lower levels.

6.4. Procurement Scope

A procurement WBS is a hierarchical breakdown of all project-specific materials, consumables, and assets to identify the procurement scope and control procure-to-pay processes. Figure 6-4 depicts this hierarchy.

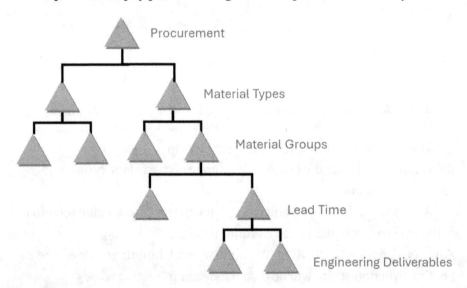

Figure 6-4. *Procurement heirarchy*

6.4.1. Material Types and Categories

The variety of materials impact the design decision for structuring the procurement WBS to the next levels. Following are the types of materials used in EPC projects.

Direct Material

The raw materials and components that are used directly in the fabrication and construction processes of an EPC project. These materials are traceable to the final products. In EPC projects direct materials typically include piping material (specific pipe types), structural materials (rebar, channels, etc.), civil material (aggregate, ready-mix concrete), electric cables, and so forth.

Equipment

Equipment refers to the mechanical systems and machinery installed within a facility that performs specific functions essential to the plant's operations. Equipment is grouped as stationary and rotary equipment:

1. **Stationary Equipment**: Equipment that is permanently installed as part of the infrastructure and does not move or rotate, such as heat exchangers, pressure vessels, boilers, and tanks.

2. **Rotary Equipment**: Equipment that has moving or rotating parts as a key aspect of its function. This type of equipment includes pumps, compressors, turbines, etc.

Consumables

These are material types that are consumed during a process but are not part of the final product. Consumables are grouped as follows:

1. **Direct Consumables**: These items are necessary for the execution of construction activities but are typically not tracked as direct materials. For example, welding material, cutting tools, lubricants, etc.

2. **Indirect Consumables**: Materials used to support the overall operations of a company but not directly involved in the production process. For example, office supplies, cleaning materials, and maintenance supplies.

Project Assets

Assets are the tangible resources acquired or created specifically for a project and used to generate project outputs. They are categorized as follows:

1. **Acquired Assets**: Project assets generally purchased or leased specifically for a project and obtained through procurement process only. For example, tools and equipment, vehicles, software, etc.

2. **Constructed Assets**: These assets are generally part of project activities. These assets include engineering, procurement, and construction tasks and can be considered under Site Preparation scope.

a. **Temporary Assets**: These are built for use during the project, such as site facilities for personnel. These assets are not intended for long-term use beyond the project's duration.

b. **Permanent Assets**: These are either part of the main scope of the project as a deliverable to the customer; for example, dormitories and workshops may be used for the project and later may continue to be used as part of the facility.

6.4.2. Integration with Finance

The accounting treatment of an asset depends on both the project lifecycle and the asset's lifespan. For instance, some acquired tools might be classified as consumables rather than assets. Conversely, constructed assets with a long duration may initially be recorded as Assets Under Construction, with different accounting treatments applied. Since WBS elements are closely integrated with S/4HANA Finance—Asset Accounting, it is essential to consider that, while configuring S/4HANA FI-AA, all aspects of the procurement WBS are covered.

6.4.3. Integration with Materials Management

The WBS elements are seamlessly linked with S/4HANA MM objects. Although not mandatory, defining material groups and material types in S/4HANA MM with the procurement structure during SAP S/4HANA implementation is highly beneficial. The closer the S/4HANA MM configuration and master data settings align with the project's material planning, budgeting, and costing requirements, the easier and more effective the reporting will be.

6.4.4. Lead Time

Another categorization necessary in procurement of material for EPC projects is influenced by the demand generated from the projects and the timely availability of the material. Materials are therefore categorized based on their lead times to optimize inventories and avoid delays.

Long Lead Item

Direct materials, consumables, or equipment that require extended procurement cycle due to various reasons, and items that are imported, have manufacturing complexity, or are identified as bottlenecks due to supplier capacity or transportation logistics are typically planned as long lead items. Long lead items also require special attention during project scheduling.

Short Lead Item

A material or equipment that can be procured relatively quickly with shorter lead times. Items that are off-the-shelf or are not falling on the critical path of the project are considered short lead items.

6.4.5. Procurement WBS Design

Considering the preceding factors, the planning engineer of the RefineX project, after gathering the required information from the engineering coordinator and collaborating with the procurement team, develops the procurement WBS shown in Figure 6-5.

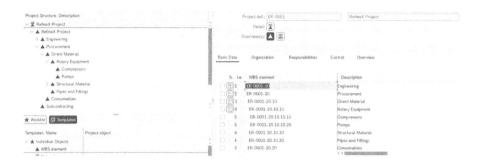

Figure 6-5. *Procurement WBS*

This procurement WBS is structured to encompass the project material delivery scope and procurement processes, including project material requirements planning, initiation of purchasing requests, managing material reservations, tracking goods receipt and issuance, and controlling procurement budget.

Similar to the engineering WBS, the last two levels of the procurement WBS—lead time and engineering deliverables—are optional.

When it comes to requirement grouping, the planning engineer of the RefineX project decides to opt out of this feature and chooses to handle the procurement planning using preliminary procurement method, explained in Section 7.3.10.

6.5. Subcontracting Scope

The subcontracting WBS is used to plan and control all subcontracting and service procurement activities. For projects where the subcontracting budget is not significant or does not require separate approval, this WBSE can be created under the procurement WBSE.

For larger projects, however, the subcontracting WBSE should be separate from the procurement WBS structure, as shown in Figure 6-6.

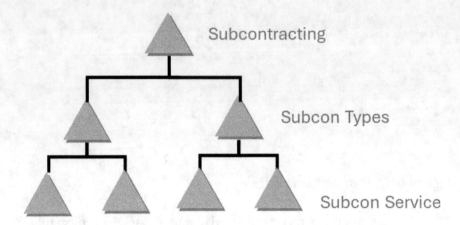

Figure 6-6. *Subcontracting WBS*

The subcontracting WBS may be expanded to lower levels to handle multiple types of services. Figure 6-7 shows the subcontracting structure created for the RefineX project.

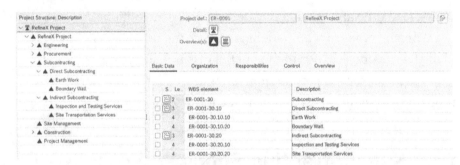

Figure 6-7. *Subcontracting WBS example*

6.5.1. Direct Subcontracting

Direct subcontracting refers to third-party services that are directly attributable to the project's primary deliverables. For examples, in an EPC project, detailed design, foundation preparation, structural welding, and earth work, when subcontracted, are considered direct subcontracted services.

6.5.2. Indirect Subcontracting

Indirect subcontracting refers to services supporting the project indirectly and are not directly attributable to primary deliverables. Indirect subcontracted services in an EPC project often include logistics and transportation, third-party testing, calibration, and so on.

6.6. Site Management

In EPC projects, site management oversees all on-site activities required to facilitate construction work. This process starts with project initiation and continues until the maintenance period ends. Site management covers a wide range of tasks. Therefore, for successful project execution, site management tasks must be wisely planned. Following are tasks that must be planned using a site management work breakdown structure, as shown in Figure 6-8.

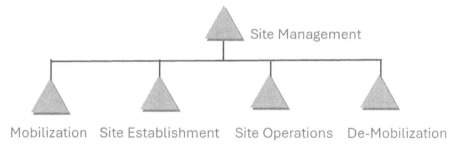

Figure 6-8. *Site management WBS*

6.6.1. Site Mobilization

Site mobilization refers to a well-planned and organized deployment of project resources. It is categorized as follows.

Personnel Mobilization

This process involves deploying the necessary workforce, including engineers, supervisors, and construction workers, to the project site. It includes arranging travel and accommodations, and ensuring the health and safety of the personnel.

Equipment Mobilization

This process involves route planning and transportation of heavy machinery and equipment, such as cranes, excavators, and generators, at the construction site. It ensures that the equipment is in proper working condition.

6.6.2. Site Establishment

Site establishment refers to the process of preparing and enabling a construction site for construction activities. This process involves preparing site access, providing site security, and constructing site facilities.

The topic of site facilities as constructed assets has been covered under the section of Project Assets, but the activities for the construction of temporary and permanent facilities will be covered under the site establishment WBSE.

6.6.3. Site Operations

Site operations refers to the ongoing day-to-day activities necessary for the timely completion of construction tasks. This includes administration of daily movement and scheduling of labor and staff, managing accommodations, transportation, and travel arrangements, and record-keeping. It also includes supervising the indirect construction and maintenance of temporary facilities and site utilities. In essence, all these elements are essential to provide an organized, safe, and cost-effective construction environment.

6.6.4. Site Demobilization

Site demobilization refers to the comprehensive closedown and cleanup of a project site. It includes personnel and equipment demobilization, clearing all the debris, removing leftover material from the site, and the closure of temporary offices, facilities, and accommodations.

   Demobilization also includes landscaping, which refers to the restoration of the project site to its original or to the contractually specified state.

6.7. Construction Scope

The term *construction* refers to the activities involved in building or assembling infrastructure at the project owner's site. Figure 6-9 provides a visual illustration of how construction projects are typically structured. It shows the work breakdown from broader categories into more detailed components.

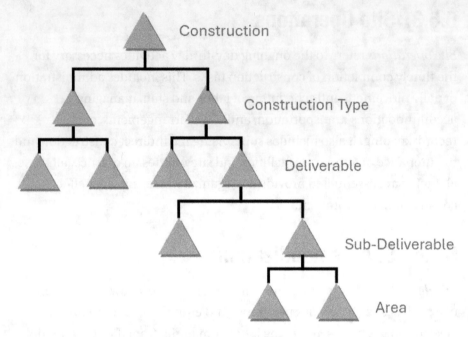

Figure 6-9. *Construction WBS*

In EPC projects, different styles of construction are adopted. Following are the three most common styles.

6.7.1. Traditional Construction

In traditional construction, all construction activities are performed directly on site. Raw materials are delivered to the site, and site construction activities are carried out using small-scale on-site workshops.

This approach relies completely on assembling and building the entire structure from scratch on site. Earth work, building construction, and so forth are some of its examples.

6.7.2. Pre-Fabricated Construction

Pre-fabrication refers to the manufacturing of components or assemblies in specialized workshops off site and transporting the assemblies and parts to the construction site. Erection refers to the on-site installation of these pre-fabricated components or assemblies to complete the structure. This method is common in large industrial and infrastructure projects, such as refineries, stadiums, hospitals, and so on.

6.7.3. Modular Construction

Modular construction uses pre-fabricated units, also called modules. The term *modules* refers to units with various components and systems assembled into a complete package. These modules are designed to be integrated into a larger system or structure. Examples of these modules include oil skids, modular offices, and so on. These modules are manufactured off site and installed on site.

6.8. Construction WBS Design

After reviewing the scope statement, the planning engineer decides to develop the construction WBS. Since the scope of work could involve a combination of traditional, modular, and pre-fabricated construction methods, and it is not possible to definitively select the construction type at this early stage, the planning engineer extends the WBS to cover all three types. This approach ensures that the WBS is flexible and comprehensive.

The planning engineer also aligns the construction WBS with the engineering and procurement WBS. This alignment ensures that on-site construction activities are coordinated with design, pre-fabrication, material procurement, and deliveries. The resulting structure, as shown in Figure 6-10, covers the entire construction scope, with each distinct deliverable enabling resource allocation, budget control, scope change control, and project schedule control.

Figure 6-10. *Construction WBS example*

6.9. Conclusion

This chapter exhibited how SAP Project System effectively converted a complex scope statement into meaningful objects that offered a clear and structured overview of all deliverables and scope items. By utilizing Project Builder's project structuring functionality, PrimeCon achieved its objectives. Further functionalities will be discussed in the following chapters, where each WBSE serves as an individual object that provides seamless integration with the other objects of S/4HANA for planning, budgeting, and performance evaluation. Each WBSE supports the assessment of internal teams, vendors, and subcontractors' performance against contractual obligations.

CHAPTER 7

Engineer-to-Order Planning

Engineer-to-order (ETO) planning in EPC projects is an integrated approach of making a detailed plan where the engineering, procurement, fabrication, and construction plans are created with the consideration of their interdependencies.

The integrated planning process begins with the creation of detailed engineering plans. These plans provide details of materials needed for subsequent procurement activities and for timely acquisition of these materials. Finally, the fabrication tasks are planned with component-level material details, followed by the delivery of assemblies to the construction site.

This section is focused on the critical aspects of creating networks and activities, the assignment of materials, and drawing within the project structure. Detailed discussion of the corresponding resource and cost planning are found in their respective chapters.

7.1. Engineering Plan

The planning engineer reviews the bid plan to assess the overall scope and timeline to identify the required man-days and planned duration for the engineering tasks. The engineering plan ensures that internal design

© Sohail Ahmed 2025
S. Ahmed, *The SAP S/4HANA Handbook for EPC Projects*,
https://doi.org/10.1007/979-8-8688-1466-2_7

engineers are adequately allocated to execute the project. This initial assessment lays the foundation for the engineering plan. The details of internal resource planning will be discussed in Chapter 8.

7.1.1. Engineering Plan Development

Figure 7-1 depicts the engineering plan for the steel structure up to the issuance of fabrication and erection drawings for the pump.

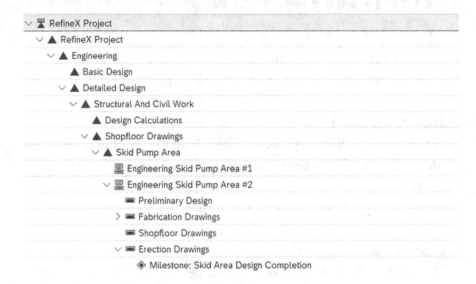

Figure 7-1. *Engineering plan development in Project Builder*

In the Skid Pump Area section, engineering activities are structured into multiple work packages, including *Engineering Skid Pump Area #1* and *Engineering Skid Pump Area #2*. Each of these packages contains activities such as Preliminary Design, Fabrication Drawings, Shopfloor Drawings, and Erection Drawings. The network activities are linked logically so that predecessor tasks must be completed before successor tasks begin.

In this case, the completion of erection drawings would trigger the billing of skid area design by setting the milestone *Skid Area Design Completion* as completed. The milestone helps track the progress of *Skid Pump Area* and ensures alignment with project billing timelines.

7.1.2. Engineering Documentation

The engineering team prepares a document control register (DCR) to list all engineering deliverables to be generated as part of the engineering plan. A simple script and a report can be developed in SAP S/4HANA using data from SAP Document Management System (DMS) module to generate a plan serving the purpose of a DCR. This plan can later be used to compare planned document release with each document created in the system.

After the DCR is handed over to the planning engineer, the planning engineer uses it as the base document for the development of the Level 3 engineering plan. The planning engineer reviews the DCR and creates the plan using internal activities in SAP PS Project Builder under thee engineering WBS hierarchy.

Engineering Document Types

The engineering team used different DMS document types, as shown in Table 7-1. These document types are configured at PrimeCon to track and control different types of engineering deliverables throughout the project lifecycle.

Table 7-1. *DMS Document Types*

Doc Type	Description	Purpose
PDD	Preliminary Design Drawings	These drawings identify the completion of holistic design and are used to initiate long lead procurement.
SFD	Shopfloor Drawings	These drawings outline the procedures for fabrication of individual parts and the process of combining these components in assemblies. To further distinguish the deliverables, separate document types may be used for fabrication drawings, shopfloor drawings, and assembly drawings.
ERD	Erection Drawings	These drawings address the installation of the assemblies on project site, such as connections and alignment.
GCD	General Construction Drawings	These drawings provide detailed instructions for the construction process, including excavation, concrete placement, formwork, etc.
ASB	As-Built Drawings	These drawings document the final version of the design as per the approved construction.

Document Part

Document Part is a great feature for engineering documents. It subdivides the main document into subdocument parts, which is especially useful with larger document structures.

The engineering coordinator, while checking-in construction drawings for Foundation of Pump B, subdivided the document into four parts: Soil Investigation Reports, Foundation Design Calculation, Reinforcement Drawings, and Concrete Mix Design.

Document Status

The S/4HANA at PrimeCon has been configured to use different statuses to clearly identify the document in different stages of a drawing, as shown in Table 7-2.

Table 7-2. *Document Statuses*

Status	Description	Significance
IFR	Issued for Review	This status identifies initial release for internal review.
IFA	Issued for Approval	This status identifies submission for customer approval.
IFP	Issued for Procurement	This status identifies the release of preliminary design drawings for material procurement.
IFC	Issued for Construction	This status identifies that the fabrication, shopfloor, assembly, or construction drawings are issued for execution.

Changes in the engineering documents will be handled through the engineering change management (ECM) process. The details of ECM will be discussed in Chapter 12.

Object Link

An object link in SAP DMS establishes a connection between a document information record (DIR) and a specific SAP business object, such as WBSE, network activity, purchase order line item, and so on. This link enables users to easily access relevant documents directly from the associated SAP transaction without a need to open the DMS transaction.

Once the engineering documents are released, the engineering coordinator links the drawings with appropriate project activity using the SAP DMS Object Link feature. Figure 7-2 shows documents from SAP DMS linked with the respective activity of the engineering work package using SAP PS Project Builder.

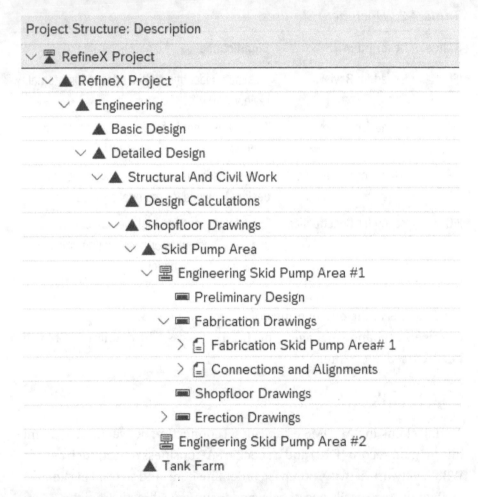

Figure 7-2. *Engineering documentation using SAP DMS in Project Builder*

This process links drawings and other related engineering documents with relevant activity and makes them available in read-only mode to the team members of other functions based on their access control.

Document Distribution Function

The document distribution function is used to distribute original files checked in to the document information record. Using this functionality, the user can send the files in an email to SAP users and email addresses.

The engineering coordinator uses the SAP DMS document distribution functionality to distribute the documents to those team members who are not directly using the DMS documents using SAP objects, such as work breakdown structure elements, purchase orders, or notifications. The team has already created different recipient lists with team members who would collaborate on the project with their access rights defined for document types.

7.2. MRP Fundamentals

Material requirements planning (MRP) is the master plan managing all project-related procurement. It encompasses the processes from requisition to issuance of material and consumables required as per project specifications, budget, and timeline. There are distinctive features of the material requirements planning offered by SAP S/4HANA that can be used independently or be combined with each other for planning materials for the project. In addition to offering different materials planning options, SAP S/4HANA uses MRP Live as a new planning tool that offers significant performance improvements.

This section explains these features so as to build a basic understanding of material requirements planning using SAP PS. Before getting into the details of engineer-to-order planning, let's first understand the basic concepts.

7.2.1. Project Stock

The procurement activities are assigned to the lowest level of the procurement WBS under the respective work breakdown structure element (WBSE). The planning engineer must identify the WBSE where each type of material is to be allocated. Organizations executing multiple projects in parallel need to identify and separate project-specific direct materials and consumables from those of other projects. Additionally, they may want to segregate different material types for inventory and budget control.

In SAP PS, each WBSE of every project within the same client can be treated as a separate project stock. As shown in Figure 7-3, SAP PS provides options to define a WBSE as a stock reference point, resulting in the creation of project stock, which can be either valuated or non-valuated.

Figure 7-3. *Valuated stock with automatic requirements grouping*

A valuated project stock allows materials to be managed for both quantity and cost, while a non-valuated project stock manages materials only for their quantity. SAP also offers the option to set a project as No Project Stock. In this case no project stock is maintained for the project, and materials are managed for multiple projects from a collective stock, known as plant stock.

It is important to note that for EPC projects, only selecting the valuated project stock option provides the desired level of control over the project procurement plan.

7.2.2. Item Categories

Item categories are used in the system to distinguish the procurement and inventory management behavior of a material. There are many item categories defined in SAP S/4HANA, as shown in Figure 7-4.

ICt	Item Category Descripti...
C	Compatible Unit
E	Enhanced Limit
L	Stock item
M	Intra material
N	Non-stock item
P	Preliminary Item
R	Variable-size item
T	Text item

Figure 7-4. *Standard item categories*

Item categories help classify materials and services based on their procurement, inventory, and usage characteristics within the system. In EPC, the following two item categories are common:

Non-Stock Item (N)

This category refers to materials not kept in inventory but rather procured directly for a project. These items are typically delivered directly to the site and are consumed immediately upon documenting the goods receipt. No inventory is maintained in the system. Non-stock items show similar behavior as externally processed network activities, so their use should be limited to items that do not require inventory control, such as water used for construction activities, concrete mix for onsite pouring, and small non-returnable tools.

Stock Item (L)

This category refers to materials maintained in SAP MM (material master). Stock items are shown in project inventory upon good receipts and are consumed only through good-issuance processes in the SAP MM module. In this book, unless explicitly mentioned, only the stock item category is discussed.

7.2.3. Requirement Grouping

SAP PS provides the functionality to group material requirements for a particular WBS element. A requirement grouping WBS element is a WBS element with valuated project stock where the requirements from several WBS elements are grouped together for the MRP. SAP provides two options for requirement grouping.

Automatic Requirement Grouping

By setting this indicator in the project definition, as shown in Figure 7-3, the root WBS element is set as the grouping WBS element. This action makes the entire project stock a single project stock. This approach combines all the project material requirements as one under the root WBSE, and all material components assigned to this project are grouped under a single material plan.

For EPC projects, however, this method is overly simplistic and often impractical due to the complexity and diversity of materials required in such projects.

Manual Requirements Grouping

For more complex requirements, where more than one WBS element is required for requirement and stock grouping, SAP allows the manual entry of WBSEs for defining the grouping WBSE, as shown in Figure 7-5. Material components can be assigned to different grouping WBS elements for more granular control.

Grouping WBS ele...	Short Description
■	Not a grouping WBS element
1	Grouping WBS element for all materials
2	Grouping WBS element for selected MRP groups

Figure 7-5. *Manual requirements grouping for a specified WBS element*

7.2.4. Procurement Types

Procurement types identify the type of demand for a material for a particular project. In S/4HANA, as shown in Figure 7-6, this behavior is controlled by providing different configurable procurement types.

Pln ≜	Description
■ PEV	Planned independent reqmnts for WBS
PF	PReq for WBS
PFS	Third party requisition for WBS
PFV	Prelim. req. for WBS
WE	Reservation plant stock

Figure 7-6. *Procurement types available for project-related procurement*

The following are the most commonly used procurement types in an EPC project.

Preliminary Requisition for WBS

This procurement type allows the user to create an initial or preliminary purchase requisition for the project stock without creating any reservations. The usefulness of this procurement type is that as the project progresses and more details become available, sometimes the material components need to be reassigned to activities more relevant to issuance. The material components before issuance must also be available in the same WBS stock.

Reservation for Network

This procurement type is used when no procurement is generated from the Project Builder or in combination with *Preliminary Requisition for WBS*. This procurement type, shown in Figure 7-7, allows the user to create reservations from the detailed activities where the materials are moved.

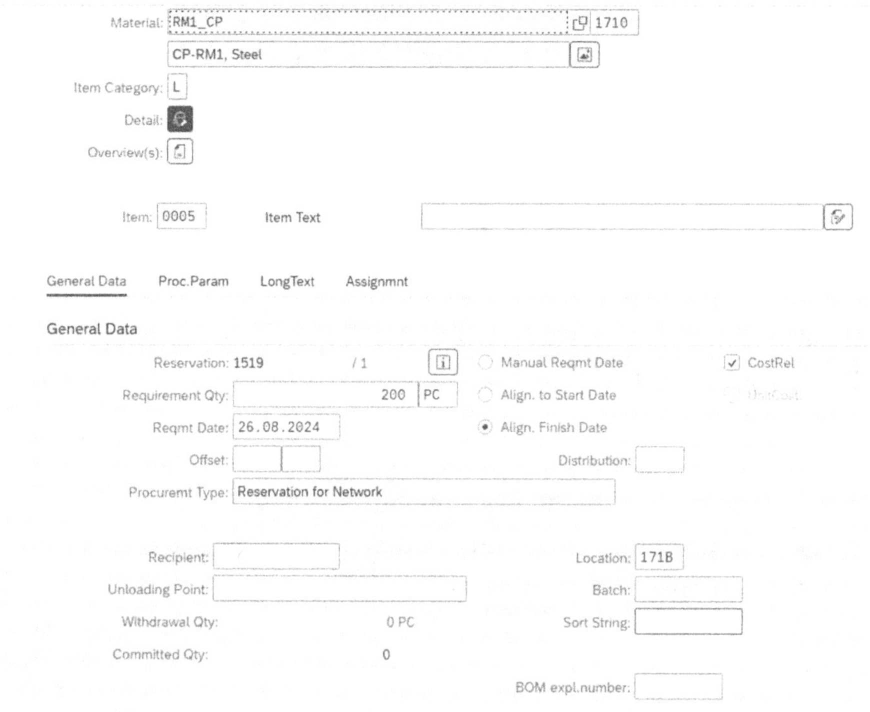

Figure 7-7. *Reservation of material for a project*

A *reservation* is a request to issue the materials against a planned material. It creates a demand for the material in the system. Unique reservation numbers are used in the SAP system to issue stock to the project.

When the demand arises for a material on a project, a reservation is created for the project. Reservations may be created manually, but for network and maintenance orders reservations are auto-generated. This demand is viewed by the MRP controller, who checks the availability of the material in stock. If the material is available, it is issued against the reservation; otherwise, a purchase requisition is created.

This procurement type is only suitable where a significant amount of procurement is required to be procured in bulk, the material management requirements are complex, and the budget control requires separate budget approvals for procurement and fabrication or construction.

Purchase Requisition + Reservation

Projects with significant bulk procurement, complex material management, or strict budget control should use the combination of preliminary PR and reservations. This procurement type allows the user to create a purchase requisition (PR) for materials needed for a specific network activity. Simultaneously, it creates a reservation with reference to the same activity. It is helpful when, at the time of PR, the user also wants the reservation to be created to ensure that the material, soon after goods receipt, is available in stock and reserved for the issuance to the same activity.

7.2.5. WBS BOM

In SAP PS, these material components are assigned to procurement activities using Project Builder. The material components can either be assigned directly to network activities using SAP Project System's Project Builder or by means of transfer of material using a WBS bill of materials (BOM).

WBS BOM Creation

In WBS BOM, the concept of a bill of materials is integrated with a specific WBS, creating a WBS-specific BOM. A WBS BOM is similar to a material BOM in its functionalities. It offers a detailed breakdown of materials required for a particular project deliverable, sub-deliverable, or drawing, tailored to the unique requirements of each deliverable.

Unlike a material BOM, which is typically used to structure a product in product lifecycle management (PLM)—and is treated as master data with limited variants in S/4HANA—a WBS BOM offers far more flexibility. It allows unlimited combinations that can be tailored uniquely for each new WBS.

To create a WBS BOM, the SAP requires both a WBS element and a material. In the EPC context, where material requirements do not follow a fixed product structure, this requirement is not meaningful. To address this, a dummy or reference material is created and used only to satisfy system requirement. This workaround allows users to set up the WBS BOM structure reusing a dummy material across multiple WBS elements. For example, in Figure 7-8 material **RM203** serves as a dummy reference that has no direct link with actual project requirements, but can be reused with multiple WBS elements, provided that each WBS–material combination is unique. The actual project-specific materials are then added within the BOM structure itself, while the dummy serves only as a technical placeholder.

Selection of activities

Project definition:	ER-0001
WBS Element:	ER-0001-20.101	to:
Sales Document:		Item:
Network:		To:

Selection profile

Profile: ZBT1   Profile: WBS BOM Transfer

Selection of BOM items

WBS Element: *	ER-0001-20.101		
Material:	RM203		
Plant:	1710	Valid from: *	26.02.2025
BOM Usage:	2	Change Number:	C000010012
Alternative BOM:		☐ Const. change number	

WBS Element	ER-0001-20.101	Pumps
Material	RM203	
	Raw Material RM203	
Plant	1710	Plant 1 US

[Position]   [Effectivity Initial Screen]

Material   Document   General

Item	ICt	Component	Component description	Quantity	Uo.
☐ 0020	N	SS20981	H-Beam, ASTM A992	12	TON
☐ 0030	N	SS20945	Steel Plate, ASTM A36 for Anchor Bolts	7	TON
☐ 0040	N	SS20561	Steel Angle, ASTM A36, HD Galvanized	2	TON
☐ 0050	N	SS20988	C-Channel, ASTM A36	2	TON
☐ 0060					

Figure 7-8. *Creation of WBS BOM*

BOM Transfer

In a WBS BOM, material components are logically grouped against a WBSE. The user can execute a detailed MRP by selecting the relevant WBS BOM required for each WBSE, rather than selecting individual materials. Once the BOM is selected, it can be assigned to an activity through BOM transfer.

Reference Point

The mapping between the WBS BOM and the activity is created by assigning the "reference point" respective network activity. The reference point must be configured and assigned in the system before executing a BOM transfer.

7.3. Procurement Plan

The objective of procurement planning using SAP PS Project Builder is to deliver project-specific direct materials and consumables in a timely manner. This plan must be closely linked with the engineering plan.

7.3.1. Initial Planning

The procurement tasks are defined as network activities in SAP PS. While detailed engineering tasks may take a longer time to finish, the procurement process must be initiated for long lead items before all engineering details are finalized. Therefore, the materials are planned in stages: first a high-level material plan based on an initial material take off (MTO), followed by the final plan based on the detailed MTO.

The network of activities in the procurement plan is used to determine the delivery dates for project-specific direct materials and consumables based on the engineering plan.

The planning engineer creates a material plan using the internally processed activities without assigning any work center, as the resources required for procurement are indirect in nature. The objective is to develop an initial material plan based on engineering documents and preliminary MTO results.

The engineering documents are reviewed to identify long lead items and bulk procurement requirements. The outcome of review is the preliminary material plan detailing the high-priority materials with extended lead times, with specifications such as material types, quantities, and required delivery dates.

7.3.2. Detailed Planning Networks

The planning engineer creates separate networks for procurement and material control. The procurement network(s) define the tasks, their duration, and the sequence in which the procurement is conducted.

The decision on the number of networks for procurement and material-issuance activities depends on the scope of the project. The activities planned for both the procurement and the fabrication networks can be standardized to expedite the planning process by using the standard network copy function. The purpose of creating fabrication network(s) is discussed later, in section 7.4.

7.3.3. Procurement Subtasks

The planning engineer, after defining the networks and activities, refines the material plan with detailed engineering drawings and procurement schedules. During this planning process, the material plan is further detailed by adding sub-activities and updated with material specifications and quantities.

As shown in the example of RefineX in Figure 7-9, network activities for the procurement of structural material are divided into activity elements: RFQ Issues, PO Issued, and Material Arrived. Additionally, specific material components are integrated into the project structure.

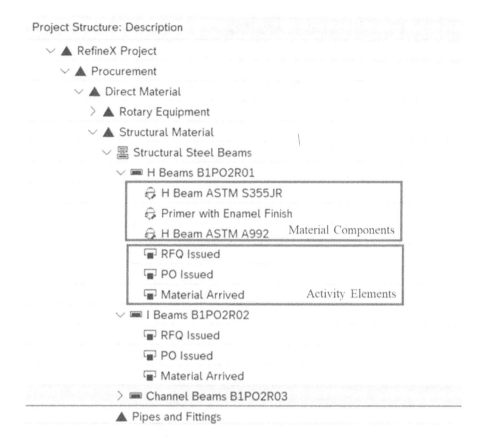

Figure 7-9. Procurement plan development in Project Builder

The planning engineer further breaks down the activities to a more granular level by defining sub-activities. This is done by assigning activity elements to the network activities of the procurement network.

For example, the activity elements of procurement activities act as subtasks and track the progress at the level that represents execution, such as material sourcing, vendor selection, RFQ issuance, and so on.

7.3.4. Procurement Dates

The material requirement dates are aligned with the start or finish date of the activity to which the material is assigned. As shown in Figure 7-10, these requirement dates can be further adjusted by adding lead or lag time—in absolute terms or a percentage.

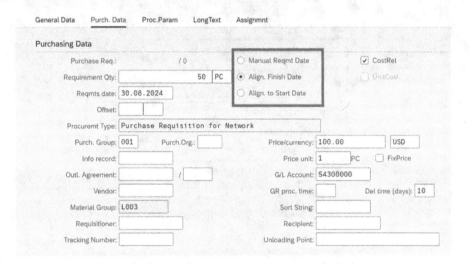

Figure 7-10. *Procurement dates alignment with network activities*

The dates from the material are then copied to purchase requisitions (PR) and subsequently transferred to purchase orders (PO) as the delivery deadline. Although material dates can be entered manually, the optimal use of PS–MM integration is to derive delivery dates from the activity dates.

7.3.5. Procurement Documentation

Procurement activities are available as object links in SAP DMS for assigning procurement-related documents. The procurement coordinator, based on the access control defined in SAP, can attach procurement-related documents—such as material specifications and special instructions to vendors—directly to procurement activities within the project structure using the SAP document management system (SAP DMS).

After the procurement activities are released and the purchase requisition (PR) is created, these documents are transferred to the PR as DMS documents. This integration ensures that all relevant documents are accessible and linked to specific procurement tasks, streamlining the document-handling process in S/4HANA.

7.3.6. Material Take Off (MTO)

An MTO is a detailed document of materials with specific quantities and technical specifications required for project execution. In SAP PS, the material components are assigned to activities using Project Builder. The material components can either be assigned directly to the network activities or by means of BOM transfer using S/4HANA WBS BOM functionality.

The term *bill of materials* (BOM) refers to a structured list of parts, components, subassemblies, and raw materials necessary to build a product or assembly. While a BOM is similar in nature to an MTO, it focuses on the hierarchical relationship between components and their quantities within a product structure.

For the RefineX project, the Planning engineer creates two types of bill of materials: preliminary BOM and detailed BOM.

7.3.7. Preliminary BOM

Preliminary BOM focuses on the bulk procurement of long lead and critical components, such as structural materials required for fabrication, packaged equipment, cables, and so on. The purpose is to initiate the procurement process in a timely manner and ensure that all necessary materials are sourced and procured according to project timelines and customer requirements.

147

The engineering team of the RefineX project creates the preliminary BOM in S/4HANA at the completion of the basic design of a particular deliverable or sub-deliverable. The details of material components and associated drawings, as shown in Figure 7-11, are extracted from the preliminary design documents, and drawings are set to status *Issued for Procurement* status in SAP DMS. The extracted list of material components is then created in the SAP S/4HANA WBS BOM by the engineering coordinator, who also creates the preliminary BOM.

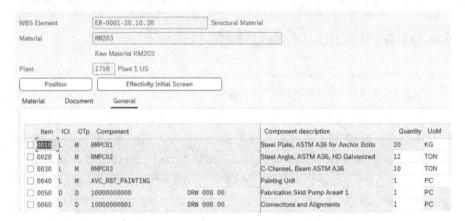

Figure 7-11. *Creation of the bill of materials and documents using WBS BOM*

A detailed BOM is created during fabrication planning after complete engineering details are issued by the engineering department. These details will be covered in section 7.4.

7.3.8. Setup Reference Points

After the procurement WBS BOM(s) and material plans are ready, the planning engineer assigns the reference point and maps activities to relevant material components in the WBS BOM. This setup, as shown in Figure 7-12, allows for effective BOM transfer and material planning for project activities.

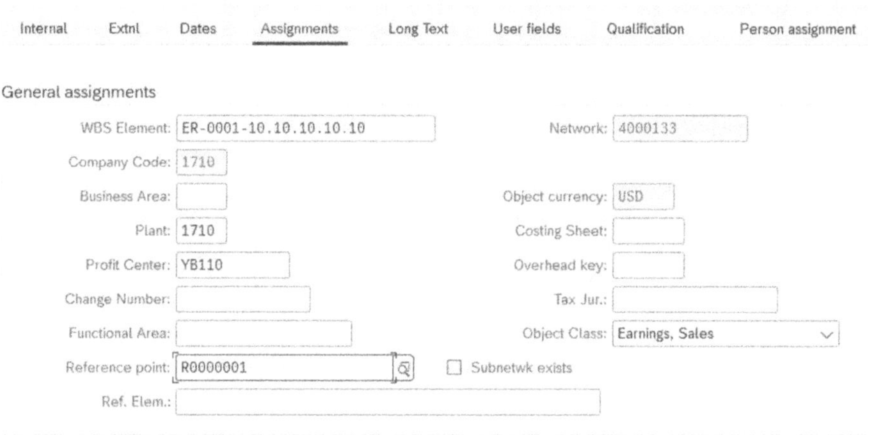

Internal	Extnl	Dates	Assignments	Long Text	User fields	Qualification	Person assignment

General assignments

WBS Element:	ER-0001-10.10.10.10.10	Network: 4000133
Company Code:	1710	
Business Area:		Object currency: USD
Plant:	1710	Costing Sheet:
Profit Center:	YB110	Overhead key:
Change Number:		Tax Jur.:
Functional Area:		Object Class: Earnings, Sales ⌄
Reference point:	R0000001 🔍	☐ Subnetwk exists
Ref. Elem.:		

Figure 7-12. Reference point on network activity for WBS BOM transfer

7.3.9. Preliminary BOM Transfer

Before executing a BOM transfer, the planning engineer also ensures that for preliminary BOM the "Preliminary requirements" indicator is activated, as shown in Figure 7-13.

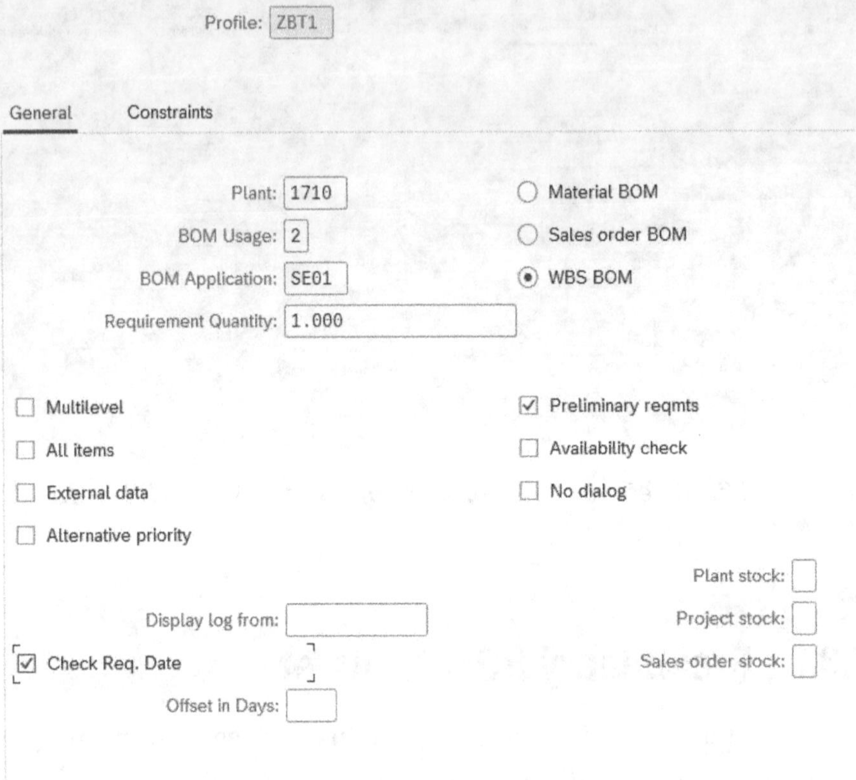

Profile: ZBT1

General   Constraints

Plant: 1710   ○ Material BOM
BOM Usage: 2   ○ Sales order BOM
BOM Application: SE01   ● WBS BOM
Requirement Quantity: 1.000

☐ Multilevel   ☑ Preliminary reqmts
☐ All items   ☐ Availability check
☐ External data   ☐ No dialog
☐ Alternative priority

                                                              Plant stock: ☐
Display log from: [   ]   Project stock: ☐
☑ Check Req. Date   Sales order stock: ☐
Offset in Days: [   ]

Figure 7-13. Preliminary requirements indicator

Selecting this option will create a preliminary purchase requisition for materials transferred from the preliminary BOM for immediate procurement initiation.

7.3.10. Preliminary Procurement

The procurement WBSE can also be set for requirements grouping to make a single project stock. If both procurement and detailed BOMs are created, then the WBS BOM must be marked for "Preliminary requirements." After all prerequisites are completed, the BOM transfer transaction is executed.

7.4. Fabrication Plan

The fabrication plan follows the procurement plan and details the generation of fabrication tasks and assembly lists.

7.4.1. Fabrication Network

The fabrication network(s) provides control over the production planning by planning and issuing material to the production teams in a sequence synchronized with the engineering and procurement plans.

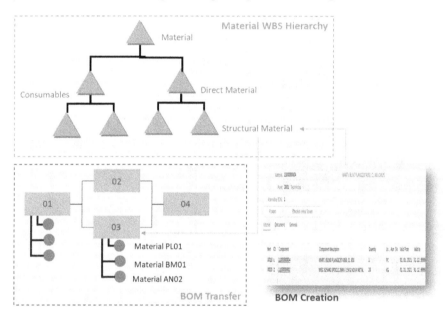

Figure 7-14. *Fabrication planning using WBS BOM and Project Builder*

This detailed fabrication plan enhances material control by aligning material issuance with specific project drawings during the fabrication process. Tekla software plays a critical role in this process, supporting the creation of detailed fabrication drawings and assembly instructions directly from the 3D model.

7.4.2. Detailed Drawings

During project execution, after the detailed design of deliverables is completed, detailed drawings are issued. These drawings are issued by engineering by setting the status of each document to "Issued For Construction."

7.4.3. Detailed BOM

The engineering coordinator converts the detailed MTO and associated lists—such as assembly lists and shipping lists—into the detailed BOM using a WBS BOM in SAP. These detailed BOMs are integrated with the network activities of fabrication networks.

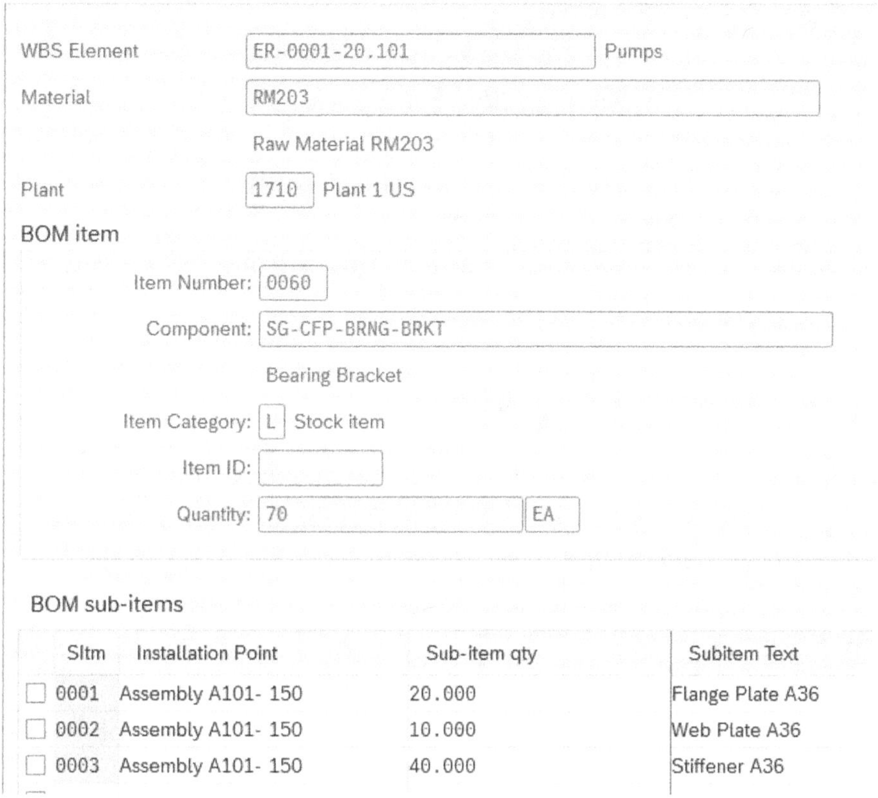

WBS Element	ER-0001-20.101	Pumps
Material	RM203	
	Raw Material RM203	
Plant	1710	Plant 1 US

BOM item

Item Number:	0060	
Component:	SG-CFP-BRNG-BRKT	
	Bearing Bracket	
Item Category:	L	Stock item
Item ID:		
Quantity:	70	EA

BOM sub-items

	SItm	Installation Point	Sub-item qty	Subitem Text
☐	0001	Assembly A101- 150	20.000	Flange Plate A36
☐	0002	Assembly A101- 150	10.000	Web Plate A36
☐	0003	Assembly A101- 150	40.000	Stiffener A36

Figure 7-15. *Detailed BOM of material components for fabrication planning*

The engineering drawings provide details of all assemblies and sub-assemblies, where each assembly comprises a main part, also known as *piecemarks*, and smaller parts, which are referred to as *marks* or *parts*. As shown in Figure 7-15, the main component is further broken down into subitems, such as flange plate, web plate, and stiffener plate.

153

7.4.4. Data Extraction

After the detailed design and approval of shop floor drawings, engineering and production planning coordinators extract details from Tekla software (see section 7.5 for details). The extracted data includes assemblies, shop floor drawings, and material components. The material take off (MTO) extraction file from Tekla must be aligned with SAP objects and features for accurate processing.

7.4.5. Material Transfer

The detailed BOM is a detailed hierarchical structure of the material components required for each assembly. It comprises subassemblies and their components and parts, with part numbers and quantities, in a structure of how individual materials are combined to form larger structures.

For each detailed BOM, material components and their subcomponents are assigned with quantities and reference points to correctly identify the work package in the project structure. This comprehensive assignment of material components to the network activities creates systematic reservation, issuance, and cost control of materials.

7.4.6. Material Issuance Control

By issuing shopfloor drawings and, where necessary, assembly drawings, the planning team can accurately determine the required materials to ensure that materials are available when needed for fabrication and assembly, control issuance of the material, and enforce production control due to design changes. The BOM change control is discussed in Chapter 12.

If the budget and material control requirements are minimal, one procurement WBSE is enough. However, if there is a need to track the issuance of each part and component during the fabrication process and the budget assignment at the procurement WBSE level is not enough to control the project, detailed BOMs are also created with the preliminary BOM.

Procurement type "Reservations only" will be created for the material components transferred from the detailed BOM to fabrication networks for the issuance of material where they are planned.

7.5. Tekla Integration with SAP

Tekla is a powerful 3D modeling software used for generating detailed models and associated drawings, including 2D views, sections, and shop drawings. In this section, we will explore how Tekla's capabilities can be effectively integrated with SAP to streamline the project's information flow.

7.5.1. Integration Points

To ensure seamless integration, the data extracted from Tekla needs to align with SAP objects. This can be achieved by creating an interface between SAP and Tekla or mapping the extracted information to an Excel file.

Fabrication Tasks

Tekla's capabilities in generating detailed fabrication drawings and assembly instructions from the 3D model ensure that fabrication tasks are aligned with design intent. These drawings and instructions can be exported to CAD formats for further detailing or modifications if necessary.

Tekla-generated fabrication tasks and material requirements are integrated into SAP PS to create networks and network activities. Each network or subnetwork within the fabrication plan represents an assembly, with network activities corresponding to fabrication tasks. Materials, drawings, and dependencies can also be assigned and updated to these activities using Tekla's strong features.

Material Codes and Specifications

For creating and managing detailed material libraries, Tekla also provides a comprehensive solution. These libraries define codes, specifications, and properties for various materials, ensuring consistency and precision throughout the design process.

Material codes and specifications from Tekla can be seamlessly integrated into SAP's material master data. Material master records in S/4HANA can be created and changed based on data exported from Tekla.

Drawings with Document Numbers and Metadata Integration

Tekla's strength lies in its ability to generate detailed 3D models, while AutoCAD is ideal for 2D drafting and detailing. By linking Tekla's 3D models with AutoCAD, you can achieve a comprehensive set of drawings. Integrating Tekla's drawings and metadata ensures that all engineering documents and drawings are accurately associated with project activities and WBS elements in SAP.

Assembly Lists

Tekla also generates assembly lists from the 3D model. These models provide details of the components and quantities needed for each assembly. These lists from Tekla can be exported to CAD software for additional detailing and visualization and sent to SAP for project execution. A typical filed mapping is shown in Table 7-3.

Table 7-3. *Filed Mapping*

Current Fields	Information	New Objects
Location of the assembly	Deliverables, Drawing Layout WBSE	SAP WBS element code
Drawing	Drawing Number, Drawing Description, Drawing Version, Sheet Number, Document Type, and Part Number	SAP DMS
Assembly	Header, Header UoM, Qty	SAP Network Activity and Finished Good Material
Material	Material Specifications Qty, UoM	Direct Material Components
Revision number	Revision number or BOM or Component	Engineering Change Number

Although more common in product lifecycle management (PLM), depending on project requirements and documentation complexity, SAP DMS's *Document Bill of Materials* functionality can be used. This feature maintains a hierarchical structure of documents that allows users to create a document structure similar to the assembly structure and easily map it when interfacing with external CAD systems.

Tekla–SAP S/4HANA Mapping

When integrating Tekla with SAP S/4HANA, data exchange is made possible through business application programming interfaces (BAPIs). These are standardized interfaces that allow external applications to interact with SAP business processes and data. The BAPIs listed in Table 7-4 are some of the commonly used BAPIs for Tekla–SAP S/4HANA integration.

Table 7-4. *BAPI List*

BAPI	Purpose
Use BAPI_BUS2002_CREATE	Create a network
BAPI_BUS2002_ACT_CREATE_MULTI	Create multiple activities
BAPI_NETWORK_MAINTAIN	Change an existing network
BAPI_MATERIAL_SAVEDATA	Create and change of material data
BAPI_DOCUMENT_CREATE2	Create documents in SAP DMS
BAPI_PS_INITIALIZATION	This BAPI is always used to initialize the system before making any changes or creating new data.

Note that this is not an exhaustive list. Additional BAPIs may be needed to meet specific requirements and scenarios. Consultants should evaluate the needs of their particular implementation and consult SAP documentation and support to identify any additional BAPIs that may be necessary for complete and effective integration.

7.5.2. Creating WBS BOM with Tekla

Integration with SAP's WBS BOM can be achieved through two primary methods:

i. Excel-based Mapping

> In this approach, assembly lists from Tekla are imported into a format compatible with SAP, such as CSV or Excel. Following this, an Excel file is prepared to map the assembly data from Tekla to SAP WBS elements. This file should define the correspondence between Tekla's assembly details and SAP's WBS BOM structure. Using SAP's data import tools or a data conversion program, the prepared Excel file can then be uploaded into SAP.

ii. Automated Mapping

> The automated integration involves extracting assembly lists from Tekla through its Open API (application programming interface). Tekla Open API enables the extraction of material data, drawing information, and other relevant details from Tekla, allowing for their seamless transfer to SAP. It also supports the automation of repetitive tasks.

For less frequent or smaller-scale integrations, a manual Excel-based approach is more suitable, involving manual data mapping and import. For more frequent or larger-scale integrations, automated integration with BAPIs offers a more efficient solution. The choice between these methods depends on the project's scale, update frequency, and integration complexity.

7.6. Network Alternatives

Under normal conditions, as well as due to varying scopes of work, non-availability of a specific material, or environmental conditions, similar work packages may require different processes or tasks to be accomplished. In all such cases, this feature in SAP PS proves to be a very effective tool for project planners.

In standard networks, predefined sets of activities are tailored to the specific requirements of a project, where each variant outlines a different combination of parameters. This combination includes activities and activity elements, sequence, duration, and work centers.

The steel structure scope of the RefineX project requires two different types of assemblies to be fabricated. Both assemblies share some common tasks, but each also has a unique requirement. The variations are managed by using multiple alternatives of standard networks, as shown in Figure 7-16.

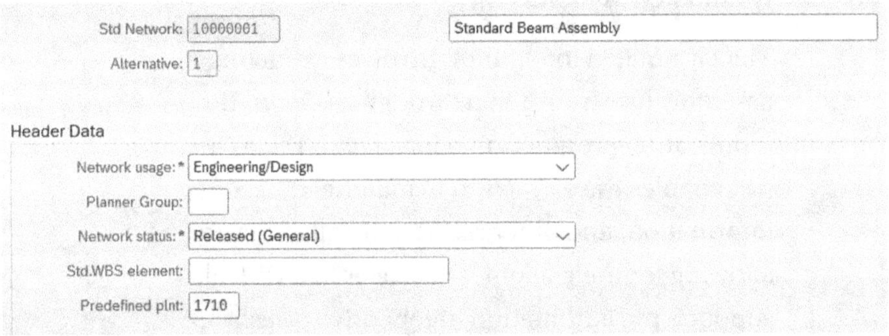

Figure 7-16. Alternative standard network: Header

Figure 7-17 further illustrates that the planning engineer of the RefineX project uses the standard network ID 10000001, *Alternative 1*, for planning the combination activities to fabricate Heavy Duty Column Assembly. The alternative has a unique combination of operations, duration, and respective effort in man-days for Fit-up & Alignment, Welding, Surface Preparation, and Protective Painting activities.

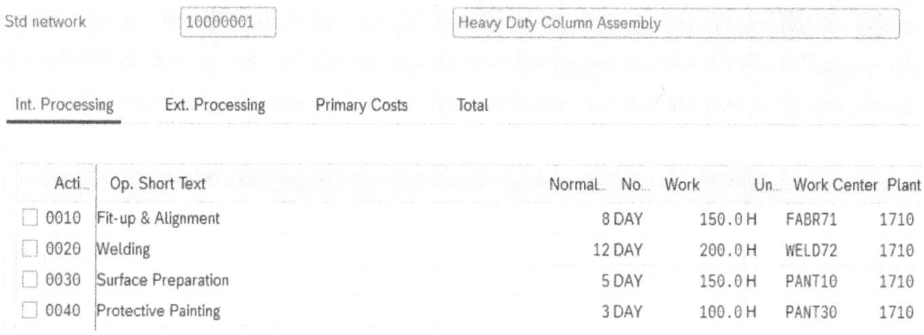

| Std network | 10000001 | | Heavy Duty Column Assembly | | | | | |

| Int. Processing | Ext. Processing | Primary Costs | Total |

Acti...	Op. Short Text	Normal...	No... Work	Un...	Work Center	Plant
☐ 0010	Fit-up & Alignment	8 DAY	150.0 H		FABR71	1710
☐ 0020	Welding	12 DAY	200.0 H		WELD72	1710
☐ 0030	Surface Preparation	5 DAY	150.0 H		PANT10	1710
☐ 0040	Protective Painting	3 DAY	100.0 H		PANT30	1710

Figure 7-17. *Alternate 1: Standard network: Detailed Screen*

Similarly, Figure 7-18 shows *Alternative 2* of the same assembly. This alternative has a different set of operations with corresponding duration and effort required to meet required specification.

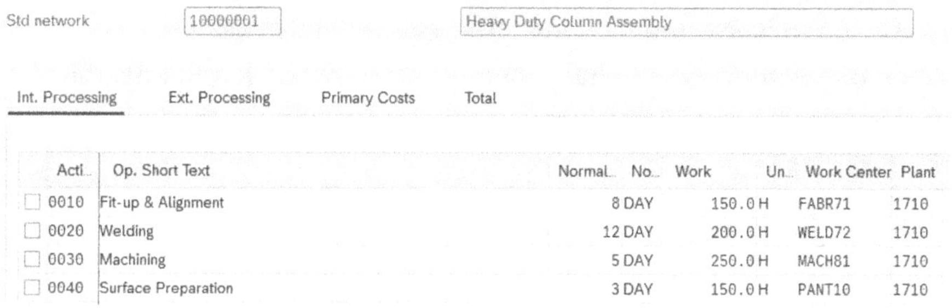

| Std network | 10000001 | | Heavy Duty Column Assembly | | | | | |

| Int. Processing | Ext. Processing | Primary Costs | Total |

Acti...	Op. Short Text	Normal...	No... Work	Un...	Work Center	Plant
☐ 0010	Fit-up & Alignment	8 DAY	150.0 H		FABR71	1710
☐ 0020	Welding	12 DAY	200.0 H		WELD72	1710
☐ 0030	Machining	5 DAY	250.0 H		MACH81	1710
☐ 0040	Surface Preparation	3 DAY	150.0 H		PANT10	1710

Figure 7-18. *Alternate 2: Standard network: Detailed Screen*

7.6.1. Configurable Standard Network

When creating the *operative networks* using standard networks, if the standard networks are used as configurable objects, then SAP PS allows copying selected network activities into the operative network based on predefined conditions. These networks, called *configurable standard*

161

networks, are generally used in product lifecycle management. However, for complex product development as part of an EPC project deliverable, or where a modular construction approach is adopted, this functionality can be useful.

7.6.2. Characteristics and Classes

Characteristics are the fundamental elements that specify these predefined restrictions or conditions. They serve as attributes that can be used to describe and differentiate the activities based on project needs.

Classes organize and group these characteristics by assigning characteristics to a variant class. You can establish a structured method to manage and apply them across different network activities, enabling a more flexible and tailored project planning approach.

The use of classes and characteristics is not only valuable for configurable networks but has other applications, such as managing materials, as discussed in Chapter 9.

7.6.3. Activity Element Variants

In projects with complex requirements, activity elements can also be a reason to create alternative standard networks. There can be an unlimited number of scenarios that can be created and saved to manage variations in the scope of work or processes. These activity elements can be assigned as subtasks or checklists for detailed progress monitoring and better control.

For example, in the RefineX project, alternatives were created not only due to different effort levels and an additional machining activity but also to accommodate variations in the Welding activity. As shown in Figure 7-19, the activity elements in Alternative 1 follow a standard manual welding process.

| Std network | 10000001 | | Heavy Duty Beam Assembly | | | | |
| Activity | 0020 | | Welding | | | | |

Int. Processing   Ext. Processing   Primary Costs   Total

Wor...	Op. Short Text	Work	Un...	Work Center	Plant	Calculation key
☐ 0040	Root Pass	50.0 H		WELD72	1710	2
☐ 0040	Fill Pass	120.0 H		WELD72	1710	2
☐ 0060	Cap Pass	80.0 H		WELD72	1710	2
☐ 0070	Slag Cleaning	20.0 H		HLP1710	1710	2
☐						

Figure 7-19. *Alternate 1: Activity elements variant*

In contrast, Alternative 2, shown in Figure 7-20, utilizes an advanced welding process with enhanced automation operations.

| Std network | 10000001 | | Heavy Duty Column Assembly | | | | |
| Activity | 0020 | | Welding | | | | |

Int. Processing   Ext. Processing   Primary Costs   Total

Wor...	Op. Short Text	Work	Un...	Work Center	Plant	Calculati...
☐ 0050	Preheating and Tack Welding	20 H		WELD71	1710	2
☐ 0060	Robotic Welding	100 H		WELD82	1710	2
☐ 0070	PWHT	30 H		PWHT01	1710	2

Figure 7-20. *Alternate 2: Activity elements variant*

These activity element variants enable greater flexibility in project planning. It allows planning teams to adapt standard networks to different execution methods or resource requirements within predefined alternatives.

7.7. Networks vs Production Orders

In EPC projects, especially those projects that require prefabrication or large-scale manufacturing, the choice between using SAP's Production Planning and Project System for planning and executing material and production significantly influences the effectiveness of project management.

Although both approaches offer distinct advantages depending on the specific needs of the project, this section will explain the reason for choosing SAP PS Network Orders instead of SAP PP Production Orders in this book.

7.7.1. Network Orders for ETO

SAP Production Planning is the *de facto* solution in all manufacturing environments. It offers production orders that contain operations, routing, and bills of material, and other such elements are fixed based on master data. Production orders in PP are used to plan and control repetitive manufacturing activities, with routings outlining the sequence of operations and BOMs listing the necessary materials and their component hierarchies.

Flexibility

Unlike production orders, network orders (or simply networks) are designed to manage the complex and customized nature of ETO manufacturing. They allow greater flexibility in defining project-specific activities and dependencies, as well as sequencing between engineering, material procurement, and subcontracting.

Integrated Planning

Although SAP S/4HANA enables the integration of production orders with the project structure, networks are necessary for this integration. In contrast, networks are the inherent part of project structures integrated with the WBS. This cohesive and hierarchical organization of project activities are visible in all standard reports, including critical path and milestone analysis.

For integrated ETO planning, networks provide direct linkages to resource planning, allowing for the detailed allocation of internal and external resources, which is essential for managing the diverse and specialized tasks found in EPC projects. Networks allow for the assignment of detailed activities and subactivities, each with its own set of dates, costs, and resources requirements.

Execution Control

Networks can also adapt to changes in scope, design, and timelines without being constrained by the predefined master data of Production Planning. The level of detail maintained in networks provides continuous control over the regular progress updates—a very strong SAP S/4HANA PS feature and a basic EPC project requirement during the project execution phase.

Networks also support the integration of SAP DMS for controlling fundamental documents, such as engineering drawings and specifications that provide direct control over the manufacturing and delivery process.

7.7.2. Production Orders for ETO

The preference of networks over production does not mean that PP–PS integration is entirely ruled out. It is strongly recommended in cases where organizations have similar assemblies, subassemblies, or components that are used across multiple projects. For example, a company that regularly manufactures modular components for large infrastructure projects should use PP to manage the production.

As another example, when production components are very high-tech and require precision in the manufacturing process, integration with material management and quality management, and the monitoring of deliveries at the batch level, using SAP Production Planning (PP) standard routings, batch management, and material BOM features offers better production control.

Material type Finished Goods (FERT) will be added to the list of master data used in defining the deliverable material or assemblies. These finished components or assemblies will then be integrated into the larger project deliverables. It is important to note that this book will discuss finished goods only in the context of deliveries from the project but not in the context of production planning and execution.

In all such cases, it is recommended to use production orders for component-level production and integrate them with networks for overall project management. This approach will best utilize the strengths of both SAP Production Planning and SAP Project System modules.

7.8. Conclusion

This chapter highlighted the importance of effective planning across engineering, procurement, fabrication, and construction in an engineer-to-order (ETO) project. It demonstrated how SAP S/4HANA enables integrated planning through various tools, planning methodologies, third-party system integration, and the management of design and execution variations to ensure adaptability without compromising control.

With engineering-driven planning in place, the next critical step is aligning the right resources at the right time. The upcoming chapter will focus on how SAP S/4HANA supports resource management by linking manpower and equipment planning directly to project plans.

CHAPTER 8

Resource Management

In project management, *resource management process* refers to the systematic process of planning, allocating, and optimizing the utilization of all resources required for timely and cost-effective execution of projects.

In engineering, procurement, and construction (EPC) projects, this process involves a detailed review of the bill of quantities (BOQ) and project-specific drawings. The planning engineer, in close collaboration with the engineering, production, and erection teams, consolidates this information into a comprehensive resource plan.

The resources are broadly categorized into manpower, machinery, materials, and subcontractor services. This chapter focuses on SAP S/4HANA's utilization in planning and controlling contractors' human resources, machines, and subcontracted work.

8.1. Internal Resource Management

In the project management lifecycle, internal resource planning occurs after detailed task planning and scheduling, as discussed in Chapter 5. As a project is structured and scheduled, and as networks and associated activities are created in SAP Project System (PS), the focus of planning shifts to defining the necessary resources for each activity.

© Sohail Ahmed 2025
S. Ahmed, *The SAP S/4HANA Handbook for EPC Projects*,
https://doi.org/10.1007/979-8-8688-1466-2_8

8.1.1. Resource Types

The resource plan identifies and aligns the resources required to perform a task during a stipulated time with the plan dates. These resources can be divided into two main types.

Direct Resources

Direct resources are actively engaged in performing specific tasks or managing activities. These resources can be directly allocated to individual tasks. In SAP PS, these resources are assigned to internal network activities. For example, both a *welder* and a *welding foreman* can have their hours logged against welding activities, making them direct resources.

Indirect Resources

Indirect resources support multiple activities and work packages without being directly attributed to any single activity in terms of time or effort. They are often treated as project overheads. For example, a *helper* who provides general support services or a *construction manager* overseeing multiple work areas is considered an indirect resource.

8.1.2. Resource Planning in SAP

Resource planning is the process of managing the balance between resource requirements and resource availability. In SAP it involves the allocation of resources by using structured master data to define resource capacities and assigning these capacities to project activities.

This is achieved through two main elements.

Work Center

The work center defines the availability of resources based on parameters such as utilization, productivity rate, and shift schedules.

Internal Activity

Internal activity calculates the resource requirement by considering planned work, activity duration, and distribution keys.

The connection between these two elements is established by assigning the *planned work* and *work center* to internal activity, ensuring accurate capacity calculations and resource allocation.

8.1.3. Work Center

Work centers in SAP are the objects created as master data to represent resources or resource groups. Work centers are assigned to internal network activities in SAP PS for capacity planning, resource cost calculation, and distribution of needed resources across the project timeline.

The resources represented by work centers can be physical or logical. A work center can represent an individual labor unit or machine as well as a team or a group of machines that performs the work, as shown in Figure 8-1. Each work center has configurable attributes that define how work is planned, resources are allocated, and activities are costed.

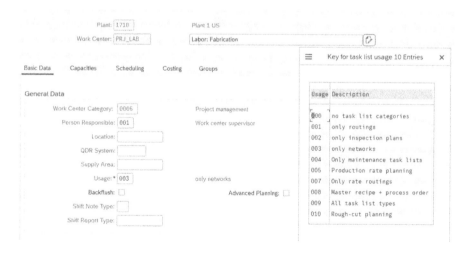

Figure 8-1. *Work center for networks*

Work Center Category

Proper categorization of resources is essential for the effective execution of project activities.

The Work Center category in SAP is a classification system used to group work centers based on the nature of the resource. For construction projects, the categories commonly used are *Project Management (006)* and *Network (003)*.

Capacity Categories

The capacity of different categories is defined in the work centers for any resource category, including multiple-capacity categories such as the following:

1. Machine capacity is calculated based on the number of machine hours available per day, considering factors like maintenance and downtime.

2. Labor capacity for work centers is calculated based on headcount and available working hours.

In SAP, resource categories are called *capacity categories*. The capacity of various resources, such as *Machine (001)* and *Labor (002)*, is defined in the work centers. A typical use of capacity categories is shown in Table 8-1.

Table 8-1. Capacity Categories

Capacity Category	Direct	Indirect
Machine (001)	Shearing machines, cutting machines, and drilling units	Forklifts, overhead cranes, and trucks
Labor (002)	Welders, fitters, and painters	Helpers, riggers

The categories align with the resources needed for different project phases, such as engineering, fabrication, and erection. Accurate classification and planning according to these types ensures proper resource allocation.

Integration with HR

Non-supervisory resources, whether direct or indirect, require detailed planning. SAP PS and SAP Human Capital Management (HCM) integration allows for assigning employees to work centers and calculating capacities using human resources (HR) master data, but this is often impractical for construction projects.

In such cases, indirect supervisory roles like *project managers* or *planning engineers* are better handled through SAP HCM's cost planning and allocation process. However, for indirect non-supervisory staff, effort planning is still necessary to develop a comprehensive resource plan.

8.1.4. Resource Requirement

The resource requirement process begins by assessing the total labor and machine hours required to complete the defined scope of work. It begins with the standard norm and then is adjusted to align with the unique project demands.

Standard Work

Standard work defines the effort needed to complete one unit of an activity. For example, if one fabricator can cut one ton of light steel structure in 1.6 hours, then the standard work for the fabrication of light steel structure is

Standard Work = 1 Person x 1.6 Hours/Ton = 1.6 Person Hours/Ton

The goal of using standard norms is to establish a baseline to calculate the total planned work that ultimately generates the resource requirements for the project.

171

Effort is calculated in terms of work hours, commonly known as manhours or person hours. As SAP PS uses *hour* as the standard unit of measurement for work, in this book person hours will be referred to simply as *hours*. Similarly, the duration of an activity will always be measured in *days*.

Planned Work

Planned work is the overall effort required to complete the scope of work. It represents the amount of time required by a worker (or a group of workers) to complete a specific activity.

Continuing with the preceding example, the RefineX project includes 300 tons of fabrication of heavy steel structure. Using the standard guidelines, the planned ork is calculated as:

Planned Work = BOQ x Standard Work = 300 x 1.6 = 480 Hours

The planned effort may vary from standards based on project-specific requirements and complexity of work. For example, the hardness of earth for excavation activity, the height of equipment placement, or the weight of the materials impacts the calculation of planned effort.

Difficulty Factor

These variations are handled using a difficulty factor. For example, for fabrication, heavy steel structure takes 50% more effort to fabricate than lightweight steel structure. In this case:

Adjusted Planned Work = BOQ x Standard Work = 300 x 1.6 x 1.5 = 720 Hours

It is important to note that difficulty factors must first be approved by the project management office (PMO) or a central governance body before calculating the planned work.

8.1.5. Available Capacity

Available capacity refers to the total number of resources available within a work center. It is determined by selecting the parameters that define that availability of individual capacities, such as the factory calendar, shift sequence, and capacity utilization.

Capacity Utilization

These parameters collectively establish the number of working days a resource is available, the number of shifts within a workday, and the start time, finish time, and break periods for each shift. Capacity utilization reflects the efficiency of a resource by accounting for unplanned breaks, idling, and downtime. For example, site safety rules restrict the overall capacity of the fabrication work center to 95%.

Capacity Calculation

Once resources are assigned to activities and the project schedule is finalized, the planning engineer will review the comparison between the planned work and the available capacity. The next step is to optimize use across the project duration.

In the RefineX project, the work center has seven fabricators. The shift starts at 8:00 am and ends at 5:00 pm, including a one-hour break. This gives a net availability of eight hours per day for this work center. The total available capacity is as follows:

Available Capacity per Day = 7 Fabricators × 8 Hours/Day = 56 Hours/Day

Based on the available resources, the fabricator work center is able to complete the adjusted planned work of 720 hours with a daily capacity of 56 hours in approximately 13 days. However, if due to any restriction the planned duration of the fabrication activity is less than 13 days, then the planning team must perform resource leveling.

173

8.1.6. Customer Enhancements

In large EPC projects, standard fields are not always sufficient to capture all the data needed for a comprehensive resource plan.

SAP PS provides the functionality in work breakdown structures (WBS) or activity elements. The functionality of customer enhancements using the user fields enables project managers to store additional information that is critical for aligning SAP with other tools, such as Primavera P6 or Tekla, but is not available as standard SAP fields.

For the RefineX project, the planning engineer uses customer enhancement to include unique attributes specific to the project, including activity codes, activity steps, BOQ quantities, standard work, disciplines (mechanical, civil, structural, etc.), and difficulty factor. These fields are used to calculate the planned work and provide additional fields required for mapping reference data for integration with external systems.

8.1.7. Pooled Capacity

Pooled capacity is the grouping of similar resources as one pool of resources. This feature is best suited for unskilled labor, such as helpers, where tracking the availability and workload of each helper is not desired; instead, a crew with similar skills and capabilities is required for different tasks.

This method is helpful in large civil construction projects where unskilled resources and a pool of similar equipment are needed. The resource pool is treated as a single unit, with capacity managed at the group level, and the tracking is managed collectively.

For example, a single work center for helpers working at 100% capacity may represent a pool of 50 helpers available for 8 hours daily, resulting in a pooled capacity of 400 hours per day (50 helpers × 8 hours). Similarly, a work center for excavators can group multiple machines, each available for 8 hours daily, to reflect the combined capacity of the entire fleet.

8.1.8. Resource Leveling

If the required capacity exceeds the available capacity, the planning team attempts to spread the resources to balance the requirement and manage the peak requirement resources. This step of resource planning is known as *resource-leveling*.

The objective of resource-leveling is to achieve a balanced workload and avoid situations where resources are either overloaded or underutilized during different periods of the project.

Schedule Adjustment

Schedule adjustment involves optimizing the duration and sequence of activities to balance resource demand across the project timeline. The planning teams smooth resource usage to prevent any period from exceeding the maximum availability of the resource. This is done by modifying the logical relationships between activities and rescheduling tasks.

This process adjusts activity start and finish dates by shifting activities and avoiding resource bottlenecks. For example, if there is a higher demand for fabricators in March compared to February, activities can be rearranged to distribute resources more evenly, minimizing peaks and troughs in utilization.

Distribution Key

While schedule adjustment helps manage the peak demand, it is not always practical or sufficient due to constraints and dependencies on other activities. There is a limit to which a project's logic and duration can be manipulated. To overcome this limitation, the planning team attempts to redistribute the resource workload.

SAP PS provides the *distribution key* as a very effective tool for resource distribution across the duration of an activity. A distribution key ensures that the resource loading is aligned with the duration constraint while staying within the overall available capacity.

The demand of this distribution varies depending on the type of resource and the nature of activities. Some activities demand high resource allocation at the beginning of the activities while others demand a peak in the middle.

Standard SAP distribution keys, such as *SAP030*, provide equal distribution of resources throughout the activity duration. By selecting the appropriate distribution key, project planners can distribute resources such as labor and costs more uniformly, minimizing disruptions and maintaining a steady workflow.

Additional distribution keys, such as bell curve, back-loaded, or front-loaded, can also be configured and assigned to work centers to support more complex project-specific scenarios.

The bell curve is the most commonly used distribution method of resources in the construction industry. This periodic distribution type, as shown in Table 8-2, provides a gradual increase in resource requirement that peaks in the middle and slows down toward the completion of the task. The cumulative curve of this distribution type is S-shaped, commonly known as the *S-curve*.

Table 8-2. *Bell Curve Periodic Distribution of Work*

Period	1	2	3	4	5	6	7	8	9	10
Value	5	8	12	16	18	18	16	12	8	5

8.1.9. Multiple Work Centers

In complex EPC projects, a single activity might require multiple types of resources working together to complete various phases.

Internal Activity Elements

For example, a fabrication activity could involve fitters, fabricators, welders, and so on. Each resource—created as a work center—is responsible for a distinct part of the activity, commonly called a subtask. In SAP PS, *activity elements* are used to create these subtasks or operations.

Instead of creating separate activities for each work center, SAP PS allows work centers to be assigned to *internal activity elements* under a single internal activity. This approach provides a structured way to manage and track resource utilization while maintaining a streamlined schedule.

In the RefineX project, *Fabrication of a Pump Skid A* is planned as a single activity. Instead of assigning one work center to the internal activity, the planning engineer creates separate internal activity elements within this activity and allocates different work centers with the distribution of planned work, as shown in Table 8-3.

Table 8-3. *Work Centers*

Activity Element	Assigned Work Center	Planned Work	Weightage
Cutting	Fabricator	144	20%
Fit-Up	Fitter	216	30%
Welding	Welder	360	50%
Total		720	

The work centers may also belong to different categories, such as instead of labor, if the cutting operation is performed using a machine, then the fabricator work center can be replaced with the shearing machine one, for example.

Activity Weightages

The *weightage* concept is also an integral part of calculating percentage of completion methods in reporting construction project progress. POC (percentage of completion) weight fields are used to assign weightage to each internal activity element to represent its relative significance within the activity. It is clear in the preceding example that welding holds 50% weightage. This means that completing this sub-activity equates to half of the activity's total effort. Misassigning can lead to inaccurate aggregation and project reporting.

This chapter has only introduced the concept of using weightages to manage resource distribution. The detailed calculation of *percentage of completion (POC),* and its application in tracking project progress, will be covered in a later chapter.

Resource Offset

Activity elements do not allow for planning duration or dates. They inherit these settings from the parent activity. It, however, offers a scheduling feature that allows maintaining *offset to start* and *offset to finish* days, as follows:

1.   **Offset to start** refers to the adjustment made in the number of days to the planned start date on an activity element with reference to the parent activity. The value in this field allows the activity elements to lead or lag from the planned start date of the parent activity.

2. **Offset to finish** refers to the adjustment made in the number of days to the planned finish date on an activity element with reference to the parent activity. The value in this field allows the activity elements to lead or lag from the planned finish date of the parent activity.

By using either of the two fields, planning and distribution of planned work can be further improved. For example, Table 8-4 illustrates how this feature can support the distribution of resource requirements of specific work centers for the same activity within the activity duration.

Table 8-4. *Distribution of Resource Requirements*

Activity Element	Work Center	Planned Work	Day 1	Day 2	Day 3	Day 4	Day 5	Day 6
Cutting	Fabricator	144	25	25	54	20	20	
Fit-Up	Fitter	216		48	60	60	48	
Welding	Welder	360			80	100	100	80
Total Planned Work			25	73	194	180	168	80

It is important to note that managing multiple work centers within a single activity presents both benefits and challenges. Therefore, it is recommended that the organization first establish planning norms and prepare master data to support this functionality. The absence of a well-defined plan, lack of coordination between team members, and frequent changes to planning and scheduling can make this feature ineffective.

8.2. External Resource Plan

In the detailed project planning and scheduling phase, the planning engineer defines the scope of subcontracted services. Once the subcontracted scope is agreed upon, the subcontracted services are mapped using service activities, as detailed in section 5.2.5.

8.2.1. Service Master Record

Organizations typically build a database of standard subcontracted services. This information is maintained in the SAP Materials Management module as service master records. The service master record is a unique identifier that allows management of recurring services. This structured approach helps maintain consistency and provides cross-project analytics.

8.2.2. Single Services

Service activities are specialized activity types within SAP PS that manage subcontracted tasks, such as printing papers, calibration of equipment, or third-party inspection.

From these simple single-service tasks to detailed multi-level bill of quantities (BOQ) scenarios, service activities can accommodate any form of complexity.

For non-standard services, where no preexisting service master record is available, descriptions and cost elements can be entered instead of selecting the service master record.

8.2.3. Service Specification Outline

In complex service contracts, the procurement of services begins when the prime contractor defines the scope of work as a well-structured, multi-level bill of quantities (BOQ). Each BOQ level represents different service groups that may include various stages, areas, or phases of the project. To support this process, the *Service Specification Outline* function in SAP PS allows service activities to be organized hierarchically. This alignment makes the BOQ easier to manage and tracks large volumes of work efficiently.

For the RefineX project, the civil work Tank Farm area, including site preparation and foundation, has been subcontracted to Earthworks LLC. The agreed scope of work, as shown in Table 8-5, is valued at USD 50,000, with the BOQ created in SAP PS using Service Specification Outline.

Table 8-5. *Agreed Scope of Work*

BOQ Level	Service	Quantity	Unit of Measurement	Unit Rate (in USD)	Price (in USD)
1	Site Preparation	1	AU	-	8,000
1.1	Site Survey	1	AU	7,000	7,000
1.2	Grading	0.5	AU	2,000	1,000
2	Foundation	10	EA	-	42,000
2.1	Excavation	100	M3	50	5,000
2.2	Lean	50	M3	80	4,000
2.3	Rebar	20	Tons	1,200	24,000
2.4	Concrete	80	M3	100	8,000
2.5	Backfill	40	M3	25	1,000

8.2.4. Model Service Specifications

SAP also offers the feature of Model Service Specification in SAP. This feature provides the option of configuring templates for standardizing service specifications. It includes configuring the predefined service specifications that can be adapted to the specific needs of a project.

8.2.5. Integration with MM

Service Entry Sheet

The service entry sheet (SES) is the primary document in SAP PS used to communicate the scope of work to the subcontracting team. It is created by copying service specifications from the *Service Specification Outline* in SAP PS into the SES in SAP MM. This process accurately conveys the service requirements and quantities outlined in the Service Specification Outline to the subcontracting department.

Service Acceptance Sheet

The service acceptance sheet (SAS) is derived from the SES and is used to track and confirm the progress of subcontracted services. It provides detailed information on the completion of work by the subcontractor.

8.3. Site Management Plan

It was evident from the engineering, procurement, and construction plans discussed earlier that direct resource plans require a high level of standardization and details. Therefore, the planning engineer developed resource plans based on a structured approach using service and internal activities supported by work centers, material masters, and service masters.

In contrast, for site management planning, the planning engineer employs a different set of network activities. For site management, cost activities and external activities are used.

8.3.1. Cost Activities for Site Management

Cost activities are used to plan tasks, such as setting up accommodations, making travel arrangements, and creating safety inductions for the construction crew. These tasks do not require capacity management but necessitate the identification, sequencing, and cost planning of the activities.

8.3.2. External Activities for Site Management

For tasks that involve non-standard or specialized external services, such as unique equipment mobilization or ad-hoc construction, external activities are utilized. Unlike service activities, external activities provide the flexibility to initiate the procurement process without relying on material or service master data.

8.4. Integration with Primavera P6

In the construction industry, where managing thousands of interdependent activities is common, Oracle Primavera P6 is known for its flexibility to handle large, complex project structure schedules. It is particularly effective in scenarios where schedules and resources need continuous adjustments based on site conditions, project progress, and design specifications. Its core features, such as schedule, resource, and risk optimization, allow project planners to easily adjust project logics, update timelines, and adopt scope changes at any level.

In contrast, SAP PS is primarily designed for logistical control and financial oversight of projects. It strictly adheres to predefined structures and is tightly integrated with other SAP modules. Before making changes to SAP PS, it is advisable to make a detailed analysis of the change and collaborate with internal stakeholders. Construction projects are usually updated on a weekly basis, and the updates are often non-binding and are intended to present the future outlook and what-if analysis. Therefore, using SAP PS for frequent and temporary changes is not practical due to its impact on financial, HR, and logistics processes.

It is advisable to integrate SAP Project System (PS) with Primavera P6 EPPM to ensure a smooth exchange of project management data at a higher frequency, such as month-end closing.

For the RefineX project, all the stakeholders, including the project owner, engineering consultant, and subcontractors, are contractually obligated to use Primavera P6 as the project management tool for monitoring project activities. All stakeholders agree to use Primavera P6 for project scheduling, resource loading, and preparing look-ahead plans of construction activities.

As an EPC contractor, PrimeCon Planning Team is made responsible for collecting project plans from subcontractors and consultants, consolidating them into a central project plan in Primavera P6, and submitting it to the project owner for review and approval.

In order to meet these obligations, as well as for internal financial and logistics controlling, the planning engineer of PrimeCon initially constructs the structure in SAP PS and integrates it with Primavera P6 for project scheduling, PERT analysis, and progress updates. The next section explains the prerequisites and technical objects required to develop this integration.

8.4.1. Initial Project Creation in SAP PS

Projects are initially established in SAP PS, encompassing the creation of work breakdown structure (WBS) elements, networks, activities, and sub-activities. Planning engineering assigns material components and work centers for labor and machine resources, as discussed in earlier chapters. Similarly, customer-defined fields may be defined to capture additional details not included in SAP's standard fields.

Mapping and Synchronization

WBS elements in SAP PS are mapped to WBS elements in Primavera P6 to maintain the project's hierarchical structure. SAP PS networks are represented as activity codes in Primavera P6, ensuring that network structures are preserved. Activities in SAP PS are mapped to activities in Primavera P6, and activity elements are mapped as sub-activities.

Data Export to Primavera P6

The project data from SAP PS are exported to Primavera P6. This includes extracting work breakdown structure, networks, and activities along with their attributes. Using appropriate Business Application Programming Interfaces (BAPI) and P6 webservices, these fields are created and/or mapped with Primavera P6 fields using unique identifiers.

Data Processing in Primavera P6

In Primavera P6, the project undergoes scheduling, resource planning, and resource leveling. Progress updates and adjustments to man-days, durations, and resource allocations are made periodically to optimize the schedule. This process provides the updated actual progress and revised activity dates, where applicable.

Data Import Back to SAP PS

The updated data, including updated schedules, relationships, dates, and durations, is imported back into SAP PS. This update reflects the latest changes made in Primavera P6.

185

8.4.2. Primavera Integration BAPIs

The integration process involves several BAPIs to facilitate interactions with SAP Project System. Each BAPI serves a specific function to support comprehensive project management. Some of the important BAPIs are listed in Table 8-6.

Data Synchronization

The user sets up periodic synchronization between P6 and SAP PS to ensure that schedule changes, resource allocations, and project updates are reflected in both systems.

Table 8-6. *BAPIs*

BAPI Name	Purpose	Fields	Direction
BAPI_ PROJECT_ GET_INFO	Retrieves detailed project information, including status, milestones, and key attributes.	PROJECT_DEFINITION, STATUS, MILESTONES, KEY_ATTRIBUTES	From P6 to SAP
BAPI_ NETWORK_ GET_DETAIL	Fetches detailed information about networks, including activities, dependencies, and status.	NETWORK, DESCRIPTION, ACTIVITIES, RELATIONSHIPS	From P6 to SAP
BAPI_ ACTIVITY_ GET_DETAIL	Retrieves details on individual activities, such as characteristics, durations, and dependencies.	ACTIVITY_ID, NETWORK, DURATION, WORK, RELATIONSHIPS	From P6 to SAP

(continued)

Table 8-6. (*continued*)

BAPI Name	Purpose	Fields	Direction
BAPI_PROJECT_CHANGE	Updates project-level details, such as attributes and status.	PROJECT_DEFINITION, WBS_ELEMENT, DATES, STATUS	From SAP to P6
BAPI_WBS_ELEMENT_CHANGE	Modifies work breakdown structure (WBS) elements, including hierarchies, attributes, and relationships.	WBS_ELEMENT, ATTRIBUTES, RELATIONSHIPS	From SAP to P6
BAPI_ACTIVITY_CHANGE	Updates activity details, including status, durations, and dependencies.	ACTIVITY_ID, NETWORK, DURATION, PROGRESS, RELATIONSHIPS	From SAP to P6
BAPI_NETWORK_CHANGE	Facilitates changes to network structures, dependencies, and activities.	NETWORK, ACTIVITIES, DEPENDENCIES, STATUS	From SAP to P6

BTP Integration Suite

SAP Business Technology Platform (BTP) is used as the middleware for integrating SAP PS and Primavera P6. SAP BTP Integration Suite handles the transformation and synchronization of data between SAP PS and P6 and manages real-time data exchange and automated error handling during the integration process.

Primavera P6 REST APIs

The P6 REST APIs allow Primavera P6 to communicate seamlessly with SAP PS by extracting key project data. These APIs provide direct access to P6 project data, such as activities and schedules. They are essential for extracting data from P6 and ensure that updates from P6 can be regularly imported into SAP PS.

8.4.3. Error Handling, Data Validation, and Reporting

The integration program must ensure that data consistency and accuracy are maintained throughout the synchronization process. Integrated reporting tools can be developed to display synchronized project data. Any errors are identified and discrepancies between the two systems are resolved. This includes the following:

1. Defining validation rules to ensure that updates (such as activity relationships, progress, and schedules) from Primavera P6 comply with SAP PS standards.

2. Data consistency checks between SAP PS and Primavera P6 to ensure field-level alignment. Error-logging mechanisms to capture integration errors, with detailed error messages.

3. A comprehensive report to view the data and error logs before updates are made in SAP PS.

Taking the preceding measures ensures that reliable integration, error handling, and data validation processes have been implemented.

8.5. Tools and Equipment Management

In large EPC projects, effectively managing tools and equipment is critical for meeting timelines and staying within the schedule. SAP S/4HANA provides comprehensive solutions to plan and monitor these assets. The integrated

S/4HANA functionalities across different departments help streamline operations, reduce project delays, and ensure resource optimization.

8.5.1. Tools Management

Tools management is the process of issuing necessary tools to workers for performing daily tasks. It is a common practice in EPC projects that tools are issued temporarily to workers and must be returned back to store after the completion of need.

Tools Issuance

In order to manage tool inventory, every tool must be created in the SAP S/4HANA MM module under the "consumable" material type. When a tool is issued to a worker, a Goods Issue document is generated to record the quantity of tools issued. Tools are typically created as non-valuated materials. Therefore, at the point of Goods Receipt, the actual cost is posted as the consumption cost.

Tool Tracking

Storekeepers are required to keep track of the tool inventory and ensure that no tools are misplaced or unaccounted for. Using the SAP inventory tracking functionality, storekeepers can check the availability and issuance status of each tool. It is pertinent to note that these materials must be created in the system as non-valuated so that the actual cost is charged at the time of Goods Receipt and only the quantities of tools are tracked during multiple Goods Issue transactions.

For example, at the RefineX project, tools are issued to workers for piping installation, equipment assembly, and so on. The *Manage Stock* app shown in Figure 8-2 can be utilized by the storekeepers to keep track of which tools are issued. By adding a customized field for selecting the employee ID from the SAP HCM module, information about to whom the tools have been issued can also be recorded.

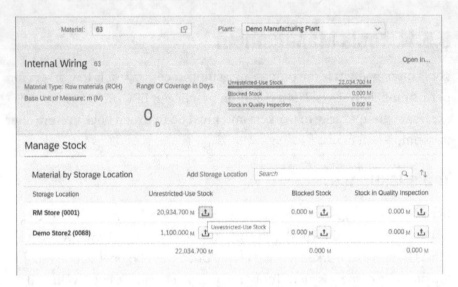

Figure 8-2. *Managing unrestricted and block stock during inspections*

8.5.2. Asset Management

SAP S/4HANA Enterprise Asset Management (EAM) offers an end-to-end approach to asset management. This line-of-business solution provides smooth asset handling of project tools and equipment. SAP S/4HANA EAM bridges the gap between the operational and financial aspects of equipment management through seamless integration with SAP Plant Maintenance and SAP Finance and Controlling modules.

In construction projects, SAP EAM plays an important role in ensuring asset availability and optimization. SAP EAM Fiori applications support project teams in planning, controlling, and monitoring asset management activities and costs.

Asset Accounting

Asset management focuses on high-value assets, such as construction machinery, specialized tools, and vehicles. Items exceeding a certain threshold value are categorized as assets. This distinction allows better asset tracking, maintenance, and costing.

SAP S/4HANA Asset Accounting supports detailed asset master data management to capture key information, such as asset classes, allocations, depreciation methods, and usage history. It governs the financial aspects of equipment management with the help of the *Manage Fixed Asset* app. This application provides a centralized platform for managing asset-related information.

Cost Capitalization

In EPC projects, significant cost is incurred by buying and maintaining new equipment. The new equipment purchasing cost is often first capitalized rather than expensed immediately. Similarly, when maintenance activities are substantial, the cost of major repairs is also capitalized to an asset under construction (AUC) using the cost settlement process. The AUC is later converted to an active asset once the maintenance work is complete. This integrated approach ensures that the cost is spread over the project life or the asset's useful life.

The *Maintenance Planning Overview* app, as shown in Figure 8-3, monitors and analyzes the status of maintenance notifications, orders, and procurement activities, including unprocessed notifications, unreleased or overdue orders, and non-stock material availability. This end-to-end visualization of project assets ensures timely and effective maintenance management.

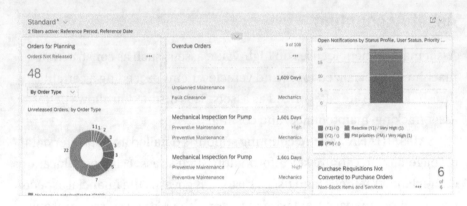

Figure 8-3. *Maintenance planning overview*

8.5.3. Technical Objects

The scope of asset management extends beyond financial tracking. It also provides operational excellence in equipment procurement. SAP S/4HANA integrates Asset Accounting and Equipment Management using the Finance, Controlling, Materials Management, and Plant Maintenance modules.

This integrated data management approach encompasses equipment planning, machine operations, and maintenance activities. In EPC projects, these operations are directly linked with projects through WBS elements and network activities. From cranes to welding plants, every piece of equipment used in an EPC project is managed through equipment master data records maintained in SAP S/4HANA. These technical objects are maintained in the SAP Plant Maintenance module with operational details.

Maintenance Request

Users can initiate the master data creation process with the *Create Maintenance Request* app to submit requests for the creation and maintenance of technical objects. The master data captures detailed information, such as equipment specifications, owner and administrator details, functional location, equipment bill of materials (BOM), and maintenance history. This structure helps maintain an organized hierarchy of equipment, sub-equipment, their locations, and details about the spare parts.

8.5.4. Equipment Planning and Administration

Equipment planning begins with aligning project needs with available equipment. Using SAP's integrated system, project managers can assess equipment availability, schedule utilization, and identify requirement gaps. These insights facilitate the timely procurement of additional equipment or allocation of resources from other projects. Purchase requisitions and purchase orders are initiated for assets. Once equipment acquisition is completed, equipment master records are created and linked with the corresponding asset master data, as shown in Figure 8-4.

Figure 8-4. *Equipment integration with asset*

In earlier SAP versions, the SAP Equipment and Tools Management
(ETM) module had been used in equipment planning and administration,
but now SAP emphasizes S/4HANA's built-in features and third-
party solution, such as seamlessly integrating into the SAP S/4HANA
architecture. In the absence of an ETM add-on, *Pool Asset Management*
(PAM) and other standard SAP S/4HANA applications can be used for
managing and tracking equipment usage.

Pool Asset Management

Pool Asset Management in SAP S/4HANA is a core component of
effectively managing shared equipment as project resources. It provides
a centralized platform for tracking equipment usage and optimizing
resource allocation for improved maintenance planning and cost control.
Key features include reservation management, usage tracking, seamless
integration with Plant Maintenance, and robust reporting and analytics
capabilities.

While primarily focused on managing pooled asset usage, PAM can be integrated with other S/4HANA modules or third-party solutions to address broader asset management needs.

Pool Asset Management ensures that the right equipment is available when needed and focuses on the reservation, availability, and tracking of shared or rotating assets—such as vehicles, tools, or equipment—that are used across different maintenance tasks or departments. In addition to PAM, SAP also offers scheduling apps that focus on who will perform the work and when.

Figure 8-5. *Maintenance scheduling board*

The *Maintenance Scheduling Board* app, shown in Figure 8-5, and *Resource Scheduling* app, shown in Figure 8-6, are designed to plan and assign maintenance operations to work centers.

Machine Resource Usage

Machine hours are planned during pool asset reservations to specify the work center of the equipment and the duration it is required for a project activity. After the activity is performed, the actual machine hours are confirmed through the Record Usage functionality. This process updates the reservation with the actual utilization data, ensuring accurate tracking of machine usage.

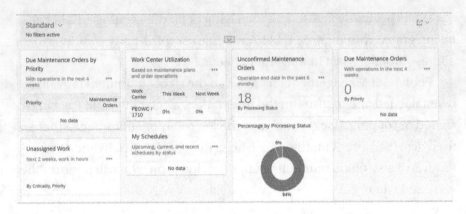

Figure 8-6. *Resource scheduling for maintenance planner*

During project execution, machine hours are confirmed to specify the actual effort spent by the equipment on a particular activity. This process posts the actual cost of the machine hours allocated to the project activity. By using PAM for machine activity confirmation, organizations ensure alignment between planned and actual machine hours while maintaining a transparent link to project or operational costs.

Fleet Management

Fleet management in SAP focuses on comprehensive tracking and maintenance of vehicles, such as trucks, cranes, and buses. Through equipment master data, maintenance scheduling, and integration with finance modules, organizations can monitor usage, fuel consumption, repair costs, and regulatory compliance. While SAP S/4HANA provides the core functionalities for fleet management, businesses requiring advanced features like GPS tracking or detailed driver logs often integrate third-party solutions to enhance operational efficiency and real-time monitoring.

Fuel Orders

Fuel requirements for heavy machinery can also be streamlined through SAP Plant Maintenance module. Fuel Orders are integrated with procurement and inventory modules to control fuel consumption, and handle real-time stock updates and cost tracking.

8.5.5. Equipment Maintenance

Equipment maintenance is the process that ensures smooth operation of machinery and reduces downtime. SAP provides tools to manage both corrective and preventive maintenance, keeping equipment in optimal condition.

Maintenance Notification

The maintenance process is initiated from the Create Maintenance Request app. It records equipment details and issue as they occur and is effective in investigating and scheduling repairs.

Maintenance Order

If the problem requires further action, a maintenance order is created to execute the repair or service. During the maintenance process, labor and machine hours, material issuance, and external services for each maintenance operation are recorded using the maintenance order.

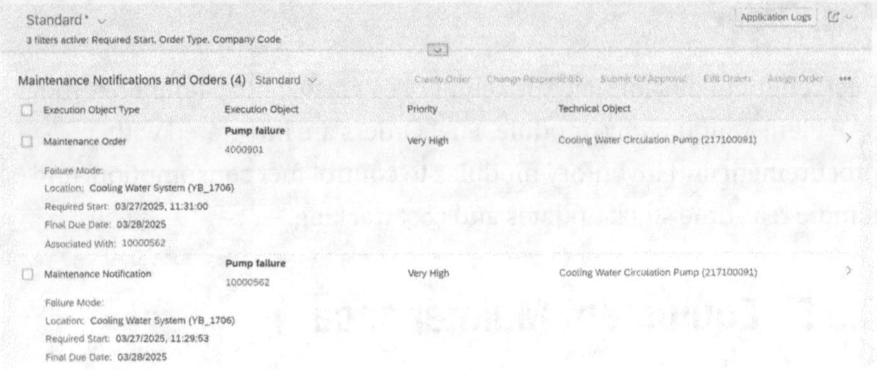

Figure 8-7. *Maintenance notification and order*

Figure 8-7 shows the details of a maintenance notification created to inspect a suspected failure in the cooling water circulation pump, along with the subsequent maintenance order issued to carry out the necessary repair tasks.

Task Lists

The task list is a set of tasks used to plan routine maintenance activities, like inspections, checks, or part replacements. These task lists are used within maintenance plans to ensure that scheduled tasks are performed consistently and in compliance with maintenance guidelines. Users can create or assign these task lists to maintenance orders or maintenance notifications.

There are two types of task lists in the SAP PM module commonly used:

1. General Task List

    The general task list is a standardized collection of tasks that can be applied to various equipment or locations. It serves as a template that can be used across different maintenance activities and is not specific to any particular piece of equipment.

2. Equipment Task List

    The equipment task list is linked to a specific piece
    of equipment and contains maintenance tasks that
    are relevant to that equipment alone. The tasks in
    the equipment task list can be tailored to the specific
    requirements of that equipment.

8.5.6. Corrective Maintenance

Corrective maintenance is performed when equipment unexpectedly
malfunctions. SAP classifies the corrective maintenance into categories
such as Breakdown, Overhaul, Modification, and Cannibalization. For
each of these classifications and categories, SAP has defined a unique
processing path and functionalities to comprehensively execute, monitor,
and report the corrective maintenance. Analytical applications such
as *Maintenance Order Costs*, shown in Figure 8-8, allow maintenance
planners to monitor the progress and cost of maintenance in real-time.

Figure 8-8. *Maintenance order cost*

SAP S4/HANA also integrates maintenance processes with the supply chain, especially when spare parts or external services are needed. In such cases, purchase requisitions are directly triggered from the maintenance order.

8.5.7. Preventive Maintenance

Preventive maintenance prevents equipment from sudden failures by scheduling routine inspection and maintenance based on manufacturer recommendations or equipment usage patterns. SAP categorizes preventive maintenance into time-based or usage-based intervals. Maintenance orders and notifications are automatically created according to the defined schedule.

8.5.8. Equipment Maintenance in EPC Projects

Maintenance orders can be integrated with project WBS elements, and maintenance plans can be linked with network activities. This means that not only cost of maintenance can be allocated to projects, but also the dates of maintenance operations can also be derived from the project schedule. With this top-down approach network activity dates guide the maintenance teams to schedule the maintenance plans according to the availability of equipment.

It is important to distinguish between internal resources managed through network planning in Project Builder, such as machine hours of an excavator assigned to construction activities, and maintenance tasks. While the former refers to the operational use of machines as project resources, the latter focuses on the enhancement of the excavator's functionality and life through repairs and servicing.

At the RefineX project, corrective maintenance occurs when a pump unexpectedly breaks down. The issue is immediately reported by the operations team. The issue is logged into the Maintenance Notification app. The maintenance team inspects the pump, and if the pump requires extensive repairs, a maintenance order is created to initiate the repair process.

To ensure that the pumps and compressors continue to operate efficiently, the maintenance team uses the SAP S/4HANA preventive maintenance process. It involves regular lubrication and inspection of pumps and compressors. A maintenance plan is set up in the SAP Plant Maintenance module to automatically schedule these activities. When maintenance tasks are due, a maintenance order is created automatically. The maintenance team receives reminders through SAP S/4HANA workflows to perform checks and replace parts if necessary. The equipment task list guides technicians in performing routine checks of each pump and compressor as per original equipment manufacture's recommendations.

8.6. Conclusion

In this chapter, we have explored how accurate forecasting, efficient allocation, and real-time tracking of resources throughout the project lifecycle enable effective project management. We also examined the comprehensive capabilities of SAP S/4HANA in managing tools and assets within the EPC project environment. From tools issuance and tracking to advanced asset accounting, SAP S/4HANA provides in-depth functionalities to address the unique challenges of large-scale construction projects and contribute toward the successful execution of projects.

CHAPTER 9

Handling Project Materials

This chapter provides a comprehensive framework for managing materials efficiently and optimizing resource utilization within engineering, procurement, and construction projects. This chapter explores the management of project materials and encompasses the material lifecycle in a project. From master data creation to the procurement process and inventory optimization to stock replenishment, special emphasis is placed on the integration of SAP functionalities and associated advanced topics, such as nesting, material traceability, project-oriented procurement, and expediting to address the unique demands of construction projects.

9.1. Material Master Data

Earlier, in Chapter 7, we explored the creation of WBS BOM based on engineering design and the transfer of BOM to project activities. The process highlighted the importance of using SAP S/4HANA during the engineering design and project planning phases. In this section, we will explore the role of SAP S/4HANA in handling material components during project execution.

© Sohail Ahmed 2025
S. Ahmed, *The SAP S/4HANA Handbook for EPC Projects*,
https://doi.org/10.1007/979-8-8688-1466-2_9

To optimize the classification process, SAP S/4HANA employs a comprehensive material taxonomy that categorizes materials based on their specific characteristics and roles within project execution. Understanding this material taxonomy is essential for project teams to efficiently manage procurement, logistics, and resource allocation. The classification depicted in Figure 9-1 provides an idea of how material attributes should be maintained in the system.

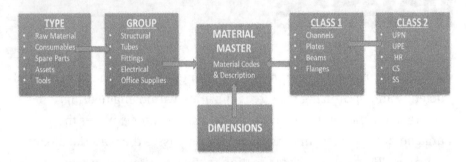

Figure 9-1. *Material classification and hierarchy in material master data*

9.1.1. Material Type

A key aspect of this process is the creation of material master records, where the user selects an appropriate material type. In EPC projects, material types are categorized based on their roles in project execution. The main material types used in EC&O industry are discussed next.

Raw Material

Materials, represented by material type ROH (raw material) in SAP material master (MM) data, are the raw materials used in project construction or manufacturing processes. This type includes both project-specific items (for example, steel plates, pipes) and non-project-specific items (e.g.,

standard bolts and fittings) that are critical for project deliverables. ROH
material types can be used as both direct and indirect material; i.e., they
are procured and issued directly against project-specific activities as well as
used indirectly through procurement and issuance by a cost center.

Consumables

Consumables, identified as HIBE (operating supplies), are used during
project execution but do not form part of the final deliverable. The HIBE
material type is required to be direct material for daily construction
activities, such as welding rods, grinding discs, or minor site works, as
shown in Figure 9-2. However, more broadly, similar to ROH, HIBE-type
materials can also be categorized as either direct or indirect materials
depending on their specific application and accounting treatment.

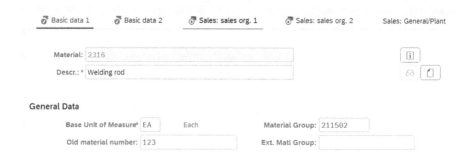

Figure 9-2. *Basic data view of material master data*

Spare Parts

Spare parts are components stored for equipment maintenance and
repair, such as bearings, seals, or replacement parts for cranes and welding
machines. The effective classification and inventory management of
material type *ERSA (spare parts)* ensures that necessary spare parts are
available in a timely manner to minimize machine downtime.

Finished Goods

In EPC projects, the FERT (finished goods) material type includes
pre-assembled items or completed modular sections that are ready for
downstream processes. In the ETO scenario, finished goods are also
created to execute the *Delivery from Project* process, discussed in Chapter 14,
where assemblies are manufactured internally, and the process is used to
track deliveries of assemblies to construction site.

Service Material

Service materials, represented by material type DIEN, should be
understood as being distinct from the service master. Unlike the service
master, which is treated as an advanced level of external network activity,
DIEN are used in SAP where services are planned and procured as physical
materials.

For example, when PrimeCon created the inquiry, quotation, and sales
order for the RefineX project, the material type used in these documents
was DIEN. The key difference between DIEN and other material types,
such as HAWA or FERT, is that DIEN focuses on delivering project services
rather than physical inventory.

Tools

Tools, represented by NLAG in SAP S/4HANA, are non-valuated materials
used for temporary purposes, such as measuring tapes, portable grinders,
or hand tools. The non-valuated material type is used to track the issuance
and return of these tools without maintaining inventory value, ensuring
utilization monitoring and accountability for issued equipment.

Trading Material

The material type *trading material* (HAWA) is utilized for materials purchased for resale without any value addition or processing. In EPC projects, HAWA items, such as pre-fabricated skids, valves, or accessories required for erection of steel structure, are sourced from suppliers and used directly in construction.

Each material type helps define the attributes and behavior of the material, ensuring proper classification, inventory management, and cost tracking throughout the project lifecycle. The following are additional ways of classifying materials.

9.1.2. Material Group

This field in material master is used to group similar materials based on common characteristics. A material group can be assigned to multiple material types, allowing for flexible classification. This relationship is particularly beneficial for reporting and procurement analysis.

For example, in EPC projects, items like bolts, plates, and piping might belong to different material types but share a common material group if they are all categorized under structural or electrical material groups.

9.2. Procurement Documents

During project execution, various categories of materials and services are required as per the procurement plan. Each of these categories has unique logistical and cost allocation requirements. As a result, organizations require different methods for the creation, review, and approval of purchasing documents.

To overcome this challenge, SAP S/4HANA provides comprehensive functionality that enables efficient transfer of requests from the requester vendor, involving key stakeholders. The procurement documents discussed in this section are purchase requisitions and purchase orders.

9.2.1. Purchase Requisition

The process of purchasing is triggered with the creation of a purchase requisition. A purchase requisition (PR) is a request or instruction to a buyer to commence the procurement process for materials or services.

This section presents a structured approach to managing various requisitioning scenarios in SAP S/4HANA for timely availability of materials, services, and assets.

Planned vs Unplanned Requisitions

Purchase requisitions may be raised for different types of materials, services, tools, and assets. These requests, coming from the projects and departments, can be either planned or unplanned.

Planned requests are triggered through MRP run by converting planned orders into purchase requisitions. Unplanned requisitions can be created directly using the PR creation transaction code or indirectly through network activities, as shown in Figure 9-3. SAP PS offers three methods to raise a PR directly from network activity, as follows:

1. Immediately when the network is saved

2. When the user releases the activity

3. Manually, as needed

Figure 9-3. *Purchase requisition from networks*

When the PR is created, it carries the information from the activity to the purchase order, including the required quantity and requirement dates, as planned during the scheduling process.

DMS Integration

During this flow of information, SAP treats purchase requisition as the main document to communicate requirements with buyers. All other documents should be treated as supporting documents and must be provided with PRs as SAP DMS attachments.

PR Approval Workflows

Organizations define signatories with limits of approvals (LOA) for each of the business scenarios just explained. All purchase requisitions must be reviewed and approved by competent authorities as per the defined authority matrix (PR release strategy) before reaching the purchase department.

9.2.2. Purchase Order (PO)

A *purchase order* is a formal request issued by a purchasing organization to a vendor to deliver a specified quantity of goods or services by a particular date. It serves as a legal commitment for purchasing of materials or services and converts internal requirements into external procurement orders.

For project-specific procurement scenarios, POs are automatically linked to WBS elements or network activities by adopting purchase requisitions created from the project or using appropriate account assignment categories directly in the PO.

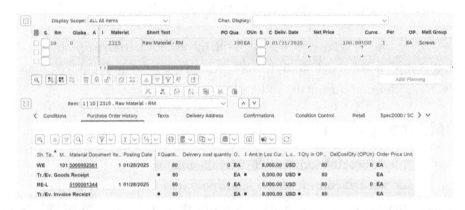

Figure 9-4. *Purchase order created with reference to purchase requisition*

In SAP S/4HANA, a PO can be created directly, with reference to a request for quotation (RFQ) or a purchase requisition (PR), as shown in Figure 9-4. Different procurement scenarios, however, require specific approaches to proceeding with the purchasing process. Procurement scenarios are discussed in detail in section 9.5.

9.3. Team Collaboration

SAP understands that team collaboration during procurement execution is equally critical. Therefore, SAP S/4HANA ensures that both internal and external stakeholders remain involved during this critical process. Key collaboration tools discussed here are release strategy and the Ariba network.

9.3.1. Release Strategy

Release strategy is a feature in SAP S/4HANA that is used to control the approval process for purchase orders (POs). It is defined to ensure that no procurement is initiated without prior approval.

It allows organizations to enforce control by specifying authorized signatories for different purchase organizations with defined approval limits based on PO values, material types, and vendors. This ensures that high-value purchases are reviewed and approved by the appropriate authority levels before being issued to the vendor. After approval, SAP can automatically send the PO to the vendor via a connected email server to streamline communication.

It is important to note that purchase and release orders are legal tender for submission to suppliers and subcontractors; therefore, if these documents must be printed, a strict policy should be applied. Using SAP S/4HANA can restrict their printing until system-based approval is completed as per the release strategy.

9.3.2. Ariba Network

SAP offers Ariba network application as a more advanced alternative for real-time communication, approval, and collaboration. If Ariba is implemented, it becomes the core tool for collaboration between the buyers and vendors for automated document exchange. Using Ariba network's self-service portal, suppliers can confirm orders, update delivery schedules, and track payments, providing visibility into the end-to-end procurement process.

9.3.3. Expediting

The process of expediting in SAP S/4HANA allows the procurement team to closely monitor the progress of material acquisition throughout the purchase order lifecycle by configuring several expediting *scenarios* and tracking the progress of key *events* for each scenario.

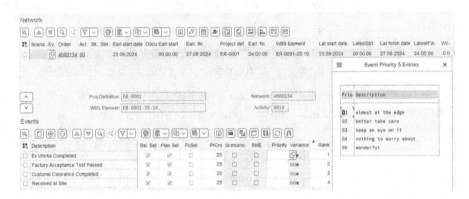

Figure 9-5. *Expediting process for procurement scenarios and event tracking*

A *scenario* ensures that all key variations in the procurement process are accounted for, while each *event* corresponds to a critical milestone within the scenario. For example, Figure 9-5 shows the event sequences of imported materials. The Event section of the scenario lists major procurement milestones, each with defined sequence and priority; the weight of each event is created as a percentage of completion (*PrCm*).

The scenario and events for locally procured material would differ, as certain steps, like customs clearance, would not be required. This structured expediting approach enables procurement teams to proactively manage supply chain risks and ensure timely material availability.

9.3.4. Project-Oriented Procurement

In EPC projects, managing large volumes of procurement-related documents can be challenging. To address this, SAP S/4HANA provides the *Project-Oriented Procurement (PROMAN) app*, as shown in Figure 9-6.

Figure 9-6. *Procurement document control with PROMAN*

Procurement Progress Tracking

PROMAN serves as a centralized procurement monitoring tool that integrates purchasing, material management, and logistics functions into a single interface. It allows project teams to execute, track, and analyze procurement activities in real-time, improving coordination between departments.

Procurement Document Tracking

The PROMAN detailed project hierarchy is integrated with various procurement documents, including purchase requisitions, purchase orders, reservations, goods issues, stock transfer postings, and deliveries. This integration provides detailed insight into requirements, improves procurement efficiency, and offers greater control to buyers and project controllers.

9.4. Outline Agreements

Outline agreements define long-term procurement frameworks or contracts that maintain preliminary terms or guidelines for an agreement for improved cost predictability and streamline repetitive purchasing activities.

An outline agreement is a contract between a customer and a vendor that outlines the terms for purchasing partial quantities or values of goods or services in recurring intervals over a specified period. An outline agreement can be created in SAP S/4HANA MM module as contracts or scheduling agreements.

9.4.1. Contract Management

Contracts are created when an organization needs to get into a long-term outline agreement for specific materials or services over a certain period of time. There are two types of contracts:

1. Quantity-based contracts

2. Value-based contracts

Quantity-based Contracts

In quantity-based contracts, the overall quantity to be purchased from the vendor is fixed. These type of outline agreements are useful when the focus is on volume buying over a long period of time. It is beneficial to secure consistent supplies of high-consumption materials, such as cement, structural steel, electrical cables, and so on. Suppliers may offer quantity discounts as an incentive for larger purchases. Using the PO history shown in Figure 9-7, procurement transactions such as goods receipts and invoice receipts can be tracked to ensure compliance with the contract.

It.. Ty.. Ca PGrP.. Doc. Date Material Short Text   Matl Group D I / Plant Locati.. Quanti.. O.. Quanti.. S.. Net Pri.. Crcy F

Supplier/Supplying Plant
Purchasing Document 4500000929
  10 NB2 F 001   10/25/2020 TG12   Trad.Good 12,Reorder Point,Reg.Trad. L001   1710 171R   10- PC   10- PC
Supplier/Supplying Plant 1000529   MM Corp
Purchasing Document 4500001896
  10 NB F 001 .ıll 12/07/2024 2307   ESPP Material (HAWA)   01   1710   1 EA   1 EA 100.00 USD

≡   PO History for Purchase Order 4500001896 Item 0...

Sh. Te.. M.. Material Document Ite.. Posting Date ΣQuanti.. Delivery cost quantity O.. Σ Amt.in Loc.Cur. L.c.. ΣQty in OP.. DelCostQty (OPUn) Order Pri
WE   101 5000002540   1 11/07/2024   1   0 EA   100.00 USD   1   0 EA
Tr./Ev. Goods Receipt   ■   1   EA ■   100.00 USD ■   1   EA
RE-L   5100001341   1 11/07/2024   1   0 EA   100.00 USD   1   0 EA
Tr./Ev. Invoice Receipt   ■   1   EA ■   100.00 USD ■   1   EA

Figure 9-7. *Purchase order history*

For the RefineX project, a quantity-based contract of 100 tons of
cement is created, which would allow multiple release orders of smaller
quantities to be issued as per the procurement plan for one year. This
agreement will provide consistency in the supply of cement, and by using
SAP S/4HANA–provided reports, the project controller will continuously
monitor the commitments against the contract.

Value-based Contracts

In value-based contracts, the overall value of the items purchased from the
vendor is fixed. These types of contracts are best suited for service-based
engagements and are less commonly used in material procurement because
they lack control over the *target quantity* to be procured.

In value-based contracts, recurring services with an upper cap on the
overall target value are controlled by setting target value using the *Limit*
field. This limit ensures that all expenses within this contract remain
within the defined threshold.

Hybrid Approach

To control both quantity and value, a hybrid approach is recommended. For example, in order to control both quantity and value, the project team at RefineX project used quantity-based contracts to control the *target quantity* and *net price,* while the overall budget was controlled using the *release budget* function, as discussed in Chapter 11.

9.4.2. Scheduling Agreements

Scheduling agreements, as shown in Figure 9.8, provide a framework for phased deliveries in line with project schedules; having multiple staggered deliveries minimizes excess inventory. Unlike quantity-based contracts that track total quantities and values, scheduling agreements in SAP S/4HANA provide granular control over the delivery schedule.

				Select All Items	Deselect All	Select Start/End of Block	Header Details	Supplier Address	Partner	More ⌄		

Agreement:	5500000038		Agreement Type:	LP		Agmt Date:	11/14/2024	
Supplier:	17300002	Domestic US Supplier 2			Currency:	USD		

Outline Agreement Items

Item	I	A	Material	Short Text	Targ. Qty	OUn	Net Price	Per	OP	Mat. Grp	P	Plnt	SLoc
10			2307	ESPP Material (HAWA)	1,000 EA		50.001	EA	01		1	1710	
20			2307	ESPP Material (HAWA)	2,000 EA		70.001	EA	01		1	1720	

Figure 9-8. *Scheduling agreement*

For the RefineX project, an outline agreement for 100 tons of cement requires weekly deliveries over one year, but the required weekly quantity is not fixed. This is where a scheduling agreement becomes important. SAP allows setting up the *Delivery Schedule Lines* field in the scheduling agreement to specify exact delivery dates and quantities through its integration with MRP, using the *MRP Area* and *Delivery Schedule* fields.

9.4.3. Release Order

A release order is a document type in SAP MM that optimizes the procurement process for outline agreements by reducing the need for repetitive creation of purchase requisitions and purchase orders.

After finalizing the delivery schedule in the scheduling agreement, the buyer can directly create a release order using the standard PO transaction by referencing the agreement number. This step ensures compliance with agreed-upon terms and provides tracking via fields like *Release Indicator* and *Target Quantity*. For example, a release order for a quantity-based contract for cement can fulfill incremental site requirements without creating new POs for each batch.

Organizations can further optimize the procurement process by defining separate release strategies for release order approval. Using the SAP DMS document type for contracts, all contractual documents should be attached to release orders using SAP DMS.

9.4.4. Ariba Contracts

SAP Ariba Contracts is a contract management tool that can also be integrated with SAP S/4HANA for executing operational tasks related to procurement. Through this integration, contracts created in SAP Ariba Contracts are linked to SAP S/4HANA outline agreements. Pricing terms and conditions defined in SAP Ariba Contracts are shared with SAP S/4HANA, enabling buyers to use these prices for order processing.

9.5. Procurement Scenarios

For engineering and construction projects, SAP S/4HANA supports multiple procurement scenarios to streamline project-specific purchasing, ensuring that each PO is aligned with the project's operational needs.

9.5.1. Assets Procurement

This scenario involves creating purchase requisitions (PRs) for assets linked to specific projects or cost centers. The process ensures that equipment and other fixed assets required for the project or departmental needs fulfill both logistics and financial reporting needs. When a department or project team identifies a need for new equipment or fixed assets, the requisition is linked to a WBS element or cost center that defines the cost allocation for the asset purchase.

For example, if a new crane is needed for a construction site, the asset management team initiates the PR for the identified asset, specifying the cost center or WBSE and the asset master record.

9.5.2. Project Materials

SAP S/4HANA offers different ways of handling the procurement of project-specific direct materials and consumables.

For example, if a project requires steel plates for structural work, these materials can be planned and converted into PRs automatically. Project materials are either created through preliminary requisitions on network activities or automatically converted from a *project MRP* run.

The planning engineer reviews the material list to ensure that all project-specific requirements are covered. Date and quantity optimization processes are employed to fine-tune the material requirements, with date optimization involving aligning material delivery with the start date of network activities and quantity optimization ensuring that only the required quantity is ordered, considering existing stock.

9.5.3. Subcontracting Orders

When specific manufacturing processes, such as painting or fabrication, are outsourced to vendors, subcontracting orders are created to manage the goods issuance of raw materials to subcontractors and handle receipt of finished goods. Subcontracting involves sending raw materials to a vendor for a specific value-adding process, such as painting or assembling. The PRs in this scenario are created for finished or semi-finished goods.

The requisition for subcontracting begins with the creation of a purchase requisition for finished goods that will be received once the subcontractor completes the value-adding process, such as assembly or painting.

During the PR creation, the bill of materials (BOM) for components that need to be sent to the subcontractor is included to ensure visibility and proper tracking of materials in transit. Once the PR is approved, it is converted into a subcontracting purchase order. This PO governs the shipment of components to the subcontractor and outlines the receipt of the finished product upon completion.

9.5.4. Non-Project Materials

Non-project materials mostly include general consumables but may include direct materials. For example, office supplies or workshop consumables are managed through this process. These materials are mostly needed for supporting regular operational needs. They are not linked to specific project requirements, nor do they depend on project design. In SAP S/4HANA, such materials are managed using standard *plant MRP* or *material MRP* procedures, as follows:

1. Plant-level MRP enables centralized planning for routine materials needed across departments.

2. Material-level MRP allows for detailed planning at the individual material level, ensuring that day-to-day operational needs are met effectively.

Both MRP runs consider current stock levels—including safety stock or minimum stock—replenishment lead times, and procurement types to generate accurate purchase requisitions as needed.

9.5.5. Spares And Maintenance Services

These PRs can be created from projects, but it is advisable to create these automatically from maintenance orders to ensure continuity of operations. By managing spare parts and external maintenance services from maintenance orders, the requirement dates of spares and services are directly linked with the maintenance dates. Later maintenance orders can be settled to the project for cost collection.

9.5.6. Departmental Requests

For materials and services required by different project support departments, PRs are created based on requests from relevant cost centers. For example, PRs for IT equipment or safety supplies are linked to corresponding IT and HSE departments (or their respective cost centers). Later, these costs are allocated to the project using standard cost allocation methods.

9.6. Requirement Optimization

After the BOM transfer process is completed, as discussed in Chapter 7, and before the material is requisitioned from a project, as discussed in section 9.2, the date and quantity of materials should be optimized to reduce unnecessary inventory accumulation. This optimization is achieved through various strategies, including nesting, stock replenishment, and efficient transfer to projects, which will be explored in this section.

9.6.1. Nesting

In ETO project scenarios, *nesting* is performed before fabrication so that the most optimized material layout is found and any available material in current stock is used. In the nesting process, the precise quantity of material required for fabrication is calculated.

While nesting is handled outside of SAP using third-party software, its outputs can be integrated into SAP through material components in the WBS BOM. The quantity of direct material transferred from the WBS BOM reflects the total designed weight, but the actual purchasing requirement is determined during the nesting process.

To incorporate nesting outputs into SAP, it is important to optimize MRP parameters for adjustments to procurement quantities based on nesting calculations, and to activate the *batch management* feature to allow proper tracking of offcuts and scrap material. Custom reports can be created to analyze how nesting impacts material requirements, providing clarity for future procurement decisions.

9.6.2. Transfer to Project

The *goods movement* process involves transferring materials internally between storage locations, such as from stores to projects or between different WBS elements. Each WBS element in SAP S/4HANA can be treated as a separate storage location. This can be done by choosing the *Valuated Project Stock* indicator.

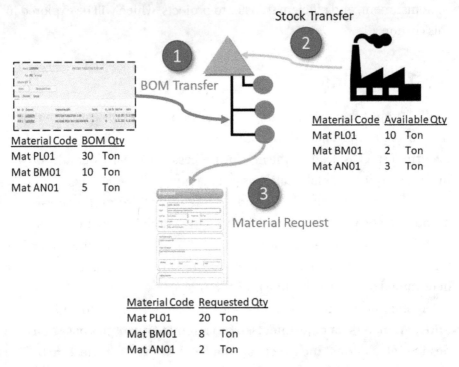

Figure 9-9. *Material requirement optimization using stock transfer*

After nesting, the material coordinator searches for unreserved stock across stores, other projects, or off-cuts. Available quantities are transferred to the direct material WBS element of the project using a *stock transfer order*. This process, illustrated in Figure 9-9, will offset BOM requirements by the quanitities transferred to the project and will generate the purchase request for the remaining quantity only.

9.6.3. Stock Replenishment

Stock replenishment refers to the process of restocking inventory when levels drop below a predefined threshold.

In SAP S/4HANA, stock replenishment is the process of continuously monitoring the stock levels and the automatic generation of requests for purchasing and production through the material requirements planning (MRP) functionality. It is an important process of reordering that ensures optimum inventory levels and prevents stockouts and disruptions.

The initial step in stock replenishment is initiated by an MRP run. When the available stock level of non-project-specific materials, planned at the plant, drops below a predefined reorder level, materials are flagged for replenishment in the next planning cycle. For project-specific items, the material procurement process is triggered upon receiving the purchase requisition.

Roles in MRP Execution

Effective execution of MRP relies on a well-structured approach where each business role has clearly defined responsibilities. A precise delineation of roles ensures smooth coordination with minimum disruptions. By assigning specific tasks to key stakeholder roles, shown in Table 9-1, businesses can enhance efficiency and maintain optimal stock levels.

Table 9-1. *Specific Tasks Assigned*

Business Role	Responsibility
MRP controller	Maintain minimum, maximum, and safety stock levels to avoid understock and overstock situations
Procurement manager	Close purchase orders or cancel unwanted PO items
Planning engineer/ maintenance engineer	Close open purchase requisitions and reservations
Warehouse manager	Monitor current stock levels

9.6.4. Material Workfront

After the shopfloor drawings are issued for fabriction and material requirements are firmed in the *detailed BOM*, the planning engineer ensures material availability for each assembly by repeating the goods movement process.

The required quantities are moved from the procurement WBSE to the lowest level WBSE using a standard *movement type*. The planning engineer can now establish a clear workfront and ensure assembly-specific material planning is accurate.

9.7. Inventory Optimization

In EPC projects, project-specific engineering and design frequently drives the need for creating new material records. Most of these are direct materials tailored for unique project scenarios, which require precise definitions and attributes in the system.

Managing material master data effectively is critical in SAP S/4HANA to prevent overloading the system with excessive records. Next, we explore key attributes and how SAP functionalities can be leveraged to simplify and streamline material management.

9.7.1. Material Description

The material code and short description provide the basic information about the material. In SAP S/4HANA, these fields are essential for searching, reporting, and categorizing materials.

For example, the description of a steel pipe could be:

Seamless Carbon Steel Pipe, ASTM A106 Gr. B, 6"
SCH 40, 6m Length, Beveled Ends

This description is perfectly correct and provides complete clarity about the item. However, due to client-driven design in EPC projects, especially when an ETO production strategy is adopted, there is a constant need for new material creation.

Defining such descriptions in material master data requires separate master records for each variation. This leads to overloading the system with data, possible data redundancy, reduced analytical capability, increased system maintenance, and higher probability of errors.

Characteristics and Class

One effective strategy for managing project materials is to limit the use of variable attributes in the material code and use a SAP S/4HANA-provided classification system that includes *characteristics* and *class*. This functionality was discussed earlier, in section 7.6. In this section, we will see how this functionality is adopted to define material attributes. *Characteristics* represent specific attributes or properties of a material, where it is assigned as a numeric or text value that makes it easier to capture specific details about a material. As shown in Figure 9-10, the *Class* groups different characteristics and acts as a categorization structure to apply characteristics to a specific material type.

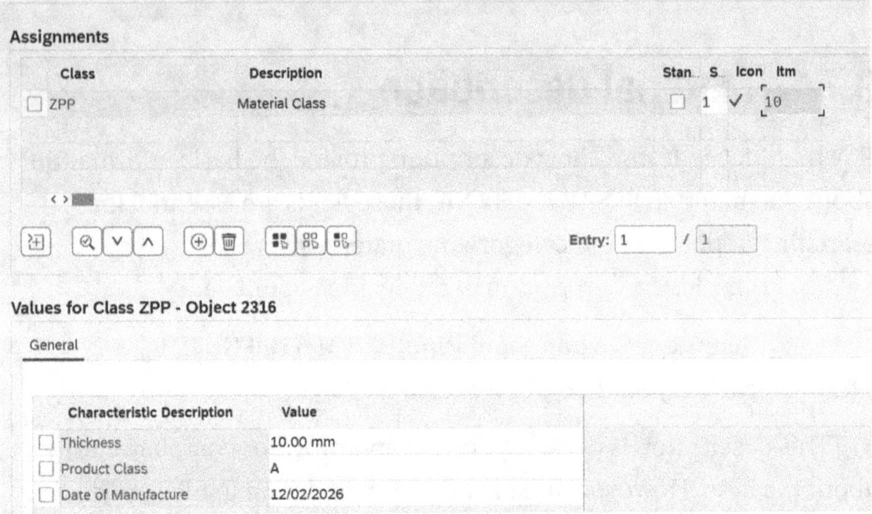

Figure 9-10. *Material optimization using material class and characteristics*

Adopting the classification system eliminates the need to embed every variation directly into the material code or its description. This reduction in the number of master records will improve both engineering and material management. For example, if carbon steel plates are needed in different lengths and thicknesses, a single material code can be created with attributes for *Length, Diameter,* and *Thickness* defined as its characteristics. By using dynamic classification, the exact specification needed for a project can be searched without needing hundreds of distinct material codes for every variation.

At PrimeCon, using the classification system, multiple classes using class type *material (001)* are created, as shown in Table 9-2.

***Table* 9-2.** *Class Type*

Class	Value
CL111	CARBON_STEEL_PIPES
CL121	STAINLESS_STEEL_PIPES
CL131	ALLOY_STEEL_PIPES

The class CL111 may encompass all carbon steel pipes used in the project, with different sizes, grades, and other properties maintained under characteristics, as shown in Table 9-3.

***Table* 9-3.** *Carbon Steel Pipes Properties*

Characteristics	Value 1	Value 2	Value 3
Material grade	ASTM A106 Gr. B	ASTM A53 Gr. B	ASTM A333 Gr. 6
Pipe diameter	6 inches	4 inches	8 inches
Schedule	40	40	80
Length	6m	12m	3m
Wall thickness	6.02 mm	5.56 mm	8.18 mm
Schedule	40	80	160
End treatment	Beveled ends	Square cut	Flanged ends

Configurable Materials

In scenarios where materials have numerous combinations of characteristics, configurable materials or material variants can also be used. Configurable materials allow for the specification of different options during the order creation stage, making them suitable for products with variable configurations. But this approach is more suited for a product development project or for an EPC project with MTO or MTS production planning strategies.

For example, a configurable material for a skid assembly in an EPC project may include options for different component sizes, layouts, and treatments, reducing the number of separate material codes.

In EPC projects, the use of characteristics and classes as just discussed allows project teams to record variable attributes without the need to manage complex configurations and data maintenance.

9.7.2. Material Traceability

Material traceability is the process of tracking a material's origin, history, and condition during different phases of a project. This capability is essential for EPC projects, as it enables project teams to ensure that all materials used are compliant with specifications and regulations.

Batch Management

SAP S/4HANA supports material traceability through its batch management functionality. The *batch information cockpit* captures important traceability attributes of a material. This functionality is primarily to handle materials that require specific tracking based on production batches during manufacturing. In the EPC context, where materials must meet design specifications and quality and safety standards, using batch management, as shown in Figure 9-11, can be extremely helpful.

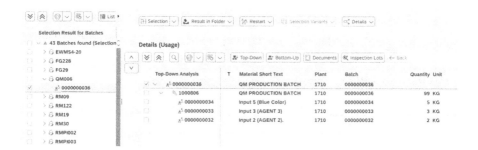

Figure 9-11. *Material traceability using batch management*

Traceability Attributes

The best use of batch management is to define key attributes as per organizational needs. These attributes are defined as characteristics and are entered into the system. Some of the examples of attributes are shown in Table 9-4.

Table 9-4. *Key Attributes*

Characteristics	Purpose
Vendor batch number	Helps track the source of the material; required for customer complaints
Heat number	Provides insight into the specific batch of raw material
Expiry date	Helpful for materials and consumables where regulations demand maintaining the information, such as perishable or inflammable items

These attributes can be added during receiving inspection, when the vendor batch number and heat number are recorded, allowing for seamless traceability of materials issued to production or subcontractors.

The traceability functionality can also be extended during quality inspection and delivery to the project site. Similarly, customer materials can be easily tracked by using the customer or sales order number as a reference attribute.

Alternate Unit of Measurement

When dealing with construction material, the measurement unit may vary based on different operational needs. For example, the scenario shown in Table 9-5 may occur where different teams require different units of measurement of the same material.

Table 9-5. *Measurment Units*

Phase	Unit of Measurement	Purpose
Engineering	Number of pieces	Bill of materials
Procurement	Tons	Bulk procurement, transportation, and inventory management
Production	Square meters	Calculating surface area
Fabrication & Construction	Linear meters	Record material issuance and quality control

In SAP S/4HANA, the SAP MM module provides the functionality to define an *alternate unit of measurement* of a material code. This feature allows flexibility in material management and provides the ability to use the appropriate measurement for its specific purpose.

9.7.3. Traceability Scenarios

Construction material often changes dimensions and properties after going through fabrication and construction processes in an ETO setup. Although they retain the same material codes, these changes in the dimensions, as shown in Figure 9-12, make these items unusable for the project they were procured for. These leftover materials not meeting the design specifications are broadly categorized as Scrap and Surplus materials.

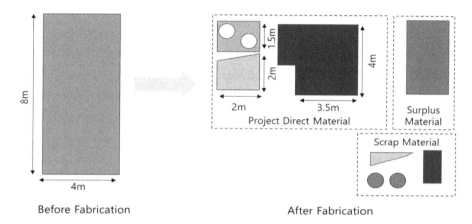

Figure 9-12. *Tracing leftover material during fabrication process*

Scrap Material

Scrap material refers to leftover, unusable, or damaged materials— resulting from manufacturing or construction processes—that cannot be utilized in their original form for project activities. These materials are often designated for disposal with some residual value.

Surplus Material

Surplus material is the leftover stock generated during the fabrication process that can be reused. These off-cut materials are not a project waste. They retain residual value higher than scrap material, so they cannot be treated as scrap. But at the same time due to their non-standard specifications, they cannot be returned to the main storage location as regular inventory. Surplus material is usually transferred to a different project if a similar requirement arises and is used during requirement optimization.

Transfer postings of the surplus material moves the surplus material to the new project with updated valuation and attributes. Both WBS elements should be configured as *valuated project stock* to keep track of the surplus stock, which ensures that the cost implications are correctly aligned with the new project cost.

In most scenarios, however, these materials are not immediately reusable. Therefore, to accurately account for the surplus material when the requirement arises, a dedicated storage location can also be set up in the system. This storage location should be distinct from regular project stock locations, allowing easy identification and segregation of surplus materials using standard SAP reports.

Additionally, changes in material dimensions and attributes that occur during on-site processes should be systematically updated and recorded. In SAP S/4HANA batch management, these new dimensions can be managed through material characteristics and batch attributes to reflect the revised material properties.

Client and Vendor Material

Keeping track of client material and vendor-returnable materials is common in EPC projects. Client material and return-to-vendor material demand specific tracking and management due to their distinct roles in project inventory, as follows:

1. *Client material* refers to items supplied by the customer for use in specific project tasks, such as specialized equipment or essential components.

2. *Return-to-vendor material* includes items sent back to suppliers for quality issues or rework.

In SAP S/4HANA, a designated storage location should be created within the operating plant to manage these materials separately from general inventory. *Storage location-to-storage location* movements should be systematically managed by using standard SAP movement types.

Site and Shopfloor Material

In some cases, large quantities of material are issued to the production floor or construction site. This material can neither be consumed within a single financial period, nor be monitored by the storekeeper daily. This situation makes financial reconciliation and material inventory quite challenging.

In SAP S/4HANA, this situation is managed by defining a designated shopfloor/site storage location. Material is first transferred from the main store to this storage location without executing the goods issuance process, which is then issued at the time of consumption.

9.8. Conclusion

This chapter explored how SAP S/4HANA can optimize the procurement and inventory management processes in EPC projects. From managing procurement contracts to reducing material wastage, it is evident that SAP S/4HANA not only offers functions and features, but also offers a comprehensive framework. For ETO scenarios in particular, material classification and traceability functions ensure compliance with internal controlling and external regulations. The focus on proactive management of surplus, scrap, and customer materials highlights the importance of using SAP S/4HANA for improving project performance and cost effectiveness.

CHAPTER 10

Quality Management

While handling project materials and services is critical to project execution, ensuring their quality is equally important for project success. In this chapter, we will explore how the SAP S/4HANA Quality Management module integrates quality control processes across the entire supply chain to ensure that products and services meet predefined quality standards.

SAP S/4HANA supports quality management (QM) processes from quality planning and inspections to nonconformance and audit management processes. The QM module interacts and integrates seamlessly with other SAP modules to deliver a unified approach to quality control by embedding quality checks and balances in the project quality control process. Key functions within the Quality Management module include inspection lot creation, sample selection, recording inspection results, and making decisions regarding acceptance or rejection of materials or processes. It also offers several tools, features, and functionalities to optimize the logistics and supply chain of projects.

10.1. Quality Planning

The quality planning process for engineering, procurement, and construction projects largely depends on client requirements and the specific stages of project execution. Quality planning establishes a standardized approach to quality control by maintaining inspection attributes for materials, inspection methods, inspection levels, standard tasks, test equipment, and work centers as master data in the SAP QM module.

© Sohail Ahmed 2025
S. Ahmed, *The SAP S/4HANA Handbook for EPC Projects*,
https://doi.org/10.1007/979-8-8688-1466-2_10

10.1.1. Quality Inspection Plan

Inspection and test plans (ITPs) in the EC&O industry define how, when, and by whom the inspection will be performed during project execution. ITP serves as a benchmark for inspections. SAP S/4HANA manages quality planning through the creation of *quality inspection plans* (QIPs) in the SAP QM module.

A quality inspection plan is a master data record that outlines the specific quality-inspection procedures for materials. The inspection plan specifies the material, plant, usage, control keys, and lot sizes. It details the sequence of inspection operations, the characteristics to be inspected, and work centers. These characteristics can be quantitative, qualitative, or both.

10.1.2. QC Work Center

It is recommended to set up dedicated work center(s) for quality-control resources, such as quality labs where quality tests will be performed, and also quality inspectors. These work centers are referenced in the QM order to track and manage quality-related activities such as inspections, rework, and defect resolutions. The QC work centers allow the allocation of labor or machine to specific tasks and report the effort and cost of quality. Every QC work center is assigned a cost center so that the costs incurred on a work center can also be recorded and monitored.

10.1.3. Quality Documentation

During inspection, SAP DMS can be used as a central repository to store and manage quality assurance manuals, procedures, and other quality control–related documents. This centralization provides the quality management team quick access to all quality-relevant documents. SAP DMS can also be integrated into quality inspection processes, such as during results recording and usage decision.

10.2. Material Inspection

In SAP QM, the inspection process follows a structured cycle, shown in Figure 10-1. It starts with the creation of inspection lots based on the criteria established in the quality plan. These lots are generated either automatically or manually, triggered by events such as goods receipt, production activities, or material issuance. This is then followed by recording the inspection results, defects recording (if any), and usage decisions and stock-posting (for stock-based inspections).

Figure 10-1. *Inspection process in SAP QM*

10.2.1. Inspection Levels

Inspection levels are predefined stages with clear definitions of responsibilities as to where and by which party inspections must be carried out. In SAP QM, the *Manage Inspection Plans* feature enables users to plan and define the inspection levels within the system and align inspections with specific project-quality requirements.

Predefined inspection levels should be configured to specify the stages of inspection. For example, for the RefineX project, the inspection levels shown in Table 10-1 are agreed upon in the ITP.

Table 10-1. *Inspection Levels*

QC Levels	Process	Responsibility
Level 0	Material receiving inspection	EPC contractor
Level 1	Final inspection at project delivery	Customer
Level 2	In-process inspection for specific materials only	Customer
Level 3	All in-process inspections done by client	Customer

Each inspection lot is linked to the material or vendor associated with the process. The SAP system records and evaluates the results of the inspections to allow users to document and make decisions about whether the materials or processes meet the required quality standards or not. As shown in Figure 10-2, the *Inspection Lot Detailed Analytics* Fiori app provides deeper insights into the quality of materials and processes.

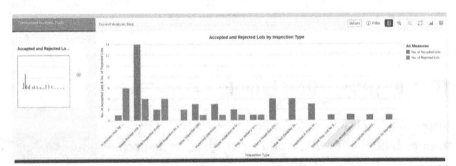

Figure 10-2. *Inspection lot detailed analytics*

10.2.2. Standard Inspection Task

QC tasks performed during inspections are defined and standardized
in the SAP QM module. These tasks, as shown in Figure 10-3, are linked
with inspection characteristics, which include the method of inspection,
sampling procedure, result recording, and tolerance limits.

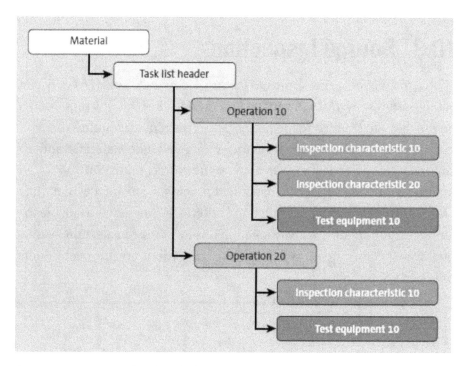

Figure 10-3. *Standard task list in QM order*

As noted earlier, these inspection characteristics can be either
qualitative or quantitative, and required qualifications for inspectors can
be assigned to ensure inspections are carried out by qualified personnel.

10.2.3. Quality Information Record

For EPC projects where contracts restrict vendor selections for materials, it is crucial to maintain a *quality information record* in SAP. This record ties the material and vendor combination together, ensuring proper inspection and verification processes are triggered.

10.3. Source Inspection

Source inspections, also known as factory acceptance tests (FATs), occur at the vendor's premises to verify that materials meet quality requirements before they are shipped to the project site. This process requires the maintenance of quality records in the system to define material–vendor combinations and trigger inspections at the correct times. SAP QM integrates with the vendor management process to ensure that materials are inspected according to predefined criteria. A program is available to automatically create quality inspection lots for source inspection, helping quality inspectors identify which source inspections are due over a defined time period.

Figure 10-4. *Quality Engineer Overview app*

As shown in Figure 10-4, the *Quality Engineer Overview* and *Quality Technician Overview* applications present centralized access to the most relevant information and any tasks related to quality inspection. The information is displayed on a set of cards, such as Inspection Lots Without Usage Decision, Top Defective Materials, Inspection Lots with Defects, and Inspection Severity of Next Inspection Stage. These cards allow quality managers and quality inspectors to focus on the most important tasks and quickly act on the information.

10.4. Receiving, Issuance, and Final Inspection

When materials are received, issued for consumption, or moved for final inspection, the SAP system automatically generates inspection lots based on the predefined inspection plans. The *Usage Decision* app, shown in Figure 10-5, allows teams to classify whether materials pass inspection and can be moved to unrestricted stock or if they should be rejected.

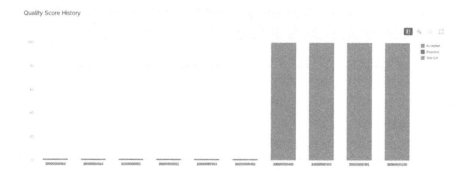

Figure 10-5. *Usage Decision app*

The *defect recording* process enables the efficient creation, recording, processing, tracking, and resolution of defects during this stage. Certified and non-certified vendors are handled distinctly, streamlining the process for material inspection and ensuring that proper procedures are followed for each vendor. Defects can also be recorded manually across categories, such as inspection lots, inspection operations, and inspection characteristics. As shown in Figure 10-6, this categorization ensures precise defect tracking at the material, process, or attribute level so that targeted corrective actions can be taken.

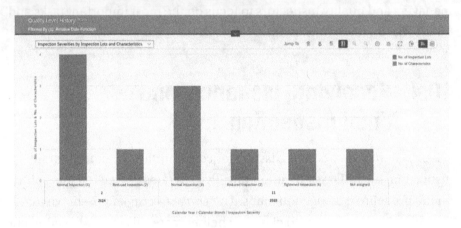

Figure 10-6. *Quality level by inspection severity*

The *Record Inspection Results* app provides access to inspection results and initiates the next steps in the supply chain or construction process based on the inspection outcome. The quality team can efficiently manage multiple inspection lots simultaneously, which is vital for time-sensitive construction projects. If a vendor has consistently and reliably been supplying quality products to a company, then the company can consider using *dynamic modification rule* (DMR) functionality to skip inspections for every good received but also ensure that inspections are *still* performed at regular intervals or frequencies.

10.5. In-Process Service Inspection

In EPC projects, in-process inspection is a critical quality control process that ensures quality standards are maintained throughout the construction and commissioning phases. These inspections are applicable to both materials and services, including fabrication, erection, and testing.

Although inspection lots require the material field, SAP S/4HANA enables service inspections through a workaround using generic, non-valuated material codes. For example, a dummy material named "Welding Inspection" can be maintained in the material master data to represent welding service inspections. Inspection lots are configured to bypass stock-related postings by associating them with non-stock items. This setup will allow service inspections without affecting inventory management.

During service inspections, the *quality inspection plan* (QIP) specifies the stages for inspections, the *quality notifications* record defects and nonconformances, and *quality code catalogs* classify defect types, root causes, and corrective actions. This standardization provides effective root cause analysis and resolution. For enhanced traceability and collaboration, these notifications are linked to WBS elements or network activities.

10.6. Nonconformance Management

Nonconformance management is a structured process designed to identify, document, and address deviations from quality standards in products or processes. This process includes the creation of nonconformance reports (NCRs), which are issued when a nonconformance instance is identified. The NCR serves as a formal record that documents the nonconformity, specifies the corrective actions required, and tracks the resolution process. This approach ensures that any nonconformities are systematically managed to maintain product quality and compliance.

When nonconformities (NCs) are detected on a project, they follow a structured process of resolution. Defects are categorized based on their severity as follows:

1. Minor nonconformance: These nonconformities require minimal rework and will trigger notifications to process owners to make necessary adjustments or submit revised requests.

2. Major nonconformance: These nonconformities require significant corrective actions. QC inspectors are required to issue nonconformance reports (NCRs) and suggest corrective actions (CAs). These suggestions are required to be implemented by the responsible person, department, or vendor.

Nonconformances, defects, or complaints identified during inspections are recorded and tracked through SAP S/4HANA's nonconformance management process. This process provides a robust framework to effectively track and manage quality nonconformance issues. It includes corrective and preventive action tracking and verification of compliance before NCR closure.

Quality catalogs define root causes, such as man, machine, and method, while *standard task lists* outline routine corrective actions with assigned responsibilities for implementation. During corrective action implementation, departments or persons responsible for the issue must close the NCR before the work can resume.

The system integrates corrective actions with notifications to ensure follow-up and timely resolutions. The *Record Defects* and *Manage Defects* apps enable detailed recording of defects, including their location, severity, and impact. The *Resolve Internal Problems* app helps streamline the resolution of internal issues, including quality, schedule, and budget discrepancies.

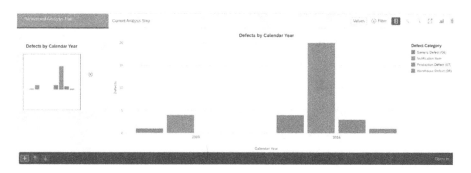

Figure 10-7. *Nonconformance Analytics app*

The *Nonconformance Analytics* app, shown in Figure 10-7, provides insights into defect trends and key quality metrics to derive informed decisions. For complex cases, the system also provides the *8D Problem Analysis* methodology, including the *5 Whys* methodology, to detect the root cause of defects.

10.7. Rework

Rework is a common occurrence during inspections when defects are identified. To ensure the detailed tracking and accountability of rework, SAP S/4HANA enables the recording of rework in a structured manner. Minor rework is recorded against the original activity, while major rework is planned and executed separately to ensure traceability.

In ETO projects where SAP S/4HANA PP module is utilized, a *rework order* can be utilized for defective material components that need rectification. A rework order is a type of production order that orders the assignment of specific routings, material, resources, and overhead costs integrated with *inspection lots* and *quality notifications* to provide a comprehensive quality control process.

245

For EPC scenarios without production order utilization, a new activity or activity element representing the rework is created. Assigning a unique work center and activity type specifically for rework tasks can further distinguish these efforts from standard activities or operations.

10.8. Cost of Quality

Monitoring the cost of quality is essential for understanding the financial impact of quality management activities. SAP QM allows the creation of QM orders that consolidate efforts and costs related to inspections, rework, and nonconformance. These costs can include materials, labor, and external services.

10.9. SAP QM Analytics

SAP QM's analytics applications enhance decision-making by providing visualizations of defect trends, root causes, and resolution effectiveness. One of its key features is the *Quality Score* app, which measures the quality of data and processes against predefined thresholds.

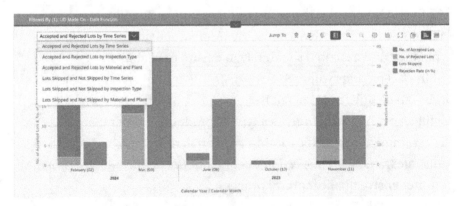

Figure 10-8. *Quality Score app and usage decision history*

These scores help organizations to maintain compliance with quality standards and to implement effective quality enhancements. The Quality Score app acts as a performance indicator that shows defect trends and root causes that offer actionable insights into the quality of products and services. The *Quality Score* app complements quality scoring by maintaining a comprehensive record of inspection results and test data. This historical data allows organizations to analyze trends, identify recurring issues, and evaluate the success of implemented corrective actions, as shown in Figure 10-8.

10.10. Quality Certificates

In EPC projects, quality certificates are used to document the compliance of materials, products, and services against predefined quality standards. These certificates include manufacturer's test certificates, third-party inspection reports (TPIs), material test certificates (MTCs), and factory acceptance test certificates (FATs), all of which can be categorized and linked to specific inspection processes.

SAP S/4HANA allows the automatic or semi-automatic creation of these certificates based on inspection results and batch characteristics, as shown in Figure 10-9. For example, when a material or equipment passes inspection, a corresponding certificate is generated, indicating its conformity to project requirements.

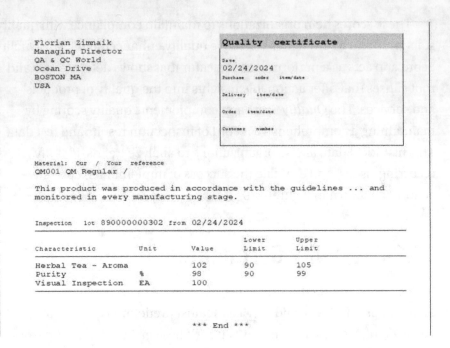

Figure 10-9. *Quality certificate*

For specific customer requirements, certificates can be customized
to include particular specifications or additional inspections. In cases
without an existing vendor–customer relationship, certificates can be
created ad hoc for inspection lots or batches, ensuring full traceability and
compliance in EPC project workflows.

10.11. Audit Management

SAP *Audit Management* is a cross-application solution in SAP S/4HANA designed
to streamline the audit process. It provides organizations with a dedicated
tool to manage audits, including audit planning, execution, and reporting,
without requiring a completed SAP Governance, Risk, and Compliance (GRC)
suite—a component of SAP S/4HANA's *Three Lines of Defense* framework
that emphasizes comprehensive governance and accountability.

The following key features of SAP Audit Management help organizations conduct compliance, safety, quality, and performance audits:

1. **Audit Planning:** Auditors can outline audit objectives, schedule audits, define participants, and use standard templates.

2. **Audit Execution:** Auditors assess compliance and record findings, using checklists and questionnaires to assess compliance for different types of audits.

3. **Audit Reporting:** Audit findings trigger corrective and preventive actions through the *Corrective and Preventive Actions* app. Corrective actions are tracked through SAP notifications and worklists for appropriate follow-up and resolution. Using tools like Smart Forms or SAPscript, SAP S/4HANA can generate structured audit reports similar to the one shown in Figure 10-10.

Additionally, audit components can be created, copied, or deleted, and relevant documents can be assigned to specific components. This solution is ideal for organizations seeking a straightforward audit management tool as part of their governance strategy, whether or not they have implemented SAP GRC.

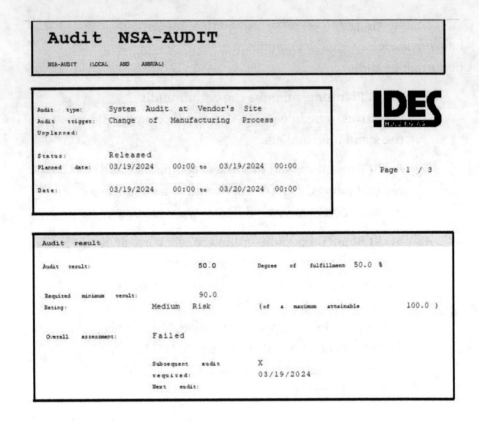

Figure 10-10. *Audit report*

10.12. Conclusion

From planning and inspections to managing nonconformances and audits, SAP QM empowers project teams with real-time insights, streamlined workflows, and centralized data management. These features help EC&O organizations maintain compliance, optimize cost of quality, and achieve their project objectives more efficiently.

CHAPTER 11

Cost Management

The primary goal of project cost and revenue planning is to establish a detailed understanding of the overall planned costs and revenues associated with a project. SAP's approach to cost management includes cost and revenue planning, cost budgeting, cost control, and cost forecasting.

SAP has a clear focus on establishing a connection between a) project cost and revenue, and b) project deliverables and their impact of resource changes. This chapter explores key concepts and planning methods and their application in engineering, procurement, and construction projects so as to demonstrate how these components work together to create a comprehensive financial plan.

Before discussing the details of cost and revenue planning, let's first understand the basic elements of cost and revenue planning in SAPS S/4HANA.

11.1. Cost Management in SAP S/4HANA

In SAP Project Systems (SAP PS), cost and revenue management revolve around several core master data objects from SAP Finance (FI) and SAP Controlling (CO), such as cost centers, profit centers, activity types, and cost elements.

© Sohail Ahmed 2025
S. Ahmed, *The SAP S/4HANA Handbook for EPC Projects*,
https://doi.org/10.1007/979-8-8688-1466-2_11

These elements are integrated within the SAP PS structure to support detailed cost planning, tracking, and profitability analysis. Understanding their functions and roles is essential for project managers and planners who want to effectively control project finances.

During financial planning, a user can assign expected costs for labor and materials to the respective network activities using predefined cost elements, functional areas, and activity types, which are automatically linked to the relevant cost centers and profit centers. As the project progresses, actual costs are posted against these planned values, enabling managers to track deviations and adjust plans accordingly.

This integrated cost structure ensures that all project-related costs are captured comprehensively, providing a clear picture of resource utilization and financial performance. Thus, these master data elements are not just definitions but integral components of SAP PS that enable detailed and effective project cost management.

11.1.1. Profit Center

A profit center is a management-oriented organizational unit used to analyze the profitability of different business areas within a company. It is designed to represent an area of responsibility, such as a product line, business division, or geographical region.

Profit centers enable companies to assess which segments are profitable and which are not by acting as "companies within the company." They are primarily used for internal reporting and decision-making, allowing for decentralized management and financial performance tracking.

In SAP PS, profit centers are assigned to WBS elements to track revenues and costs, helping to assess the profitability of the business unit executing the project, the project itself, or part of the project.

11.1.2. Project to Profit Center Mapping

Profit centers can be mapped to projects using either a one-to-one (1:1) or one-to-many (1:N) relationship. This mapping influences how costs, revenues, and profitability are tracked and reported in balance sheets and profit and loss (P&L) statements.

One-to-One mapping

In a one-to-one (1:1) mapping, each project is itself a profit center, so one profit center is created for every new project. This approach is suited for mega projects that run over multiple years, and organizations or business units need detailed project-specific financial reporting for managerial and statutory reporting. This scenario is also applicable where a separate balance sheet is required to capture the assets and liabilities of each project.

One-to-Many Mapping

In a one-to-many (1:N) mapping, multiple projects are assigned to a single profit center. This practice is useful for organizations looking to consolidate financial data across related projects. The P&L statement aggregates revenues and expenses from all the projects tied to the same profit center, while the balance sheet consolidates assets and liabilities for the entire group of projects. For example, an engineering firm managing multiple small-scale projects might use one profit center to oversee financials collectively. These mapping strategies allow organizations to balance detailed project-level tracking and consolidated financial reporting.

In the example of the RefineX project where separate divisions of PrimeCon—engineering, construction, and manufacturing—are contributing to the project, each division can be represented as an individual profit center in SAP S/4HANA. The business unit to which the RefineX project is assigned, and to which the project is directly contributing profitability, has a profit center assigned directly to the WBS elements. SAP PS captures and reports profitability at this division. Other business units contributing to the project are handled through intercompany or intracompany financial transactions.

11.1.3. Cost Center

A cost center is an organizational unit within a company that records and accumulates costs associated with a particular location or function. Cost centers serve as cost collectors for monitoring and managing expenses in specific areas of the business.

In SAP PS, cost centers represent a clearly defined location where costs are incurred, such as a production department, maintenance workshop, or administrative unit.

At PrimeCon, each production unit is structured as a cost center. The type of resources that operate in each production line determines the activity types that can be created for work centers within that cost center. For costing purposes, one cost center is typically associated with a single *activity type*. This structure allows the allocation and tracking of the cost of each resource type. The rates for labor, machines, or any other cost elements can be uniformly tracked and analyzed at the cost center level.

The cost centers allocate costs, such as labor, utilities, and machine usage, to WBS elements and network activities. For example, at the RefineX project, the labor and machine cost of fabrication and assembling is allocated to the network activity through the cost centers Fabrication Unit and Assembly Unit.

The link between the cost center and network activities in this case is through the use of work centers, which are assigned to a cost center. As labor and machine hours are utilized in these areas, the costs are captured and tracked against each activity. This process enables detailed visibility and analysis of costs associated with each activity based on the rate defined by the activity type.

11.1.4. Activity Type

An activity type classifies and quantifies the activities provided by a cost center, such as labor and machine hours. Activity types are assigned to cost centers, as shown in Figure 11-1, and are used to plan and allocate the costs of activities performed in network activities and WBS elements. They serve as the basis for planning and calculating the cost of work by providing the rate at which specific activities are set within a cost center. Activity types are linked to a cost center by calculating the activity rates based on the relevant direct and indirect costs associated with the resources.

Figure 11-1. *Activity type*

Activity types provide to the network activity the rate of specific activities' costs as set within a cost center. They represent measurable efforts in terms of rate or price for calculating the overall cost of internal activities.

Activity types are linked to a cost center for the purpose of activity price calculation, and while creating the work centers, activity types are assigned to a work center. Therefore, similar to work centers that provide resources, the combination of cost center and activity type provides the rate per hour of the resource.

11.1.5. Cost Element

A cost element functions like a general ledger account in SAP, representing the type of cost or revenue incurred in an organization. The main cost categories in SAP S/4HANA are the following.

Primary Cost Element

Primary cost elements represent core business activities and are directly linked to financial transactions. For example, the costs for concrete purchased, salaries paid to project team, and revenue recorded from services are classified under primary cost elements.

Secondary Cost Elements

Secondary cost elements are used for internal allocations between cost objects. Common examples of secondary cost elements, as shown in Figure 11-2, include allocation of overhead costs from cost centers to project WBS, or assigning costs from internal projects to cost centers.

Figure 11-2. *Secondary cost and revenue elements*

These are used for internal cost allocations and do not represent actual cash outflows. They facilitate the redistribution of costs among different cost centers or projects. For example, using secondary cost elements, the cost of the project management office could be allocated from different cost centers to relevant project work breakdown structures based on the planned cost distribution predefined in the system.

During cost planning in SAP PS, cost elements define the type of expense being planned. By specifying cost elements for different WBS elements or network activities, organizations can achieve detailed cost categorization. For example, "Direct Labor Costs" and "Subcontractor Costs" might be used in separate WBS elements, enabling precise reporting on labor versus subcontractor spending.

Cost Element Group

A cost element group is a collection of related cost elements grouped for planning and reporting purposes. In SAP PS, these groups simplify cost planning by allowing users to plan and analyze multiple cost elements simultaneously.

Cost element groups are used to organize cost elements into meaningful categories, such as "Direct Costs," "Indirect Costs," or "Overheads," making it easier to manage complex cost structures.

Figure 11-3. *Cost element group*

For example, the RefineX project includes extensive travelling and administrative costs. A cost element group named "Overhead Costs," as shown in Figure 11-3, includes cost elements for travel expenses, office supplies, and indirect payroll expenses. By using this group in planning, total overhead cost can be planned across relevant WBS elements. The actuals are posted at individual cost elements, and the comparison of planned and actual cost can be drilled down and reported at the level of individual cost elements.

11.1.6. Functional Area

A functional area serves as an essential account assignment characteristic within SAP PS. It categorizes operating expenses according to their specific functions within a project.

Functional Area

Search and Select	Define Conditions

Search	Q

Items (55)

	Functional Area	≞	Functional Area Name	Validity End Date	Validity Start Date	
☐	YB10		Sales Revenue			
☐	YB15		Sales discounts and allow			
☐	YB18		Cost of Goods Sold			
☐	YB20		Production			
☐	YB25		Consulting/Services			
☐	YB30		Sales and Distribution			
☐	YB35		Marketing			
☐	YB40		Administration			
☐	YB50		Research & Development			

Figure 11-4. *Functional area list*

This classification is important for effective financial tracking and reporting. While the work breakdown structure (WBS) adheres to the project hierarchy, for an organization's consolidated analysis and reporting at company level the assignment of functional areas to cost elements or WBS elements provides the necessary breakdown. Figure 11-4 shows a list of functional areas typically used.

Within the same work breakdown structure element (WBSE), if the actual cost of labor posted includes both direct and indirect labor—such as a welder representing direct labor and a helper representing indirect labor—the functional areas assigned to each cost category differ. As a result, the costs associated with direct and indirect labor cost elements across all projects that share the same functional area can be consolidated for comprehensive reporting.

During the posting of transactions, the system derives the functional area from the master data of the assigned objects, thereby enabling financial reporting from a dimension that is distinct from the project structure. This dual-layer reporting capability is critical for organizations to assess financial performance holistically, facilitating better resource allocation and informed decision-making.

By leveraging functional areas, project managers can gain insights into specific cost drivers, enhancing budget control and enabling more strategic financial planning throughout the project's lifecycle.

In conclusion, these building blocks create the foundation for accurate planning, monitoring, and control of project finances. These components ensure that project costs are well defined, efficiently allocated, and closely monitored for project profitability.

11.2. Cost Planning Methods

SAP PS offers a wide range of cost planning methods, where each method provides its own unique features and functions. This range of features allows users the flexibility to adopt a method that fits the type of project or fulfills the need of different stages of a project.

In Chapter 4 we discussed the use of financial planning for project bidding using SAP S/4HANA Commercial Project Management. In this section, we will discover more cost planning methods.

11.2.1. Hierarchical Cost Planning

Hierarchical cost planning is the simplest form of cost planning. It is structured at the WBS element level, where costs can be planned as total values for the project or divided into fiscal year–specific values. This method is primarily used at a very early stage of the project for rough cost estimations without any reference to SAP financial or logistics objects.

It requires minimal planning effort and expertise, but in the EPC environment, it is only suitable for developing preliminary plans. This method can be applied in creating the initial budget—particularly for preliminary procurement and team mobilization activities. This planned cost is not integrated with any other SAP module, and in EPC projects should be used as an ad-hoc method when the detailed plan is under preparation.

11.2.2. Cost Element Planning

Cost element planning provides a higher level of detail as compared to hierarchical planning. It associates costs with specific cost elements to link SAP PS data with SAP FI and SAP CO modules. In this method, costs are not only planned for individual WBS elements but are also reported in the general ledger. This method is particularly effective when detailed planning and comparison against actuals are required.

In EPC projects, cost element planning is primarily used for overhead planning and in scenarios where logistics master data objects are not available or not required. This method allows accurate planning of internal costs that are not directly impacted by the changes in the logistics master data but are important for project control in SAP Controlling.

11.2.3. Unit Cost Estimates

Unit cost estimates can be used for cost planning when a cost breakdown is needed. It uses quantity-based calculations and uses master data. This method is best suited for projects that involve the extensive use of materials or services where quantity-based tracking is essential.

The unit cost estimate method can be used in conjunction with other cost planning techniques discussed next. Unit cost estimates can also be used in methods discussed later.

A unit cost estimate is a tool for quantity-based calculation of costs. It assigns costs to predefined units of a resource, such as materials, activity types, and services. This tool requires extensive master data in the system, and the planning is performed using these objects.

There are several key material master objects required for planning project cost based on individual resources.

Material Cost

Costs are calculated using material codes, plant, and planned quantity. The system calls unit prices and measurement units from the master data, using automatic account determination to assign the appropriate cost element.

Services Cost

For subcontracted services, the system calculates the total value based on service master data (e.g., unit price and measurement unit). Costs are transferred from the service master's record.

Internal Activity

This covers internal labor and machine costs. The system determines the cost based on cost centers and activity types and evaluates planned quantities based on predefined rates.

Variable Item

This is similar to cost element planning in a way, as while using the unit cost estimate tool if the master data is not available or required, the user can still plan the cost. In addition to the unit cost and quantity, the user can also enter the description of the item and the cost element manually to calculate the total value of the item.

11.2.4. Base Planning Object

Base planning objects (BPOs) are the backbone of unit costing. They are predefined templates that provide standardized cost structures. BPOs can be easily copied and applied across multiple projects or WBS. By using BPOs, users can maintain consistency and control in cost planning while reducing manual setup efforts.

BPOs can incorporate unit costing to specify cost allocations based on specific units. This method is particularly effective for complex projects that require structured cost templates, ensuring that all cost categories are accounted for uniformly.

11.2.5. Easy Cost Planning (ECP)

The distinguishing factor of easy cost planning (ECP) as compared with other models is its data entry process. It is designed for cost estimations using *cost models*.

The cost models use predefined templates that outline standard cost structures, along with formulas and characteristics to automate cost calculations. The cost models enable project estimators to define variables, such as dimensions, derivation rules, unit rates, and quantities, and then use these variables in formulas to derive specific cost estimates for each component. In ECP users can call a cost model from SAP CO and assign it to a WBS element in SAP PS to estimate project cost.

11.2.6. Network Costing

Network costing is a detailed and activity-based method for using networks and activities. Network activities are assigned to work breakdown structures; therefore, the costs planned at activities are aggregated to the assigned WBS elements and subsequently roll up to the highest-level WBS.

Integration with Other SAP Modules

The network costing method is best suited for EPC projects where the planning and distribution of costs across multiple periods is essential. Since SAP objects like material, services, and work centers are assigned to network activities, the cost from master data of other SAP modules—such as purchasing info records, service master data, and activity type—are automatically transferred to the respective network activities. This integration provides a high level of control, standardization, and transparency over the planned cost of the project.

Cost Distribution

This planning method also supports cost breakup for the period and cost element. When the networks are scheduled the logistics data assigned to network activities are also distributed over the project timeline based on the dates of the activities, activity elements, and material components. If the price, distribution, or schedule changes, the planned costs are redistributed automatically to accommodate these changes. Network costing supports the use of distribution keys to allocate labor costs across multiple periods, ensuring accurate period-based costing.

11.2.7. EPC Project Costing

In the RefineX Project, cost planning follows the completion of resource allocation and capacity optimization, as discussed earlier, in Chapter 8. The planning engineer used network costing to establish the main resource cost plan, covering labor, machinery, and materials.

Each cost item was derived based on the planned hours and corresponding standard rates, providing a detailed view of direct costs linked to specific activities.

For overheads, such as administrative expenses or logistics support, the unit costing method within a designated general cost activity was used. This method enabled the user to categorize expenses by individual cost elements, link them to logistics data and network activities, and distribute the costs across different periods throughout the project lifecycle.

11.2.8. SAC Planning Models

SAC planning models are designed to provide a structured framework for budgeting, forecasting, and resource allocation across projects, tightly integrated with SAP S/4HANA. These models are powered with S/4HANA live data connections to dynamically adjust project parameters for accurate and real-time cost projections.

For example, when managing an EPC project, SAC planning models can be integrated with the SAP Plant Maintenance module to track the cost of equipment distributed over the project timeline. This integration enables the calculation of costs related to equipment depreciation, capitalization, and maintenance based on equipment usage. Any changes in equipment usage or maintenance schedules are reflected in the project's financial outlook through planning models. Financial managers can simulate the financial impacts of these factors on the overall project budget and predict future costs.

11.3. Indirect Cost Allocation

Cost planning of indirect resources on a project is performed using one of two options.

11.3.1. Planned Cost Distribution

This method allocates the costs of indirect resources that contribute to multiple projects or non-project activities, whose efforts cannot be directly attributed to a specific project or activity.

These costs are planned by directly distributing them to the respective work breakdown structure elements (WBSEs) of the project.

For example, at PrimeCon the quality control team operates as an indirect resource, working across multiple projects. The costs associated with the quality control team, such as salaries and overheads, cannot be directly attributed to a single project activity. Therefore, to allocate the cost of quality control, the team's monthly salary of $50,000 is distributed using the inherent integration of SAP HCM with WBSE. The cost is distributed based on a predefined breakup, as shown in Table 11-1.

Table 11-1. *Quality Control Team Costs*

Project	Planned Cost Breakup	Distributed Cost
ER.1001	30%	$15,000
ER.1002	50%	$25,000
ER.1003	20%	$10,000

SAP S/4HANA supports cost distribution through cycles for both planned and actual costs. Both follow the same logic of allocating shared costs across WBS elements based on predefined percentages.

11.3.2. Plan Cost Splitting

In this method, the costs of indirect resources or overheads are integrated into the rate of a direct resource by assigning such costs to the splitting structure of activity types, as shown in Figure 11-5.

```
Display status      Total for all periods

Cost Object                    Planned (COArCurr) Crcy

ATY 3110101/MCH01                 1,840,000.00  PKR
ATY 3110101/UTLT01                  580,000.00  PKR
CTR 3110102                                     PKR
ATY 3110102/UTLT01                   63,333.34  PKR
ATY 3110102/ZLAB                     63,333.34  PKR
ATY 3110102/ZMACH                    63,333.32  PKR
CTR 3100000000                                  PKR
ATY 3100000000/LAB01                230,000.00  PKR
ATY 3100000000/MCH01                240,000.00  PKR
```

Figure 11-5. *Plan cost splitting*

Using this method, the indirect costs are accounted for in the overall cost calculation of direct activities, which allocates all costs associated with the activity where the direct cost is planned to use the work center and activity type. For example, instead of allocating the cost of the QC team directly from SAP HCM, if the indirect cost is allocated using cost splitting, the cost element of QC would be made part of the activity type splitting structure. The costs incurred by the QC team would then be included in the overall calculation of the network activity. The cost of the QC team would then be directly charged to the fabrication activity based on the total number of direct hours consumed.

11.4. Direct Resource Allocation

There are different methods available in SAP to define and allocate the rates of internal resources. The rates can be planned manually by entering values manually, or be planned by calculating the planned values based on historical actual costs. The system also supports the use of costing sheets to distribute costs automatically, enabling cost rates to be derived from the previous period's actual values.

For example, PrimeCon decides to define the planned rates manually at the start of the fiscal year and update these rates annually to incorporate inflation, budgetary approvals, overall strategy, and so on. Once these rates are updated, they are applied to all future cost planning activities to keep consistency in financial analysis.

11.4.1. Machine Hours

To determine the cost of machine operation per hour, it is essential to break down the various cost components that contribute to the overall expense. Table 11-2 outlines these key cost elements of calculating the machine-hour rate.

Table 11-2. *Machine Cost*

Cost Component	Monthly Cost	Description
Salaries of machine operator	$10,000	Direct labor cost for machine operation
Indirect labor	$5,000	Indirect labor (e.g., helpers)
Supervision staff	$4,000	Allocated cost of floor supervisors
Depreciation	$6,000	Depreciation cost of the machine
Insurance	$2,000	Insurance cost for the machine
Maintenance	$3,000	Monthly maintenance cost charged to cost center
Fuel cost	$1,500	Monthly fuel consumption
Total monthly cost	$31,500	

If the number of normal available hours per month is 260 hours, the formula to calculate the rate is as follows:

Rate per Machine Hour = Total Monthly Cost / Normal Available Hours
= \$31,500 / 260
Rate per Machine Hour = \$121.15

11.4.2. Labor Hours

The key cost components that contribute to overall labor are shown in Table 11-3. A comprehensive understanding of these components is essential for accurately determining labor costs per hour.

Table 11-3. *Overall Labor*

Cost Component	Monthly Cost	Description
Salaries and benefits	\$20,000	Wages and benefits for direct production staff
Overhead allocation	\$6,000	Administration, utilities, and other general costs
Total monthly cost	**\$26,000**	

If the number of normal available hours per month is 260 hours, the formula to calculate the rate is as follows:

Rate per Labor Hour = Total Monthly Cost / Normal Available Hours =
\$26,000 / 260
Rate per Labor Hour = \$100

11.5. Material Cost Plan

The cost of material components assigned to internal activities is calculated as the product of required quantity and price, with the price obtained from purchasing information records (PIRs). PIRs contain essential data about materials and suppliers, ensuring accurate cost planning.

11.5.1. Valuation Strategy

To ensure the latest price is used for material cost calculation, SAP offers different *valuation strategies*. The valuation strategy is configured with the desired sequence. For example, the following sequence must be maintained in the system so that the latest quoted price take precedence over the purchase order prices, while in the absence of both latest quoted and last purchase price, the system will check the material master data for the moving average of commercial price:

1. Gross quotation price

2. Gross purchase order price

3. Moving average or commercial price

If none of the preceding prices are applicable, then manual updates are required for the planned material component.

11.5.2. Unplanned Material Cost

During material cost planning, if details of material components are partially available, the total estimated cost for a group of materials can be planned at the activity level. For rough-cut cost planning until the exact material is known, the planned cost of material can be maintained using the *Unplanned Material Cost* field for internal activities. With the assignment of these components, these preliminary costs will be automatically deducted from the total planned amount until fully utilized or exceeded.

Accurate material cost planning is vital for maintaining the project budget, as these costs often represent a significant portion of overall expenditures.

11.6. Material Value Flow

SAP S/4HANA PS reports show different material values related to various phases of material handling within the supply chain lifecycle. Each phase represents a different stage in the procurement and usage of materials, and the associated cost values are reported as illustrated in Table 11-4.

Table 11-4. *Material Values*

Stage	Material Planning	Purchase Requisition	Purchase Order	Goods Receipt	Goods Issued/ Consumed
Cost Type	Planned Cost	PR Commitment Cost	PO Commitment Cost	Statistical Actual Cost	Actual Cost
Value	$ 1000	$ 800	$ 700	$ 600	$ 100

11.6.1. Planned Cost

At the beginning of the supply chain process, the material planning phase defines the *planned cost* for the required materials. This is the estimated cost that serves as the baseline for further procurement processes.

11.6.2. Purchase Requisition Commitment Cost

Once a material requirement is identified in the project builder, the purchase requisition is created. The *purchase requisition commitment cost* represents the projected cost of the material requested. It indicates the anticipated financial obligation for the purchase that has not yet been executed.

11.6.3. Purchase Order Commitment Cost

The *purchase order commitment cost* represents a formal commitment to the vendor. It reflects the agreed-upon purchase price of the materials. Figure 11-6 shows the *PO commitment line item* report in SAP PS. This value might differ slightly from the purchase requisition due to changes in material pricing during vendor negotiations.

Doc.	Debit Date	OTy	Object	Cost element	UM	₨	Plan/TC
POrd	11/12/2020	W.	ONG.004	51600000	PC		1,000.00
	11/18/2020	W			PC		360.00
	11/23/2020	W		54300000	PC		1,000.00
			ONG.004		♙	■	2,360.00
₤᠑O						■■	2,360.00
♙						■■■	2,360.00

Figure 11-6. *PO commitment line items for project*

11.6.4. Statistical Actual Cost

Once the materials are received, SAP records the goods receipt (GR). At this point, the system reports the *statistical actual cost*. This cost reflects a goods receipt event and represents the value of the inventory but does not impact the financial accounting directly.

11.6.5. Actual Consumption Cost

The final stage occurs when materials are issued or consumed during the project execution stage. At this point, the system records the *actual consumption cost,* as shown in Figure 11-7. This cost directly impacts financial accounting. It reflects the realized cost of the materials as they are consumed against the activity where they are issued.

Doc. Date	OTy	Object	Cost Element ⌐	Val/COArea Crcy COCr ⌐	Value TranCurr TCurr
11/30/2022	WBS	00000000000000000149TTO	65009000	1,000.00 USD	1,000.00 USD
03/31/2023	WBS			500.00 USD	500.00 USD
03/31/2023	WBS			500.00 USD	500.00 USD
		00000000000000000149TTO ⌂	▪	2,000.00 USD ▪	2,000.00 USD
09/01/2022	WBS	00000000000000000155TTO	41000400	2,000.00- USD	2,000.00- USD
		00000000000000000155TTO ⌂	▪	2,000.00- USD ▪	2,000.00- USD
06/30/2020	WBS	00000000000000000170TTO	65009000	2,000.00 USD	2,000.00 USD
		00000000000000000170TTO ⌂	▪	2,000.00 USD ▪	2,000.00 USD
06/30/2020	WBS	00000000000000001854TTO	65009000	1,000.00 USD	1,000.00 USD
		00000000000000001854TTO ⌂	▪	1,000.00 USD ▪	1,000.00 USD
05/20/2020	WBS	00000000000000001940TTO	94308000	560.00 USD	560.00 USD
		00000000000000001940TTO ⌂	▪	560.00 USD ▪	560.00 USD
11/12/2020	WBS	ONG.004	51600000	900.00 USD	900.00 USD
11/16/2020	WBS			100.00 USD	100.00 USD
11/18/2020	WBS			180.00 USD	180.00 USD
11/18/2020	WBS			180.00 USD	180.00 USD
11/12/2020	WBS		54300000	1,000.00 USD	1,000.00 USD

Figure 11-7. *Actual cost line items for projects*

11.7. Project Budgeting

The project budget represents the approved financial ceiling for executing a project. As discussed earlier, the cost plan provides estimates and serves only as guiding principles for project expenses. Project budgets, however, are binding frameworks that regulate project expenditures.

11.7.1. Original Budget

The budgeting process in SAP PS starts with the planned cost *Copy View* function. This function enables users to select any planned cost version prepared during project estimation or the planning phase and use it as the basis of setting the original budget.

Original budgets can exceed the planned cost, or they can be created without reference to the project planned cost; however, for better transparency and consistency, it is recommended that the original budget always be created using a planned cost version. The original budget thus created will form the cost baseline of the project for future reference.

11.7.2. Budget Distribution

Unlike cost planning, which adopts a bottom-up approach, project budgeting is top-down, as depicted in Figure 11-8. It involves distributing approved costs to WBS elements while ensuring the consistency and accuracy of budget allocation.

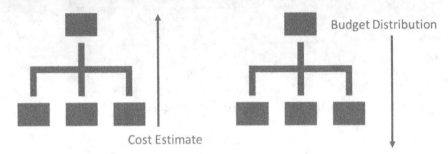

Figure 11-8. *Budget distribution in SAP PS*

Project budgets are hierarchically allocated to work breakdown structure elements to ensure that the entire project scope is approved and actively controlled during the project lifecycle.

The top-down allocation reflects the level of funding available for the project from a higher-level WBSE to its lower-lever WBS elements. The project budget can be distributed hierarchically to ensure effective cost control and monitoring.

The *distributed budget* refers to amounts allocated to subordinate WBS elements, while the *distributable budget* indicates the portion of the budget that remains unallocated and available for further distribution as needed.

The project budget provides the following controls for the distribution process:

1. The total amount distributed cannot exceed the distributable budget.

2. Budget distribution is limited to child WBS elements within the same project hierarchy and cannot be allocated to other WBS elements.

Although SAP PS allows budget distribution to the last level of the hierarchy, while distributing the budget an optimal balance should be maintained between cost oversight and operational efficiency. Restricting the entire WBS hierarchy with budgetary control may affect the flexibility needed to execute the project.

11.7.3. Release Control

After the original budget is allocated and distributed as per the project requirement, the *release budget* functionality comes into play, which allows funds to be spent or committed incrementally. The release budget allows partial budget releases, leaving room for contingencies and management reserves. While the original budget function serves as the baseline for monitoring project expenses, the released budget function prevents overspending by restricting the commitments and actual costs by the amount released for execution.

Although SAP does not restrict the release of 100% of the original budget at once, and the decision to release the budget is governed by management's decisions and budget control policies, it is recommended to use the budget release function for maintaining budget reserves.

A portion of the original budget should be kept in *reserve* and be released at a later stage of the project. This staging ensures cost plan alignment with project progress and allows incremental funding with an additional layer of governance to ensure expenditures remain within approved limits.

11.7.4. Availability Control

The availability control feature in SAP PS enables users to define tolerance limits and specify the action the system should take when the tolerance limits are exceeded. These settings are configured in the *budget profile*. Specific types of transactions within SAP are categorized into business transaction groups to define which transactions are subject to budget availability check.

Business Transaction Groups

The transactions defined in the settings refer to transactions included for monitoring budget consumption. During the availability control check, the system evaluates whether the commitment item and the actual cost posted by these transactions cause the budget to exceed predefined tolerance thresholds or not.

Tolerance Limits

The tolerance limit settings for projects result in sending alerts to the users when the budget exceeds the defined threshold. Based on these settings, when a project's budget exceeds defined thresholds, the system can trigger the following responses:

1. When 80% of the budget is consumed, the system displays a warning message.

2. When 90% of the budget is consumed, the system sends an email notification to the project manager (assigned as an SAP User).

3. Once 100% of the budget is utilized, the system blocks all commitments and actual cost postings.

11.7.5. Project Updates

After the budget is released for execution, if additional funds are needed during project execution, the budget is updated. These updates can take a few forms in SAP PS.

Budget Transfer

If one WBS element exceeds budget limits, budget is transferred between WBS elements within the same project. Budget transfers are attempts to shift budget between WBS elements. Budget transfers cannot be transferred within the same WBS hierarchy (i.e., parent-to-child); use the budget distribution function instead.

Budget Supplements

In case of cost overrun, additional funds can be supplemented to the existing budget. If the transfer process is restricted or does not fulfil the required needs, a supplement allocates extra funds either within the project or from external sources; as shown in Figure 11-9, the original budget is supplemented for Earth Work and Boundary Wall.

E.. Lev	WBS Element	Supplement	Tran.	Current budget	Distributed	Distributable	Remainder	
1	RefineX Project	15,000.00	USD	245,000.00	245,000.00		245,000.00	
2	Engineering		USD	25,000.00		25,000.00	25,000.00	
2	Procurement		USD	45,000.00		45,000.00	45,000.00	
2	Subcontracting	15,000.00	USD	75,000.00	75,000.00		75,000.00	
3	Direct Subcontracting	15,000.00	USD	55,000.00	55,000.00		55,000.00	
4	Earth Work	5,000.00	USD	30,000.00		30,000.00	30,000.00	
4	Boundary Wall	10,000.00	USD	25,000.00		25,000.00	25,000.00	
3	Indirect Subcontracting		USD	20,000.00		20,000.00	20,000.00	

Figure 11-9. *Budget supplement in SAP PS*

Budget Returns

In case of overbudgeting, which usually happens in case of descoping or change of design and specifications, budget is returned.

As a result of the preceding changes, the original budget is changed to the *current budget*. The current budget reflects the updated allocation after adjustments derived by using the following formula:

Current Budget = Original Budget + Supplements - Returns ± Transfers

11.7.6. Budget Currencies

SAP PS budget features offer the flexibility to prepare budgets in various currencies to offer flexibility in executing and controlling global projects. Budgets can be prepared in controlling area currency, company code currency, or object currency. *Object currency* refers to the currency assigned specifically to accommodate budgeting requirements of projects operating in different countries or stakeholders. While the budget is managed in any of the designated currencies, it does not restrict users from executing transactions in any other currency. SAP automatically converts transactional currency to the project's object currency for accurate cost reporting.

11.7.7. Integration Scenarios

SAP *Project Budget* function provides a framework that controls project costs throughout the project lifecycle. It can be integrated with SAP S/4HANA PPM for cross-project governance and SAP Investment Management (IM) for controlling capital expenditure projects. To further enhance its capability, workflows can be created in SAP Build Process Automation to automate the budget approval process and streamline budget approval, release, and update processes.

11.8. Revenue Planning

In SAP PS, the revenue planning features allow users to estimate and distribute expected revenue across project periods based on WBS elements and cost structures.

Revenue planning is allowed only for the WBS elements flagged as *revenue elements*. Revenue planning can be done by methods similar to hierarchical and cost element costing methods.

Cost elements define the types of revenue being forecasted. For projects with multiple revenue streams, individual cost elements can be used to segregate revenue categories such as Direct Sales and Variation Orders.

This stage is independent of project billing and serves as a projection tool to anticipate project cash flow and profitability.

In EPC projects, there is usually one Sales Order line item reflecting the entire contract value. This line item in SAP SD is mapped with one revenue element in SAP PS. Therefore, the entire revenue planning task can be done at the top-level WBSE.

However, if a project's scope includes deliverables with distinct revenue streams (e.g., different types of services or deliverables with separate billing requirements), breaking down the revenue planning into multiple revenue elements will provide better visibility of the revenue.

11.9. Billing Plan

Unlike revenue planning, project billing is the process of invoicing customers as the project progresses when contractual milestones are completed. In simple terms, revenue planning is a forward-looking exercise for anticipating revenue, while billing is a transaction executed based on contractual agreement.

Revenue planning and billing are integrated through the use of sales order account assignment, where the planned revenue values at the *sales order line Item* is integrated with the billing element of the project to generate project billing.

Figure 11-10. *WBS integration with sales order*

To align revenue planning and billing, SAP PS uses a *milestone billing plan*. The total planned revenue value is split and mapped to billing milestones. As shown in Figure 11-11, each milestone is assigned a weightage reflecting its contribution to the total revenue.

Figure 11-11. *Billing milestones with associated invoicing percentage*

As these milestones are reached, the corresponding revenue values are realized by confirming the network activity as completed. This action triggers the billing event, thus maintaining synchronization between forecasted and actual revenues.

For example, in the RefineX project, the root WBS element is used as a single revenue element and the project's direct revenue is planned with one cost element, *direct sales from project*. The total revenue is planned and distributed periodically to ensure the revenue plan is aligned with the corresponding billing milestones. This alignment ensures that when any of the following milestones is marked as completed, the corresponding billing milestone is automatically unblocked in the sales order for generating the invoice. The planned revenue is structured around the following milestones, and their respective weightages are shown in Table 11-5.

Table 11-5. *Planned Revenue*

Milestone	Weight	Billing Amount
Basic design completion	15%	$150,000
Equipment delivery completion	25%	$250,000
Construction work completion	50%	$500,000
Commissioning of equipment	10%	$100,000
Total		$1,000,000

11.10. Conclusion

Cost management is central to the financial success of projects. This chapter demonstrated how SAP S/4HANA enables detailed planning, budgeting, and tracking of project costs through integrated tools and real-time data. These capabilities support project controllers in maintaining financial visibility and control throughout the project lifecycle.

A well-managed cost structure not only ensures accountability but also enhances the project's responsiveness to evolving conditions. The upcoming chapter builds on this foundation by addressing how projects can further strengthen control through structured handling of risks, issues, changes, and claims in an engineering-to-order environment.

CHAPTER 12

Risks and Change Management

The complex and dynamic nature of engineering, procurement, and construction projects often causes deviations from the original project plan. These deviations can originate from unforeseen events or client requests and result in resource bottlenecks or delays in deliveries. These impact project schedule and budget. Addressing these deviations requires a robust application that can perform a complete risk management cycle. From risk identification to implementing the risk response, risk management plays an important role in project execution.

SAP Commercial Project Management (CPM) provides dedicated functionality for risk, issue, and change management to effectively and quickly manage project risks and deviations as needed to ensure project continuity and control.

In this chapter, we will learn what advanced risk, issue, and change management tools and applications are offered by SAP CPM. This chapter will also explore how issue and change management address the structured approach to evaluate issues, perform adjustments, and control resulting changes during project execution.

© Sohail Ahmed 2025
S. Ahmed, *The SAP S/4HANA Handbook for EPC Projects*,
https://doi.org/10.1007/979-8-8688-1466-2_12

SAP S/4HANA Claim Management, which supports documenting and processing claims, will also be covered to provide a solution for an organization not opting to use SAP CPM. Finally, we will dive into the Engineering Change Management (ECM) feature of SAP S/4HANA, which focuses on design and engineering changes.

12.1. Risk Management

Project risk refers to a situation that, if it occurs, will negatively affect project outcomes. Risk management processes involve risk identification, analysis, risk planning, and responding to risks. In SAP CPM, these processes are enhanced through centralized tools, automated workflows, and analytics for better visibility and control.

12.1.1. Risk Identification

Risk identification is the process of identifying the probability of a risk's occurring and its impact on project timelines, costs, outcomes, or quality.

Risk Register

A single source of truth for managing risks is provided by employing a *risk register* in SAP CPM, as shown in Figure 12-1. Risks identified at any stage of the project are effectively documented, shared, and managed within the SAP CPM system. The risk register enables teams to centrally log and track risks in a structured format. Each risk entry includes details such as risk type (cost, schedule, or quality), probability, impact, and current status. It enables the categorization and prioritization of risks. Risks can be integrated and referenced to SAP S/4HANA objects within SAP CPM through the *master project structure*.

Figure 12-1. *Risk register in SAP CPM*

12.1.2. Risk Analysis

Risk analysis involves evaluating potential events that could impact a project. This process uses both qualitative and quantitative approaches. SAP CPM integrates these methods to provide a comprehensive understanding of risks and informed decision-making.

Qualitative Risk Analysis

Users can assess risks using a *risk matrix*, which helps to categorize risks by severity and to prioritize mitigation plans accordingly. The risk matrix is a tool for analyzing project risks by evaluating their probability and impact. It organizes and displays the number of risks corresponding to different combinations of impact and probability levels. Users can define custom thresholds for risk impact, such as setting a high impact when the actual cost exceeds budget by 10%.

Similarly, the *opportunity matrix* is used to analyze identified opportunities. It mirrors the functionality of the risk matrix but focuses on the probability and impact analysis of opportunities.

Quantitative Risk Analysis

CPM integrates tools to calculate risk impact numerically. The sensitivity analysis enables stakeholders to simulate risk outcomes and their potential project implications. Risk managers can input the estimated financial impact of cost overruns, scope changes, or scheduling delays.

In addition to the inherent analytical capabilities of SAP CPM, integrating it with SAP SAC enables real-time monitoring and advanced analytics. Customized key risk indicators further highlight new or escalating risks for enhanced and more advanced risk management.

12.1.3. Risk Response

Risk response is the process of implementing risk mitigation plans to reduce or eliminate the impact of identified risks and issues. In CPM, risk response is facilitated through structured workflows, where each risk is assigned a risk response owner. Mitigation plans define specific actions required to minimize impact, and workflows ensure that approvals are secured for high-risk scenarios.

Risk Versions

SAP CPM supports iterative and dynamic risk management for complex projects. It allows users to create multiple risk versions to monitor changes in risk exposure and evaluate how risk management efforts have impacted project outcomes

Risk versions allow users to document a snapshot of selected risks, including potential impacts, responses, related activities, and object references, and to compare risks at a specific point in time to analyze how effectively the risk response plan worked.

12.1.4. Risk Closure

Once risks are mitigated, transferred, or accepted, SAP CPM allows users to close risks in the risk register. In cases where the risk leads to further issues, the system links the unresolved risks to issue and change management processes, enabling continuous monitoring and resolution.

12.2. Issue and Change Management

In the issue and change management process, the first step is identification and logging the issues as they arise. Once the issue is logged by the user, each issue is evaluated to determine its potential impact on the project. If the issue is deemed irrelevant by the reviewer, or if it does not result in any changes to cost or timeline, it is archived for future reference or analysis. However, if the issue leads to changes in project scope, schedule, or time, for example, it triggers the transition to the *change management* phase.

12.2.1. Issue Management

The Issue Management feature in SAP CPM provides a structured approach to document and resolve project-related issues, which may arise due to unexpected changes, supplier delays, or operational challenges. The *Manage Project Issues* app, as shown in Figure 12-2, serves as a central repository for logging and managing issues, offering transparency and accountability across project teams.

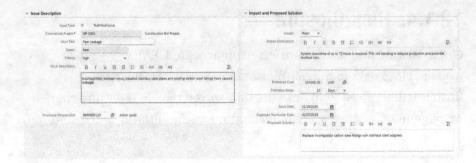

Figure 12-2. *Manage project issues in SAP CPM*

Issue Classification

The process begins by documenting each issue's details, including its ID, description, type, priority, and status. Each issue can also be linked to relevant business partners and reference objects, such as project items, purchasing documents, or other SAP objects. This integration allows users to view the area or stakeholder impacting the project.

Activities

SAP CPM employs a structured approach for its issue resolution process. Actions or measures are defined by implementing activities. *Activities* represent the individual steps necessary to address and resolve an issue. Activities can be created as the following:

1. **Automatic:** Activities are initiated as a standard response based on predefined rules without manual intervention.

2. **Manual:** Steps are created manually for unique or complex issues where predefined rules are not enough. For recurring issues, consistency in implementing measures can, however, be applied by using standard templates.

Approval Workflow

Activities are customizable and can include specific partner assignments and automated email notifications to inform stakeholders of their roles in the resolution process. Approval workflows allow project teams to enforce structured approval processes for complex issues, ensuring that changes impacting scope or budget are reviewed by relevant stakeholders before implementation.

Evaluating and Tracking Issues

Risk or issue owners assess each issue's potential impact on project timelines, costs, and resources. By documenting impact assessments and proposed solutions, project managers prioritize high-impact issues and set clear resolution timelines. Furthermore, the document history feature in SAP CPM maintains a log of all changes made to each issue, including updates to status, descriptions, and assigned responsibilities. This historical record supports accountability and provides a complete audit trail, ensuring that all actions taken to resolve the issue are transparent and traceable.

SAP Analytics Cloud (SAC) integration

CPM integration with SAC provides real-time visibility into issue trends and open issue counts, helping project managers identify recurring issues and bottlenecks that may require further analysis or escalation.

12.2.2. Change Management

In change management, a formal change request is generated, which includes a thorough estimation of the costs and impacts associated with the change. Depending on the nature of the change, it may require external approval from stakeholders or clients. Once the change request is approved, the project's scope, timeline, and/or budget are updated to reflect the new conditions, and the necessary work is carried out according to the revised plan. In Chapter 6, we discussed the creation of separate WBS element(s) for scoping and identification of separate revenue items.

Change Requests

A change request in SAP CPM is created using the *Change Request* app, as shown in Figure 12-3. This integration streamlines the transition from issue to change management for better project tracking. When an issue is escalated into a change request, relevant data from the issue is copied to the change request.

Figure 12-3. Change request in SAP CPM

SAP CPM Change Management provides the functionality to document, evaluate, approve, and implement changes triggered during the project. Change requests can be created independently, copied from existing requests, or generated based on a linked project issue to maintain a seamless flow between issue and change management.

In large projects where multiple related changes occur, collective change requests can also be created for the approval of change.

Integration with Planning Workbook

A key feature of Change Management in SAP CPM is the ability to develop and evaluate multiple *cost estimation alternatives* for each change request. These alternatives provide flexibility in financial planning, allowing project teams to explore various approaches for accommodating project changes.

Each alternative can be developed using SAP CPM's Planning Workbook, which enables detailed financial planning and analysis. Cost estimation alternatives are entered in the change request, where they are evaluated based on their projected impact on the project's budget. Project managers can compare these alternatives, determining the most viable option for moving forward.

Change Approval

After a cost estimation alternative is developed, it can be marked as ready for approval by setting its status within the change request. Once a specific alternative is approved, its values are integrated with the project's overall financial plan, providing a unified view of the project for tracking against overall planned values. Once the cost estimation is completed, the alternative is marked as "Ready for Approval." If a change request impacts client deliverables or contractual terms, external approvals from stakeholders may be required, in addition to internal approvals. The project manager reviews the proposed changes and approves the plan. Approval workflows ensure that each change request is reviewed and authorized before implementation. The approval of the change request is followed by the processes of budget updates and schedule updates, as covered in Chapter 11 and Chapter 13, respectively.

Dispute Resolution

The issue and change management processes are closely connected, as the evaluation of an issue directly influences whether it leads to a change request. If the change is rejected, it may trigger a dispute resolution process. Meanwhile, approved changes result in project updates that help the project to adapt to evolving conditions and to continue progressing.

12.3. Claim Management

In the absence of SAP CPM, SAP S/4HANA Claim Management can serve as an alternative for tracking and managing claims within project environments. It provides a structured approach for documenting and handling unexpected events or changes that affect a project, such as delays, cost deviations, or specification changes.

12.3.1. Claim Types

Claims can involve both internal issues and external factors, which can take the following forms.

Variation Orders

In the case of variation orders, a complete scope of work is added to the project as it is treated as a sub-project. The standard WSE hierarchy explained in Chapter 6 provides the WBSE for variation orders.

Back Charges

If a claim arises from a vendor or subcontractor, it is treated as a back charge, and the claim is created in the system on behalf of the vendor.

12.3.2. Claim Order

Claims can be separately estimated, approved, and monitored throughout project execution. Using the *Create Claim Order* app in SAP S/4HANA, activities, services, and material components are directly assigned within claim orders. A claim order clearly identifies the parties involved in each claim, whether they are the ones claiming or being claimed against.

Claim Approval

Claims go through approval workflows with automated notifications, ensuring smooth review and decision-making processes. The system also provides detailed reports, such as the *Claim Overview* and *Claim Hierarchy* reports, to assess the status and financial implications of claims.

Integration with Project Objects

Claims can be linked directly to specific WBSEs to capture their potential cost impact in the project structure and to evaluate the financial impact of the claim against the overall project cost plan. Estimation and planning processes are also followed to the level of detail required. This ensures that claim-related costs are accurately tracked in the project's financial plan.

If the client accepts the proposed changes, and the change is billable, a new sales order line is created according to the cost specified in the claim order. If the client does not accept the proposed changes, the claim order is modified and resubmitted for approval.

12.4. Engineering Change Management

In the engineering, construction & operations (EC&O) industry, projects are highly complex and involve multiple levels of material management, document control, and project execution. During project execution, changes in designs, material specifications, and work processes are inevitable. Engineering changes during project execution can be grouped under internal and external change control.

SAP engineering change management (ECM) offers a structured and integrated solution for controlling and documenting changes. It ensures change traceability and control and provides a central framework to manage changes to key elements, such as WBS BOM, documents, materials, and project activities. This functionality allows engineering and planning teams to handle project changes systematically through defined processes. SAP ECM offers key features, like revision management using change numbers, effectivity, impact analysis, and workflows, to ensure that changes are accurately implemented, approved, and documented.

12.4.1. Revisions vs Versions

The engineering change management process provides the control mechanism for controlling both internal and external changes. Revision numbers and version control have an important role in tracking changes to project documents, materials, and structures. However, they both serve distinct purposes and operate differently.

Version Numbers

Versions are typically used by engineering teams for internal document control and are often created without the need for a formal change request. A version reflects internal updates and reviews that help the project team track the incremental progress of engineering development that is going through an iterative process of modification without officially locking in the change history or recording the formal review and approval process.

For example, when a team updates a drawing internally to reflect potential design changes but has not yet submitted it for external approval, they create a new version. These versions can be continuously updated until the changes are formalized and are ready for external approval.

Revision Numbers

Revision numbers, however, are tied to external control and require a formal change number. A revision is created when an official change has been approved and is ready for formal issuance. A key point is that revisions represent the final, approved state of an object that will be implemented in the project.

In industries like EC&O, revisions typically follow workflows and approvals and are part of formal documentation for external use. This ensures that all stakeholders, including contractors, clients, and suppliers, are working off the same set of instructions or documents.

Consider the example of the issued for construction (IFC) drawing of the RefineX project. The IFC drawing is issued after all internal reviews are completed and all necessary approvals from the project owner and consultant have been received. This drawing is now ready for actual construction work. To represent this final, approved state, the drawing will have a revision number, ensuring that all external teams (e.g., contractors) use the latest, validated version. Any changes to the drawing or its associated bill of materials will follow the formal engineering change management process.

Note that the versioning discussed in this chapter pertains specifically to document and engineering change controlling and should not be confused with other version types covered in this book.

12.4.2. Engineering Change Request (ECR)

An engineering change request (ECR) initiates the ECM process. The ECR details the nature of the changes required and the objects affected by the changes. ECRs pass through defined workflows for review and approval before any change is formalized. This ensures that all changes are subject to necessary validation by key stakeholders.

An ECR is generated in SAP to formally document the proposed change. The ECR details the specific modifications required, outlines the objects that require changes, and specifies the validity for the changes. This formal request links back to the original notification, ensuring that the issue is tracked throughout the change process. The ECR then undergoes a structured workflow for approval as per the defined hierarchy. Key departments or engineering disciplines are often defined as reviewers and approvers.

12.4.3. Engineering Change Number (ECN)

The engineering change number (ECN) is the core of the SAP ECM process. It acts as the unique identifier that links all objects affected by changes. Whether they are documents, material components, or WBS, the change number ensures that any change that occurs in these objects is traceable and auditable across the entire project lifecycle.

In an EPC project, a change number is assigned to identify a revision. For example, if a design is revised due to any reason, as shown in Figure 12-4, the drawing number along with the new material specifications and updated procurement and work instructions all are tied to the same revision number. The entire team then follows the same revision number of the WBS BOM and associated documents. This coordinated approach prevents errors caused by miscommunication or incorrect material use on site.

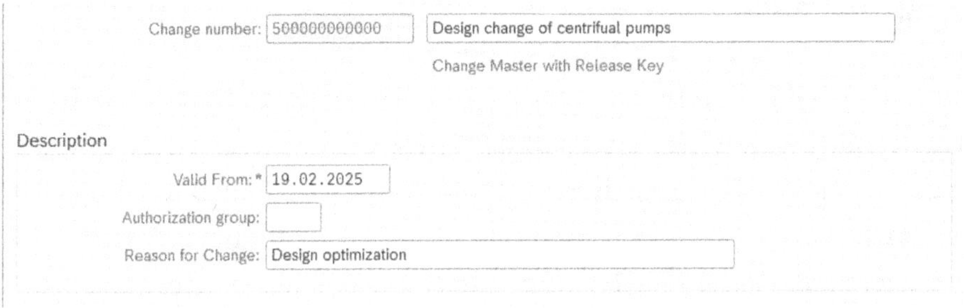

Change number: 500000000000   Design change of centrifual pumps
                                Change Master with Release Key

Description

Valid From: * 19.02.2025
Authorization group:
Reason for Change: Design optimization

Figure 12-4. *Engineering change number*

The change number also facilitates the creation of multi-level BOMs, where complex assemblies are broken down into manageable components, each linked by the same change number to maintain consistency and traceability.

12.4.4. Change Validity

Validity refers to the date from which a specific WBS BOM—either its header or its objects—are valid for use. Validity ensures that the changes made through the revision are implemented only after the specified date, aligning the revision's applicability with project timelines.

Valid-from Date

For example, if a new revision of the WBS BOM is created due to a change in the type of steel, and this change is valid from a specific phase of construction, the *Valid-from date* is set to a future date. This means that procurement and construction activities can only use the new steel specifications starting from this date. Until then, ongoing activities will continue with the existing WBS BOM.

Valid-to Date

The valid-to date is a key concept used to define the end of a revision's applicability or validity. In EPC projects, the valid-to date is typically not required, as revisions remain applicable for the duration of the project unless another revision supersedes it. In contrast, product lifecycle management uses both valid-from and valid-to dates to determine the applicability of revisions across different product versions.

12.4.5. Change Notification

In the standard SAP ECM processes, the change process starts with the creation of an ECR. The process can be improved for effectively managing the workflow by creating a custom notification type that precedes the ECR.

This is done so that every ECR initiation and assessment of changes is properly documented and justified before a formal change request is initiated.

The notification captures the details of the problem, including the affected objects and any supporting documentation. The notification serves as a preliminary document reviewed by relevant stakeholders to assess its validity and impact. If the notification is approved and deemed significant, it triggers the subsequent step in the ECM process. It covers steps of documenting the issue, such as referencing the instruction from the customer and attaching relevant documents.

12.4.6. Engineering Change Order (ECO)

Once the ECR is approved, it is converted into an engineering change order (ECO). An ECO authorizes and facilitates the implementation of the changes within the project. The ECO ensures that the proposed changes are executed according to the specifications outlined in the ECR, and it continues to track the modifications throughout the project lifecycle.

12.5. Engineering Change Process

Separating the ECR and ECO brings a structured and controlled approach of managing engineering changes. The ECR focuses on proposing and reviewing changes, while the ECO deals with the actual implementation of those changes.

For each document, the changes can be distinguished between header-level and object-level changes. This segregation is important for accurately identifying the scope of modifications and tracking the stage of the change document.

12.5.1. Header-Level Change

At the header level, the overall progress of the engineering change request (ECR) or engineering change order (ECO) is tracked. This level deals with the broader aspects of the change process and indicates the current stage of the document.

12.5.2. Object-Level Change

At the object level, individual components or items affected by the change are identified. For example, if a WBS BOM is being modified, the object-level status ensures that each individual material component or associated document is accurately tracked within the WBS BOM.

This dual approach helps to maintain clarity, especially in complex projects with multiple layers of materials, documents, and activities that require individual status tracking.

12.5.3. Change Management Status

Throughout this process, status management tools in SAP help monitor the progress of the ECR and ECO and ensure that it transitions smoothly from initiation through approval to implementation.

Statuses are applied at both the header and object levels, offering detailed control and traceability throughout the change process.

ECR Status

The different statuses that an engineering change request can have throughout project lifecycle are:

1. **Created:** This status indicates that the ECR has been initiated but has not yet been reviewed or approved. It is in the initial stage where details are entered.

2. **Check ECR:** The Check status indicates that the ECR is undergoing initial review to assess the feasibility of the change. By setting this status the system triggers a workflow that allows relevant team members to review and make decisions on the change for each object identified in the ECR.

Object-Level Status

At the object level, statuses apply to the specific components being modified, such as the WBS BOM, materials, or documents. These statuses show whether individual objects are available for change or if they have already been modified as part of the ECO. For example:

1. **Change possible:** This status indicates that the object is currently in a state where modifications can be made, and the change order is approved or in progress.

2. **Change unnecessary:** This status indicates that no changes are required to this added object. This means that the object has been added to the system, but no modifications are necessary at this time. The object might be added as a placeholder or for future reference.

3. **Change impossible:** This status indicates that changes in the objects are not possible. Once the status is set, the object is blocked for changes, even if the request is approved. This status is typically used for critical components when restrictions are imposed on the modifications due to its impact on other objects or the entire system.

Change Decisions

The different decisions that can be taken on an engineering change request (ECR) are:

1. **ECR Checked:** This status is set at the header level to indicate the completion of a decision and moves the workflow to a decision point if the changes are possible.

2. **Approve ECR:** This status indicates that the ECR has been formally reviewed and the decision about the changes at the object level has been the changes approved after review by relevant stakeholders. It is ready to be converted into an engineering change order (ECO) for implementation.

3. **Convert ECR:** When the ECR moves from planning to implementation, it is converted into an ECO, reflecting the transition from a proposal to an actionable order.

4. **Complete:** This status indicates that the ECO has been completed and the decision on the change request has been concluded, even if no changes are implemented.

5. **Release ECO:** This status indicates that the changes have been implemented, and the ECO is fully or partially ready to be implemented.

12.5.4. BOM Comparison

The BOM comparison is a powerful tool that enables users to effectively compare two versions of WBS BOM and provides the comparison to show the changes implemented at each component. The tool highlights the similarities and differences between WBS BOM versions and allows users to identify which parts of the BOM have been changed, added, or removed.

It supports single-level and multi-level comparisons that allow users to examine changes across the entire WBS BOM hierarchy or focus on individual components. making it easy to identify the specific changes that have been made. This information is essential for understanding the impact of changes on the project and for ensuring that they are implemented correctly.

12.6. Conclusion

Managing project risks, issues, and changes is crucial for the success of EPC projects. SAP S/4HANA provides tools to address deviations from the scope, project schedule, and design specifications, ensuring the project keeps on time and its budget is on track. While this chapter focuses on managing and controlling deviations, the next chapter will explore tools and techniques for tracking project performance and addressing time- and effort-related issues.

CHAPTER 13

Project Monitoring and Control

The project planning phase relies heavily on estimations and historical data to define how the project is intended to progress. However, miscalculations, changes, and force majeure events can lead to deviations from the original plan. Achieving the project objectives is only possible if these variances are identified early and corrective actions are implemented in a timely manner.

This chapter will explore how effective monitoring and management of project progress and performance require continuous access to real-time information across all stages of EPC projects.

13.1. Progress Monitoring

Progress refers to the process of moving forward toward defined project objectives, measured by comparing actual performance with the planned values, such as scope, cost, time, and schedule.

Progress analysis is the process of monitoring and measuring the progress of activities in real-time. It provides insights into both works completed and resources spent.

© Sohail Ahmed 2025
S. Ahmed, *The SAP S/4HANA Handbook for EPC Projects*,
https://doi.org/10.1007/979-8-8688-1466-2_13

By measuring key metrics, project managers can assess project efficiency and compare performance against planned targets. It is also used to compare cost and schedule variances early to steer the project in the right direction.

13.1.1. Progress Monitoring Metrices

Before getting into the details of progress tracking and performance analysis in SAP S/4HANA, it is important to understand the following key metrices.

Earned Work

In project management terms, earned work represents the value of work physically completed at the status date regardless of the effort spent. It is the portion of the project that is confirmed as partially or fully completed.

$$\text{Earned Work} = \text{Planned Work} \times \text{Percentage of Completion}$$

Actual Work

Actual work, in project management terms, represents the total effort spent on a project activity, regardless of how much of that activity has been completed.

Percentage of Completion

During progress analysis, percentage of completion (POC) plays an important role in calculating the planned and earned work at a given status date.

$$\text{POC} = \text{Work Completed as of status date} / \text{Total Planned Work}$$

Status Date

In project management, the term *status date* refers to a specific point in time at which the current progress of a project is measured and analyzed.

Efficiency

Efficiency is a metric that focuses on comparing the actual work done by the internal resources with the actual hours spent on an individual activity. It provides insights into the operational efficiency of resource deployed and allows comparisons between actual work and earned work.

$$\text{Efficiency} = \text{Earned Work} / \text{Actual Work}$$

By comparing earned work with actual work, project managers can assess whether the actual progress aligns with planned work within given timelines.

Activity Confirmation

Activity confirmation is the process used to record the progress of completion (POC) of work of a specific internal network activity. The POC is entered for each activity to reflect how much of the task has been completed. The POC of an activity is calculated for both planned and actual values for comparing the progress:

1. **Planned POC:** If the POC is determined for planned values, then it is called planned POC. For example, the planned POC of an activity at the status date is 5% because the work planned is 50 out of 1000 units.

2. **Actual POC:** If the POC is determined for the actual values, then it is called actual POC. For example, the actual POC of an activity is 3% because the progress made is 30 out of 1000 units.

The units used in the POC calculation depend upon the measurement method. The following section discusses different types of measurement methods offered by SAP S/4HANA for POC calculations.

13.1.2. Measurement Methods

A measurement method in SAP S/4HANA determines how the system calculates the percentage of completion for an object, such as a work breakdown structure element and internal network activities.

For EPC projects, POCs are measured as network activities or activity elements and then aggregated to the WBSE for overall project tracking. The selection of an appropriate measurement method depends on the required accuracy and the agreed-upon terms between the owner and contractor for project monitoring and analytics.

Several measurement methods are available in SAP, each offering distinct ways to assess progress; however, using the same measurement method for both planning and actual progress tracking in not required, as shown in Figure 13-1. In fact, it is not a common industry practice, as different criteria are often used for engineering, procurement, and construction phases—for example, engineering progress may be tracked based on document approvals, procurement on cost, and construction on physical completion of work.

Figure 13-1. *Measurement methods for plan and actual progress tracking*

Some of the key measurement methods available in SAP PS are discussed next.

Time Proportionality

In this method, POC is calculated based on the ratio of the total duration completed up to the status date to the total planned duration of the project.

This method is not commonly applicable in EPC projects because project activities progress along a non-linear curve. Using time proportionality in EPC projects may not accurately reflect the actual status of work planned or completed. This method should instead be used for calculating the progress of indirect tasks where work is linear and predictable.

Cost Proportionality

In this method, progress is based on the ratio of cumulative costs incurred or planned up to the status date to the total project cost. Planned costs are used for planned POC calculations, while actual costs are employed for actual POC. In procurement-intensive projects, this method is particularly effective because costs tend to have greater significance than the physical progress of activities.

Milestone-Based

In this method, POC is tied to the completion of predefined milestones. Each milestone has a set percentage showing its contribution to the overall project progress. Milestones are assigned to activity so that they follow the planned and actual finish dates. This method is effective in milestone-based contracts where payments or deliverables are tied to specific milestones.

Degree of Processing from Confirmation

This method does not use a formula. Instead, POC is calculated based on actual work of an activity confirmed in the system. This provides a real-time reflection of progress as work is completed and confirmed.

Secondary Proportionality

This method reflects the POC of objects referenced in the network activities. The progress of the linked objects is copied to the network activities. These objects include other network activities or subnetworks, quality orders, and production orders. It is most effective when project progress relies heavily on other functions and SAP users have a clear understanding of interdependencies between these objects. It is best suited for cases where sub-projects are created, or for engineer-to-order scenarios where large quantities of production and quality management orders are created and linked with project activities.

Quantity Proportionality

This method requires predefined schedule key figures (SKF) as master data. In this method, POC is based on the ratio of completed quantity of units to the total planned quantity. SKFs represent the measurable quantity of units that represent the basis of progress. For example, in engineering projects, if progress is calculated based on number of drawings completed, an SKF representing *drawings* is created to track the progress of drawing delivery.

Estimates

Estimates is another method to plan POC of an activity that allows users to estimate planned percentage of completion for each period. An estimated value of the actual percentage of completion can also be entered for each activity using this method. This method gives a higher degree of control to the user, in a way, than system-calculated POC.

In addition to the detailed measurement methods discussed above, SAP S/4HANA also provides simpler percentage of completion (POC) calculation methods, such as start-finish, and actual = plan. However, these methods may not be suited to the non-linear nature of EPC projects.

13.1.3. POC Aggregation

POC aggregation involves progressively accumulating the POC values from lower-level activities to higher levels of the WBS until the project's overall progress is calculated. Only the progress of internal activities is considered in the POC aggregation.

SAP S/4HANA allows users to configure a POC measurement method that suits project needs. With the exception of the degree of processing from confirmation method (which cannot be used for planned POC), most POC measurement methods can be set up for automatic aggregation. Depending on the nature of the project and agreements between project owners and contractors, the criteria for aggregation may extend beyond SAP-provided methods.

13.1.4. POC Weight

In SAP S/4HANA, the POC weight reflects the significance of individual activities or WBS elements in determining overall project progress. SAP S/4HANA supports the following:

1. **Automatic aggregation:** Where POC is aggregated based on selected measurement method

2. **Manual aggregation:** Where POC weight is assigned manually to each object

Manual POC Weight

In all cases where the automatic aggregation does not provide desired results, manual assignment of POC weight, as shown in Figure 13-2, should be considered.

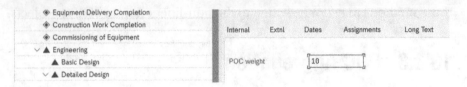

Figure 13-2. *Manual POC weight for progress aggregation*

The following scenarios require manual POC weight assignment:

1. If multiple criteria of weightages are required for different deliverables of the project; for example, using the quantity proportional for engineering deliverables but cost proportional for procurement deliverables.

2. If the planned POC is required to be aggregated based on planned work, no specific measurement method can be applied. The direct proportionality method cannot be used for planned POC, and the estimate method requires manual periodic entries.

POC Weight for Standardization

POC weight can also be effectively utilized with *standard networks*. For example, Table 13-1 illustrates that while activity elements have a fixed contribution in an activity across projects, the weights of activities (assemblies) vary due to design differences.

Table 13-1. *Activity Elements*

Internal Activity	Variable Weightage(Tons)	Calculated Weightage	Standard Activity Element	Fixed Weightage(Effort)
Assembly A201	0.60	60%		
Assembly 202	10	10%	Cutting	10%
			Fit-up	25%
			Welding	50%
			Painting	15%
Assembly 203	30	30%		

13.2. Time Management in SAP S/4HANA

SAP S/4HANA provides two functionalities to capture actual time. Depending on the complexity of reporting, one or both options may be used.

1. Time and attendance
2. Time sheet management

13.2.1. Time and Attendance

Time and attendance is the process of recording the physical availability of employees for a project during any given period. This functionality involves employees clocking in and out using time logging machines installed at production floors and project sites.

311

SAP HCM Time Management

SAP HCM time management's functionality allows organizations to manage employee attendance and working hours.

Time-in and time-out data of employees can be entered in the system manually, using an upload program, or by installing biometric or face-recognition machines at production floors and project sites where employees mark their attendance.

SAP SuccessFactors Time Tracking

For organizations using SAP SuccessFactors Employee Central as the core module for HR operations, SAP provides a user-friendly interface for managing employee time and attendance known as *SAP SuccessFactors Time Tracking*. This software offers self-service options for employees to maintain time and attendance. It provides real-time visibility into labor availability for accurate day-to-day planning and resource management.

13.2.2. Cross-Application Time Sheet

SAP S/4HANA provides Cross-Application Time Sheet (CATS) functionality that allows users to enter detailed time entry of resources. CATS is typically used when tracking of working hours of individual employees against specific internal network activity is required.

In EPC projects, the primary purpose of this process is to calculate the efficiency of a particular labor type, group, or individual employee. Using CATS, employee actual hours spent during a particular shift are assigned to specific cost centers or internal network activities.

In SAP S/4HANA, the key distinction between earned work and actual work lies in how they are measured and recorded. Earned work represents the percentage of a task completed and is calculated based on activity confirmations. Actual work, meanwhile, is recorded through the CATS system, where employees log hours to reflect the effort invested.

It is important to note that there is no distinct standard field for *earned work* in SAP PS. Instead, the system treats both earned and actual work as *actual work*. Actual work data from CATS overrides the progress-based calculations from activity confirmations.

This behavior can sometimes lead to confusion in interpreting earned and actual work—both key project performance metrics. Therefore, EPC projects may require customization to capture the earned work separately.

13.2.3. Payroll & Resource Cost Allocation

SAP HCM Payroll allows organizations to configure time data collection from either time and attendance or CATS, or both—with some restrictions. These configurations ensure flexibility in managing different employee groups or job types.

Direct Resources

Using CATS, organizations can capture regular working hours, overtime, and shift differentials, along with other wage types for direct labor. Each of these objects can be tied to specific project activities or cost centers, ensuring accurate allocation of employee labor costs.

Indirect Resources

This process of booking hours can be extended to include indirect employees, such as those from engineering, project management, and production control teams. Timesheets for these resources can be booked either by providing them with direct access to the SAP SuccessFactors Time Tracking app or by using SAP CATS for granular reporting. Alternatively, an administrative user can be created to enter hours on behalf of these employees.

13.2.4. Integrated Time Management in the RefineX Project

The RefineX project utilized CATS to centralize time management, as illustrated in Figure 13-3. Labor hours are captured via time-logging machines and integrated into CATS, followed by *time evaluation* in SAP HR before approval. Machine hours are recorded by scanning the work order for each machine. Once approved, both labor and machine hours, along with directly entered engineering hours in CATS, are posted to SAP PS. This integration ensures accurate time tracking and cost allocation within SAP PS.

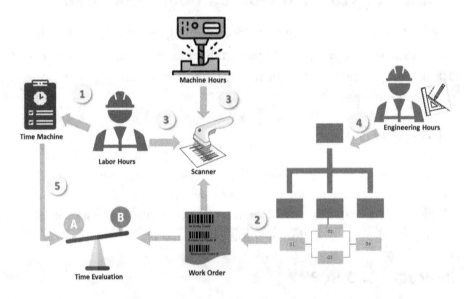

Figure 13-3. *Integrated time management using HCM, PS, CATS, and machine integration*

13.3. Project Execution

The RefineX project serves as a case study to illustrate how various execution metrics, such as earned work, percentage of completion (POC), and actual work hours, are applied in real-world EPC projects. In the following sections we will see how progress and effort ae measured, gaps are identified, and the plan is updated based on the data entered in the system.

13.3.1. Progress Tracking

The contractor's internal workforce has been assigned to the internal activity *Assembly A101*. This activity is further divided into two activity elements: *fabrication* and *welding*.

Planned Values

The project in the execution phase and the planned values are as shown in Table 13-2.

Table 13-2. *Planned Values*

Planned Work for Assembly A101	Planned Work at Activity Element
Fabrication	50 hours
Welding	50 hours
Total planned work	100 hours

Actual Work from Activity Confirmation

The amount of work earned on Assembly A101 during the week is based on the percentage of work confirmed in the system. During the week, the planning engineer confirms 30% progress in SAP PS, resulting in Actual Work = 30% x 100 = 30 hours.

Actual Work from CATS

Meanwhile, the project administrator collects daily time sheets from workers and logs time against the internal activities. For the employee working as a fitter, a time sheet looks like Table 13-3.

Table 13-3. *Time Sheets*

Assembly A101	Actual Work from CATS	Time & Attendance	Variance
Fabrication	15 hours	45 hours	−5 hours
Welding	25 hours		
Total logged hours	40 hours		

This example in Table 13-3 shows a negative variance of five hours. This variance represents unutilized or non-productive time. During this period the resource was idle and could not be assigned to project activity. As a result, the fitter's efficiency is calculated as 75%, based on the comparison of earned work (30 hours) and actual work (40 hours). The cumulative efficiencies of all resources result in the project efficiency. In this example, the remaining five idle hours will remain unallocated and will be considered as non-productive time.

Non-Productive Time

Non-productive or *idle time* refers to the effort spent without any direct or indirect work due to the unavailability of a work front or other reasons. If these hours are booked against the originally planned activity, they can distort project efficiency, leading to an inflated standard rate. This issue not only affects the project's contribution margin but also provides inaccurate data for future project estimations. To address this, organizations can establish a separate cost center to track and monitor non-productive hours.

When a resource is available at the shop or project site, but no work is assigned, time is booked against the idle cost center rather than the project. For a more decentralized approach, when idling costs are to be considered part of the project's profit and loss statement, a dedicated WBS element can be used instead of a central cost center, with the remaining idle hours recorded against this WBSE in CATS.

13.3.2. Time and Work Approval

This variance can be sent to the project manager for approval. Organizations should establish a policy to determine whether to adopt the hours confirmed from the confirmation or those recorded by the time logging machine. This process can be fully automated by using SAP build process automation on SAP BTP, which will be discussed in section 13.5.2 in detail.

13.3.3. Schedule Update

Once the progress of a project is updated based on actual work and earned work, the project schedule is updated to reflect the latest progress at a defined cut-off date. A schedule update run recalculates the remaining duration of activities and revises the overall project completion date.

Schedules are typically updated weekly or monthly, depending on the size, duration, and complexity of the project. The frequency of these updates must be documented in the project charter through an agreement between the project owner and the consultant.

Regular schedule updates help in forecasting the remaining resource requirements and provide insights for comparison with the baseline schedule. For every update, a project version will be saved in the system for comparison reports.

13.4. Version Management

Version management is a fundamental concept in project management that all software uses. It tracks and compares the current progress of a project with various baselines over the project lifecycle. SAP PS, part of the S/4HANA Enterprise solution, integrates various types of version management that provides controls at project and higher organization levels.

The following sections provide details of how organizations can capture snapshots of key project metrics at specific points in time and make informed decisions throughout the project lifecycle.

13.4.1. Project Version

A project version is a snapshot of the entire project. It maintains a static version of a project by preserving project structure, dates, progress, milestone trend, and financial figures at a specific point in time. It serves as a record of the project for comparison between different updates and adjustments.

This feature makes it an essential tool for tracking project evolution. There are no limitations on the number of project versions that can be created. Therefore, saving the current version of the project after every schedule update helps with comparing multiple updates of the entire project. The project version helps maintain a detailed history of the project and makes every update a reference point for the future.

It is important to understand the difference between *project versions* and the *progress version*. A progress version is a type of CO version pre-configured by SAP. CO versions are discussed in the next section.

13.4.2. Controlling Version

Controlling version is a concept in SAP S/4HANA that creates different versions of cost plans in the SAP CO module. These versions can also be used for project controlling for tracking and comparing project-related financial data.

For project monitoring, each CO version in SAP PS represents a distinct financial snapshot, capturing planning, forecasting, or actual cost data. Organizations can configure different CO versions to meet their specific reporting requirements. It is not recommended to create project-specific CO versions. The number of CO versions should be determined based on the organization's reporting needs during the system design and configuration.

The following are some of the important pre-configured CO versions in SAP PS for project monitoring.

Network Version

Network version, configured as version 0, is a standard version in SAP that records actual costs and revenues directly associated with the project. This version also captures planned cost for network activities, which enables detailed monitoring against actuals.

Progress Version

This version, configured as version 100 in the system, is specifically designed for tracking EVA data in progress analysis reporting. All progress-related KPIs (POC, SPI, CPI, etc.) are stored as SKF in this CO version.

Forecast Version

Forecast versions, configured as version 110, are used to manually input future costs and revenues of network activities. These values may differ from the planned values of *network versions* and are helpful to evaluate future needs based on actual costs incurred and changes in the project or market conditions.

Cross-Project Version Management

In addition to standard versions, an EC&O organization can configure additional CO versions to capture consolidated reporting at various organizational levels. These versions provide a consolidated view of projects at the profit center, controlling area, or company code.

While SAP PPM provides detailed insights and control at the portfolio level, which is ideal for tracking strategic project performance across multiple portfolios, the CO-version approach in SAP PS offers direct integration with SAP FI and SAP CO modules.

In the case of PrimeCon, the company has configured CO versions for quarterly budgets. The CO version Q1, for example, establishes an initial budget at the start of the first quarter. Throughout the first quarter, PrimeCon monitors consolidated actuals against the baseline values set in CO version Q1. At the end of the quarter, the company uses the actual data to extrapolate projections for the upcoming quarters and adjusts the baseline as needed for strategic reporting and decision-making at the organizational level.

13.4.3. Simulation Versions

In addition to static versioning using project versions, dynamic and scenario-based versioning is also offered by SAP S/4HANA. These versions are called *simulation versions*, where projects are created as simulations without modifying the original operative projects.

These versions enable the project team to simulate a change and evaluate multiple possible outcomes of the same project. Operative projects are first transferred to simulation projects to create a replica of the ongoing project.

For new projects, the process starts with creating multiple simulation versions. Different possible scenarios are created and saved as different versions. These versions are then compared, and the most optimal version is converted to the operative project.

Visualize Outcomes

Simulation versions allow project managers to visualize the impact of a change on the resources, budget, and timeline, especially if additional resources are required to compress the timeline.

For example, in an EPC project, if a delay in procurement activities threatens the overall project deadline, the planning team might try to crash the project by shortening the duration of construction activities. Without modifying the operative project, they can create multiple simulation versions to visualize the possible outcomes.

Resource Optimization

The estimation engineer can also use simulation projects for workload projection of upcoming projects. By creating potential projects as simulations, the resources requirement of the future can be compared with the available capacity. The sales team can evaluate the probability of completing the proposed projects with available resources or identify the need for additional capacity. Such evaluations assist management in making informed decision on whether to buy or rent resources.

13.4.4. Predictive Analytics

SAC is a comprehensive solution for business intelligence, planning, and predictive analytics. It enables business users to generate interactive and insightful reports. It is a strong tool for handling complex forecasting and scenario-based analysis.

Data Visualization

Stories are the central component of SAC reporting. They are interactive reports or dashboards that combine data from various sources into a cohesive narrative. In a SAC story, data is visualized through widgets. Widgets are the building blocks of SAC stories. They include charts, tables, maps, and other visual components that help users interactively analyze the data.

Predictive Scenarios

SAC empowers business users to perform scenario-based analysis and what-if models, reducing reliance on IT and manual tools like spreadsheets. SAC allows predictive scenario-based simulations to evaluate how different changes can affect a project. By testing multiple potential outcomes, project managers can assess risks, opportunities, and impacts without altering the original planning framework.

In contrast to simulation versions, SAC is more dynamic in planning and forecasting. These models are not limited to simulating operative projects in isolation. Instead, they work on live data from S/4HANA for real-time analysis of a project's performance.

What-if Analysis

With SAC What-if Analysis, financial managers can simulate the impact of delayed receivables on cash flow. Similarly, project managers can test different cost performance index values in earned value analysis to calculate the Estimated At Completion cost of the project. By understanding the effects of scenario-based planning, stakeholders can take proactive measures and adjust strategies to mitigate risks.

13.5. Progress Analysis Automation

Using the SAP S/4HANA Business Technology Platform (BTP), organizations can automate this otherwise time-consuming process and achieve real-time information, eliminating the risk of human error and bias.

Time and attendance machines can be integrated with SAP S/4HANA by connecting physical time-tracking devices with SAP S/4HANA. BTP tools extract attendance data from the time-logging machines and securely transfer it to SAP HCM.

13.5.1. SAP BTP Integration Suite

Actual working hours are directly transferred from attendance machines to SAP S/4HANA HCM for real-time attendance data collection. SAP S/4HANA powered by BTP uses APIs on Cloud Platform Integration (CPI) to ensure seamless data transfer between time-logging machines and SAP S/4HANA.

In a similar way, machine hours can be captured by deploying PC workstations and scanners on shop floors. SAP S/4HANA can generate QR codes for work centers (machines) and network activities. In the absence of PC workstations, the production engineer can print work orders for each internal activity or activity element and issue RFID cards for each machine.

When an activity at a work center is started or completed, both the work order and the RFID cards are scanned to log the actual hours spent by the machine on that activity. SAP BTP CPI automates the process by integrating SAP S/4HANA with the scanners.

13.5.2. SAP Build Process Automation

Organizations can achieve further automation by employing SAP BTP build process automation. Following are two very strong automation platforms provided by SAP to automate the entire process.

SAP Intelligent Robotic Process Automation (iRPA)

This can be deployed to collect data from timesheet entries via optical character recognition (OCR), QR code scanners, and time and attendance machines.

The SAP BTP iRPA bot can be designed to first validate the extracted data by cross-checking it against SAP S/4HANA master data. For large organizations managing multiple projects across different locations, this automation can significantly reduce the required team size for progress confirmation and CATS data entry.

The bot can be deployed centrally to enhance process efficiency by communicating with decentralized project teams. It can be scheduled to run at scheduled times or can request users to unlock the necessary network activities for activity confirmation.

It can also verify budget availability at WBSE and send notifications to users, prompting them to provide additional budget if needed and prevent financial discrepancies between actual work and actual cost.

Workflow Automation

SAP BTP workflow automation can be implemented to approve time variances. The workflow can include steps for reviewing discrepancies, which might involve automated notifications to relevant managers or team leads when a variance occurs. Integrating this workflow with SAP Intelligent Robotic Process Automation (iRPA) further enhances the efficiency of the process by automating routine tasks such as data entry, validation, and reporting.

For example, if the human resources (HR) policy states that the hours recorded by the time-logging machine take precedence unless they differ by a 10% threshold, the bot can analyze the data accordingly. If a variance falls within the acceptable range defined by the policy, the bot can accept the time recorded by the time-logging machine without human intervention. However, if the variance exceeds this threshold, the bot can generate a report summarizing the differences and send it to the designated user for further review and approval. The bot will log these decisions and actions for auditing purposes, ensuring compliance with HR policies.

13.6. Earned Value Analysis

Earned value analysis (EVA), a key component of EVM, is used to evaluate project performance at specific points by comparing planned progress against actual progress in terms of cost.

This section covers how the critical EVA metrices convert the data entered into the system during different transactions in SAP PS, CATS, and other modules as progress, actual hours, or actual cost to measure the variance and forecast future trends of the project. The EVA metrics can be categorized as follows:

1. Progress indices

2. Cost indices

3. Schedule indices

4. Predictive indices

13.6.1. Progress Indices

Progress indices are the key metrics in EVA used to assess project performance in terms of planned, earned, and actual work. Following are three key metrices:

Budgeted Cost of Work Scheduled (BCWS)

BCWS, also called planned value (PV), represents the planned cost for the work scheduled by a specific date, providing insight into planned versus actual schedule adherence.

$$\text{BCWS} = \text{Total Planned Cost} \times \text{Planned POC}$$

Budgeted Cost of Work Performed (BCWP)

BCWP, also called earned value (EV), measures the planned cost for the completed portion of work, regardless of actual costs, allowing comparison of planned work value against project progress.

$$\text{BCWP} = \text{Actual POC} \times \text{Total Planned Cost}$$

Actual Cost of Work Performed (ACWP)

ACWP, also called actual cost (AC), represents the total actual costs incurred in completing the work by a specific date. In SAP S/4HANA, ACWP includes cost calculated from transactions in activity confirmations, cross-application time sheets, material issuance, service acceptance, and so on.

Planned Cost vs Budget in EVA

In SAP PS, the terms *planned cost* and *budget* are distinct concepts, each having specific meanings, as discussed in Chapter 11. Understanding this difference is important, as the system relies on planned cost values rather than project budget while calculating metrices such as BCWP and BCWS to align with earned value management terminology.

13.6.2. Cost Indices

The following indices are key metrics in EVA used to evaluate a project's financial health. They indicate whether a project is on budget by comparing the planned cost and the actual cost of completed work as of the data date.

Cost Variance

CV is the difference between earned value and actual cost of work performed. This index identifies cost overrun or savings.

$$CV = BCWP - ACWP$$

A negative CV value shows cost overrun, while a positive CV value shows savings from planned cost as of the status date. CV shows the variance in absolute terms. For example, a −$10,000 variance shows the amount of budget overrun on the status date.

Cost Performance Index

CPI indicates cost efficiency, showing the ratio of the value of completed work to the actual cost incurred.

$$CPI = BCWP/ACWP$$

A CPI value above 1.0 indicates cost efficiency, while a value below 1.0 signals cost inefficiency. For example, CPI 1.2 means 120% of the work has been earned compared to the actual costs incurred.

13.6.3. Schedule Indices

The following two indices indicate a project's schedule health. They measure how efficiently a project is progressing in terms of time. They show how much work should have been completed compared to the planned schedule on the data date.

Schedule Variance (SV)

SV is the difference between earned value (BCWP) and planned value (BCWS). This metric shows if a project is ahead of or behind schedule in monetary terms.

$$SV = BCWP - BCWS$$

A positive SV value indicates that the project is ahead of schedule, while a negative SV value signals delays. For example, an SV of $5,000 means the project is progressing faster than planned by that amount as of the status date.

Schedule Performance Index (SPI)

SPI is the ratio of earned value to planned value, measuring schedule efficiency by comparing actual progress to the planned schedule.

$$SPI = BCWP/BCWS$$

An SPI above 1.0 indicates the project is progressing efficiently, whereas an SPI below 1.0 shows delays. For example, an SPI of 1.1 means the project is achieving 110% of planned progress, advancing faster than anticipated.

13.6.4. Predictive Indices

The following two indices provide valuable insights into a project's financial and schedule health, allowing for proactive decision-making.

Estimated Cost to Complete (ETC)

ETC forecasts the cost required to finish the remaining work. ETC considers current cost performance and helps project managers anticipate future expenditures based on the performance data gathered to date. The simplest form of calculating ETC is as follows:

$$\textbf{ETC} = \textbf{Total Planned Cost} - \textbf{BCWP}$$

Large EPC projects may require that consideration of project cost and schedule efficiencies be built into the projections. In this case, the ETC formula can be adjusted and added to standard SAP PS reports to consider the project's cost performance index (CPI), schedule performance index (SPI), or both.

For example, depending on the desired accuracy, risks, and assumptions about projects' future performance, adjusted ETC can be calculated using any of the following formulas:

$$\textbf{ETC}_1 = (\textbf{Total Planned Cost} - \textbf{BCWP}) / \textbf{CPI}$$

$$\textbf{ETC}_2 = (\textbf{Total Planned Cost} - \textbf{BCWP}) / \textbf{SPI}$$

$$\textbf{ETC}_3 = (\textbf{Total Planned Cost} - \textbf{BCWP}) / \textbf{CPI} \times \textbf{SPI}$$

If the CPI is less than 1.0, for example, the ETC_1 calculation assumes continued cost inefficiency unless corrective actions are taken. The value of ETC_1 will show a higher projected cost to complete the remaining work compared with the ETC. This adjustment helps project controllers anticipate future budget requirements based on past performance trends.

Estimated Total Costs at Completion (EAC)

EAC projects the total expected project cost by combining actual costs to date (ACWP) with the forecasted estimated cost to complete (ETC).

$$\textbf{EAC} = \textbf{ETC} + \textbf{ACWP}$$

In scenarios where future performance is expected to continue with current cost and/or schedule trends, EAC can also substitute ETC with ETC_1, ETC_2, or ETC_3.

For example, Figure 13-4 suggests that despite increasing forecasts for the final revenue, the project's expected revenue and costs at completion remain below their initial planned values. And the final forecast suggests that for both revenue and cost, the estimate at completion is less than the planned values.

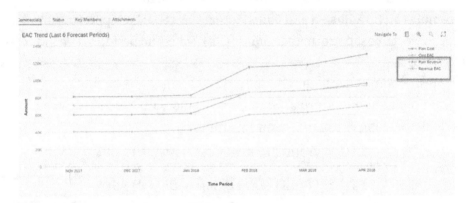

Figure 13-4. *Estimate at completion trend*

13.6.5. Cost Forecasting With EVA

EVA is also a valuable tool for forecasting the estimated cost to complete a project. By analyzing the actual values recorded to date, rescheduling based on the remaining project duration, and planning the remaining work, project teams can use EVA to calculate the ETC and EAC.

For example, in this six-month project, after completing the first month, a cost overrun of $400 was identified. The breakdown of the initial budget, actual costs, and the revised forecast is presented in Table 13-4.

Table 13-4. *Budget Forecast*

Versions	Total	Jan	Feb	Mar	Apr	May	Jun
Initial budget Ver 0	$2,500	$200	$300	$500	$500	$750	$250
Actual cost		$500					
Revised plan Ver 1	$2,400		$400	$500	$500	$750	$250

The budget based on bid estimate = $2500

Actual cost incurred during the first month = $500

Revised/forecasted plan for remaining periods (Ver 1) = $2400

Estimate at completion (EAC) = 2400 + 500 = $2900

Cost overrun = ($400)

After completing all necessary process steps and maintaining appropriate project cost versions, SAP EVA reports provide detailed cost analysis of the project at both the WBS element and cost element levels.

13.7. Conclusion

In this chapter we explored how SAP S/4HANA progress and time-tracking capabilities bring transparency to evaluating a project's health with the help of business process automation. These tools, based on proven best practices, increase the accuracy of forecasting time and budget risks by providing automation and supporting risk mitigation proactively.

In the following chapter, we'll learn how this real-time data can be visualized and analyzed through SAP's advanced reporting and analytics tools. These tools empower project managers to dynamically manage resources, control costs, and make timely adjustments, driving better outcomes across the project lifecycle.

CHAPTER 14

Financial Performance

At every period end, SAP PS plays a critical role in managing closing tasks. This process ensures that project costs are accurately posted, variances are identified, and project performance is reported. In this chapter, we will explore the key functions performed during period-end closing to effectively reconcile project costs and align them with financial accounting requirements.

14.1. Rate Revaluation

Revaluation is a functionality in SAP PS that adjusts and updates the interim actual costs of internal activities with the actual costs accurately after period-end processing.

During project execution, when internal activities, such as labor or machine usage, are confirmed, SAP calculates an interim actual cost during the month based on the following formula:

$$\text{Planned Rate of Activity Type} \times \text{Actual POC}$$

© Sohail Ahmed 2025
S. Ahmed, *The SAP S/4HANA Handbook for EPC Projects*,
https://doi.org/10.1007/979-8-8688-1466-2_14

14.1.1. Revaluation Process

This interim cost provides a tentative estimate of labor and machine costs so that the cost controller can assess budget tolerance. The cost controller can use this information to monitor potential cost overruns and decide whether to implement cost control measures or initiate a budget revision.

At period end, after payroll is executed for labor resources and maintenance, depreciation, and operational costs are booked for machine resources, the revaluation transaction is executed by the financial controller. This transaction replaces the interim costs calculated during the month with actual costs posted during the period-end processing.

14.1.2. Revaluation Methods

SAP offers different methods for activity price calculation. Each method is designed to address specific project requirements and cost structures. For EPC projects, where diverse labor crafts and equipment types are involved and the price has the potential to vary between different periods, the following two options are best suited to cater to specific project complexities:

1.   Periodically differentiated price method

2.   Equivalence number method

By understanding the unique scenarios where these methods are most suitable, organizations can select the approach that aligns with their operational and financial reporting needs.

Periodically Differentiated Price Method

The periodically differentiated price method is suitable for projects where labor rates and machine usage fluctuate significantly over time. This method reports actual costs separately for each period. It calculates actual prices at the end of each period based on the total costs and activities confirmed for that period. This approach allows for precise reflection of cost changes over time and is ideal for scenarios where labor rates or machine costs fluctuate significantly.

In EPC projects, where different labor categories contribute jointly to complete an activity, or in a multi-year construction project where the labor rate varies periodically due to change in task types, shifts in demand, or overtime, the SAP PS revaluation process ensures accurate cost allocation.

For example, if multiple work centers, such as welders and fitters, confirm their hours against the same activity in CATS, the system initially allocates costs based on the planned activity rates of each work center. Since the activity price of each resource is different, the system calculates a differentiated actual price for each resource based on the specific actual costs incurred by their respective cost centers. At period-end, if the actual labor cost exceeds the planned cost, the cost center shows a positive balance for each work center, whereas if the actual labor cost is lower, it reflects a negative balance. The revaluation process adjusts the cost center for each work center to reflect these cost changes, and the WBS element is updated accordingly to ensure that the actual costs of the activity are accurately captured and aligned with financial reporting requirements.

Equivalence Number Method

The equivalence number method is suitable for projects with diverse labor categories or equipment types that require proportional cost allocation. This approach is particularly useful in scenarios such as structure assembly or equipment installation, where workers from multiple crafts, such as riggers, welders, and electricians, collaborate on activities such as panel installations or structural assembly.

This method simplifies the revaluation process by eliminating the need to differentiate between individual crafts or resources. Instead, it produces a weighted average rate, distributing costs proportionally based on the nature and quantity of resources used.

For example, when multiple crafts like welders and fitters work on the same activity, welders might be considered twice as valuable as fitters, so the equivalency number of welder is 2 and the equivalency number of fitter is 1, and their combined resource usage determines the equivalent rate.

While this method reduces complexity, it may not provide the same level of precision in capturing specific cost variances.

14.2. Results Analysis

The financial performance of a project is analyzed by comparing the actual values with the planned values. This process, known as *results analysis* in SAP PS, encompasses the calculation of earned revenue and profit margins, and assesses and forecasts the project's final outcome. This functionality provides insight into the project's profitability and cash flow.

Results analysis (RA) enables organizations to make informed decisions about project adjustments and financial reporting by comparing planned values with actual performance data. Results analysis integrates key project data to calculate critical metrics such as cost, revenue, and profit.

Revenue Recognition

Revenue recognition is a fundamental accounting process that determines when and how revenue from projects should be recorded and reported. It is integrated into the project management framework of the SAP Project System module and is aligned with the globally accepted International Financial Reporting Standard (IFRS) 15.

Performance Obligations

A performance obligation (POB) represents a promise in a contract to deliver a specific good or service to the customer. POBs are central to the revenue recognition process. They are usually satisfied over the duration of the project. This means that milestones or deliveries in the project contract (created as work breakdown structure) are identified as *performance obligation*s.

Compliance with Standard

IFRS 15 establishes principles for reporting revenue from contracts and specifies that revenue is recognized only when the POB is satisfied. The revenue is recognized based on how and when performance obligations are fulfilled.

This obligation fulfillment can occur at various points during the project lifecycle or at a single point. The SAP PS module offers flexibility to handle distinct project obligations as defined in the contract with multiple revenue recognition methods.

14.2.1. Revenue Recognition Types

In an EPC project, multiple interdependent phases and milestones signify the progress and performance of the project, and since most EPC projects span several months or years, using different methods to recognize revenue at different stages of the project is necessary to reflect the work completed.

The selection of revenue recognition method depends on the project's nature and the contractual agreement. The following two revenue recognition options are applicable in EPC projects.

Over-Time

Revenue is recognized as the project progresses. This type is common in long-term EPC contracts where the customer progressively and simultaneously receives and benefits from the goods and/or services. The risk and benefits are transferred to the customer over the duration of the project.

For example, at the RefineX project, two skids are commissioned at different time intervals and are handed over to the customer and treated as two performance obligations delivered over time.

Point-In-Time

Revenue is recognized at a single moment when control of the goods or services is transferred to the customer. This typically occurs when the performance obligation is fulfilled in one step.

For example, pumps and compressors are procured, and upon delivery the performance obligation is considered fulfilled.

14.2.2. Results Analysis Parameters

Results analysis in SAP PS offers detailed analysis of project performance by comparing actual and planned values at every period end. It provides

- automatically calculated revenue based on predefined methods,
- discrepancies between actual billing and revenue recognition, and
- visibility into project profitability by calculating key metrics, such as capitalized profit, surplus revenue, and work-in-progress inventories.

It is essential to develop a reliable understanding of the project's financial health to accurately report revenue and profit. To fully comprehend the calculation methods used in SAP PS results analysis, it is crucial to first gain a clear understanding of all the parameters involved in the calculation.

Planned Values

Planned values define project expectations and are used to assess project performance during results analysis. They are derived from the project plan and serve as the baseline against which actual performance is measured. They include the following:

1. **Planned Revenue:** The total revenue expected to be earned from the project as per the contractual terms and pricing.

2. **Planned Cost:** The estimated total cost of completing the project, including materials, labor, subcontracting, and overhead.

3. **Planned Work:** The anticipated total effort required, often measured in terms of man-days or hours.

4. **Quantities to Be Delivered:** The total expected output, whether produced or procured, to be delivered as it is produced or procured.

5. **Project Duration:** The scheduled timeline for project completion.

Earned Revenue

The *earned revenue* represents the revenue that corresponds to the progress achieved or costs incurred in the project. In SAP PS results analysis it is categorized as *revenue affecting net income*. The earned revenue reflects the completion of actual work or the fulfillment of obligations.

The earned revenue, or the revenue affecting net income, is determined from different POC methods of results analysis valuation, calculated as follows:

$$\text{Earned Revenue} = \text{POC} \times \text{Total Planned Revenue}$$

Actual Revenue

The *actual revenue* in SAP PS is the amount billed to the customer during project execution. It is also called *billed revenue*. The actual revenue can only be recorded against the WBS element marked as a *revenue element* linked with a sales order line item in SAP SD. At month end, billing is managed through SAP SD.

Actual costs are incurred from various expense categories and are recorded against project WBS elements marked as *account assignment elements*.

14.2.3. Revenue Recognition Methods

SAP PS results analysis offers various methods to calculate and report cost, revenue, and profit. The percentage of completion (POC) plays a central role in defining these methods. During results analysis, revenue is calculated using different POC methods to reflect the financial progress of the project.

RA Keys

Different results analysis keys (RA keys) are available in SAP PS to determine revenue recognition. Each RA key function provides a unique approach to calculating project results. Organizations have the flexibility to select a method based on the project's contractual terms and the way cost, revenue, and progress are monitored.

In this section, we will discuss the most common RA key functions applicable to EPC projects, using project scenarios to demonstrate how different revenue recognition methods in SAP PS influence the timing of revenue and profit recognition, as well as their impact on overall revenue reporting. The RA is typically executed at every month-end. After executing the RA, the system returns project results. Based on the method used, the system shows the values discussed for each revenue recognition method.

The planned values shown in Table 14-1 are consistent across all methods and are used for the comparative analysis of revenue recognition methods:

Table 14-1. *Planned Values*

Planned Values	
Planned revenue	$200,000
Planned cost	$120,000
Quantities to be delivered	10 equipment
Planned work	1,000 man-days
Project duration	4 months

Cost-based POC Method

This method uses the *cost proportionality* measurement method, where the POC is derived as the ratio of actual cost to planned cost. In this method, the POC is calculated as:

$$POC = \frac{\text{Actual Cost}}{\text{Total Planned Cost}}$$

Table 14-2 demonstrates how this cost-based method calculates the percentage of completion and revenue affecting net income over the project's timeline.

Table 14-2. *Project Cost and Revenue*

Parameters	Cumulative Values			
	Month 1	Month 2	Month 3	Final Billing
Actual cost	$10,000	$80,000	$90,000	$130,000
Actual/billed revenue	$0	$100,000	$170,000	$200,000
Percentage of completion	8.3%	66.7%	75.0%	100.0%
Results Analysis				
Revenue affecting net income	$16,700	$133,300	$150,000	$200,000
Cost affecting net income	$10,000	$80,000	$90,000	$130,000
Profit	$67,00	$53,300	$60,000	$70,000
Revenue in excess of billing	$16,700	$33,300		
Revenue surplus			$20,000	

The *revenue surplus* indicates that the actual revenue billed to the customer exceeds the revenue recognized by the system. This usually occurs when the billing is made up front, while the corresponding work based on performance obligations is not yet earned.

The *revenue in excess of billing* parameter quantifies the amount by which the recognized revenue exceeds the actual revenue billed to the customer. It indicates unbilled receivables and highlights potential future cash inflows from unbilled receivables. This typically happens when

1. work is completed ahead of schedule or without prior authorization, or

2. costs are incurred before they can be billed.

In this method, the *actual cost* is aligned with the POC; therefore, it is directly recognized under the *cost affecting net income* component, and no additional adjustments or deferrals are made to the cost.

The *profit* is calculated as the difference between revenue affecting net income and cost affecting net income. The results analysis does not allow the POC to exceed 100%, even though there are actual cost overruns in this use case. At final billing, when the actual cost surpasses the planned cost, the profit is adjusted downward to reflect the cost overrun.

Quantity-based POC Method

This method uses the *quantity proportionality* measurement method, where POC is calculated as the ratio of actual progress to planned progress.

$$POC = \frac{\text{Qty Delivered}}{\text{Total Planned Cost}}$$

Table 14-3 demonstrates how the quantity-based method calculates different values over the project's timeline.

Table 14-3. *Quantity-based Method*

Parameters	Cumulative Values			
	Month 1	Month 2	Month 3	Final Billing
Actual cost	$10,000	$80,000	$90,000	$130,000
Actual/billed revenue	$0	$100,000	$170,000	$200,000
Actual work [qty] completed	200	400	800	1000
Percentage of completion	20%	40%	80%	100%
Results Analysis				
Revenue affecting net income	$40,000	$80,000	$160,000	$200,000
Cost affecting net income	$24,000	$48,000	$96.000	$130,000
Profit	$16,000	$32,000	$64,000	$70,000
Revenue in excess of billing	$40,000	$0	$0	$0
Revenue surplus		$20,000	$10,000	
Capitalized cost		$32,000		
Unrealized cost	$14,000		$6000	

The *cost affecting net income* in this case may differ from the actual cost. It is calculated by applying the POC to the planned cost. It represents the cost recognized in the profit and loss statement based on project progress, and only the cost relevant to the earned work is accounted for in the financials.

The *capitalized cost* is calculated as the difference between the *actual cost* and the *cost affecting net income*. In any given period, if the difference is positive, it represents the cost that is not recognized in the profit and loss statement but is instead retained on the balance sheet as work-In-progress (WIP).

However, if the difference is negative, it represents *unrealized cost* that refers to the portion of project costs that exceeds the actual incurred cost but is not yet recognized in the financial statements. It typically reflects a provision for anticipated costs yet to be incurred or adjustments for potential discrepancies in cost reporting during the project lifecycle.

Revenue-based Method with Profit Realization

This method calculated POC based on actual revenue from billing recorded for the project and the planned revenue.

This method differs from the other two POC methods as it ties the revenue recognition directly to customer billing events rather than the progress or costs incurred.

$$POC = \frac{Actual\ Revenue}{Total\ Planned\ Revenue}$$

Table 14-4 shows how this method calculates the percentage of completion and revenue affecting net income over the project's timeline.

Table 14-4. *Percentage of Completion and Revenue*

Parameters	Cumulative Values			
	Month 1	Month 2	Month 3	Final Billing
Actual cost	$10,000	$80,000	$90,000	$130,000
Actual/billed revenue	$0	$100,000	$170,000	$200,000
Percentage of completion	0%	50%	85%	100%
Revenue affecting net income	$0	$100,000	$170,000	$200,000
Cost affecting net income		$60,000	$102,000	$130,000
Profit	$0	$40,000	$68,000	$70,000
Capitalized cost	10.0	20.0		
Unrealized cost			$12,000	

This method is particularly suitable for projects where billing milestones align directly with the delivery of goods, services, or manpower. For example, in delivery-based projects, revenue is recognized as invoices are issued, reflecting the revenue and profit realization accurately in alignment with billing.

In this method, the revenue recognized is based on the project's POC; therefore, *revenue affecting net income* aligns with the *actual revenue* throughout the project lifecycle. This ensures that only the appropriate portion of the revenue is accounted for in the financial statements.

Completed Contract Method (CCM)

This method recognizes revenue and profit only when the project is fully completed and all the performance obligations under the contract have been fulfilled. In CCM, the entire project must be delivered before any revenue can be recognized, and the revenue and profit would not be reported until the handover of the performance obligations.

Table 14-5 shows how this method calculates a project's financial performance over the project's timeline without periodically recognizing the revenue or calculating the percentage of completion.

Table 14-5. *Project Financial Performance*

Parameters	Cumulative Values			
	Month 1	Month 2	Month 3	Final Billing
Actual cost	$10,000	$80,000	$90,000	$130,000
Actual/billed revenue	$0	$100,000	$170,000	$200,000
Percentage of completion	0%	0%	0%	100%
Revenue affecting net income	$0	$0	$0	$200,000
Cost affecting net income	$0	$0	$0	$130,000
Profit	$0	$0	$0	$70,000
Revenue surplus		$100,000	$170,000	
Capitalized cost	$10,000	$80,000	$90,000	$0

This method is best suited for projects where

1. the outcome is uncertain until the very end,

2. the performance obligations are tightly interdependent and cannot be segmented into smaller milestones, or

3. the project is planned to be completed within a single accounting period.

While CCM ensures absolute certainty in revenue recognition, it delays financial reporting until the project concludes. It does not reflect the ongoing financial health of the project during its execution phase. This makes it less commonly used in industries where stakeholders demand periodic reporting of performance or progress.

14.2.4. Settlement Rule

In SAP PS, a project WBS is a temporary cost collector during project execution. Before the financial closure of the project, all financial values must be transferred to permanent objects through a process called *cost settlement*.

Allocation Structure

A *settlement rule* is configured in the system to specify how the cost incurred on a project is distributed or transferred to permanent financial objects. Settlement rules define the allocation structure, which determines how the costs or revenues are distributed to the settlement receivers. This includes specifying which cost elements or revenue elements are included in the settlement process.

Settlement Sender

In the cost settlement process, the actual costs posted against network activities and WBS elements are transferred to the superior-level WBSE during settlement, as shown in Figure 14-1. At period end, the accumulated costs, depending on the nature of the expense, are settled to the appropriate permanent objects.

Figure 14-1. *Settlement rule in SAP PS*

Settlement rules are created and maintained at the level of WBS elements or network activities. To define a settlement rule, the user specifies the receiver object and assigns the allocation structure.

Settlement Receivers

Settlement rules can include a percentage allocation to split costs or revenues among multiple receivers. The financial values on the temporary objects are allocated to the appropriate receivers, such as general ledger (GL) accounts or assets under construction (AUC).

Costs directly associated with project execution, such as procurement, labor, and subcontracting, are generally settled to GL accounts for accurate revenue and expense matching. In this case, the cost settlement is executed for the billing element WBS used for the results analysis to align the revenue recognition and cost allocation calculated during the results analysis process.

For costs incurred for the construction of site facilities or other capitalizable infrastructure, the settlement is directed to an AUC account. Costs settled to AUC are recognized as assets under construction until the project is completed. These costs can later be capitalized or transferred to the final asset accounts.

This dual-settlement approach helps EPC projects manage their complex financial structures effectively.

14.3. Delivery From Project

The *delivery from project* process in SAP PS is the structured way of managing the dispatch of finished or semi-finished deliveries, such as assemblies or sub-assemblies, from a project. This functionality integrates logistical activities into the project lifecycle to enhance collaboration between planning, quality, and logistics teams.

14.3.1. Delivery Planning

The process begins when the engineering team identifies project deliverables and classifies them as finished goods (FG) in the SAP material master data. Assemblies and sub-assemblies are defined in the detailed BOM and transferred into the project WBS, as discussed in Chapter 7. During project planning, a shipping activity is already assigned to the WBS elements to specify delivery dates and the weightage for delivery planning and scheduling. After delivery is executed, this same activity can be used to monitor the cost of deliveries.

14.3.2. Delivery Creation

Deliveries are created by selecting material components associated with the project. The planning team identifies these components based on project definition and the WBS elements where the material is assigned.

14.3.3. Shipping Documents

A *shipping document* is the central element for handling transportation planning and shipment completion. This document contains all the information necessary for carrying out transportation, such as load transfer points, service agents, goods for handling and creating shipment, and planned and actual transportation deadlines.

Delivery Notes

SAP S/4HANA supports both in-house and externally procured materials, ensuring flexibility for diverse project needs. *Delivery notes,* generated by SAP S/4HANA, list materials to be dispatched with necessary details, such as shipping points and planned goods issue dates. For partial deliveries, the system calculates delivery quantities based on available stock and outstanding requirements.

14.3.4. Delivery Document Control

SAP S/4HANA also provides centralized document management for delivery data and associated documentation through SAP DMS integration. Packing lists, inspection certificates, and other essential records can be securely stored and retrieved. This functionality provides easy access to key delivery-related information and reduces the risk of errors.

14.3.5. Collaboration Using Workflows

Workflow items in SAP PS Project Builder are triggered by events such as the completion of shipping activity or setting system status. Once triggered, the workflow generates a work item that appears in the relevant users' Fiori launchpad. The work item contains the project activity number as the reference and the list of materials requiring inspection, and, optionally, document information record-object link. System status is automatically updated either by marking it as completed or by triggering follow-up actions, such as recording inspection results, closing punch lists, or approving the dispatch.

14.3.6. Delivery Quality Control

Workflows in particular play an important role in notifying the quality assurance team when a dispatch is ready for inspection. In the SAP S/4HANA QM module, inspection lots can be triggered automatically or manually for outgoing quality compliance and dispatch approval. These inspection lots facilitate detailed quality checks before materials are dispatched.

Good Issuance

After QC approval, a goods issue (GI) is posted to reduce the inventory level of the issued materials. The materials assigned to the network activity show a corresponding decrease in available stock, reflecting that the material has been delivered.

14.4. Customer Billing

Customer billing in project management can vary depending on the contractual agreement and payment schedule. It involves generating invoices based on progress or delivery milestones achieved throughout the project's lifecycle. There are generally two scenarios.

Progress-based Billing

This billing method calculates billing based on the approved progress derived either from the actual percentage of completion or the completion of a milestone during the month. This approach aligns billing with the actual progress of the project.

Delivery-based Billing

This billing method is based on the overall weight or quantity of assemblies or sub-assemblies delivered in a particular month. The project execution team delivers these items according to the client's priorities, and revenue is calculated accordingly.

Customer Invoice

The final step involves creating a customer invoice in the system to capture the actual revenue of the project, particularly when the delivery method of revenue recognition is adopted.

14.5. Conclusion

This chapter provided an in-depth exploration of financial performance in EPC projects, detailing how SAP S/4HANA manages period-end closing, cost allocation, and revaluation methods for updating labor and machine costs. We also examined various IFRS-15–based performance obligation and revenue recognition methods. Additionally, different billing methods along with the management of finished and semi-finished goods' delivery from projects were explored.

In the next chapter, we will build on this foundation by examining tools like the SAP Project Information System and Core Data Services (CDS), and SAP Analytics Cloud (SAC) for performance tracking and reporting.

CHAPTER 15

Performance Analysis

The capabilities of SAP S/4HANA discussed in the previous chapter establish a foundation for monitoring project progress and performance. The next critical aspect in project management is the analysis of this information. Performance analysis in SAP S/4HANA is supported by the standard and structured approach of earned value analysis (EVA).

In this chapter, we will explore SAP S/4HANA Project System (PS) reports along with tailored SAP Analytics Cloud (SAC) stories and Core Data Services (CDS) views designed specifically for the EC&O industry. These tools provide detailed and multi-dimensional views of project key performance indicators (KPI).

15.1. Project Information System

The SAP Project Information System is part of the classic SAP GUI reporting environment. It is a flexible and comprehensive information system that is designed to evaluate individual projects, partial projects, or multiple projects simultaneously.

© Sohail Ahmed 2025
S. Ahmed, *The SAP S/4HANA Handbook for EPC Projects*,
https://doi.org/10.1007/979-8-8688-1466-2_15

15.1.1. Classical Reports

Classical GUI offers comprehensive project reporting through a hierarchical project structure and cost structure views.

Hierarchical Reports

The hierarchical reports allow users to view a clear hierarchy of project phases and tasks to ensure visibility into each level of project scope. Project managers can visualize and manage WBS elements and network structures to maintain oversight of the project hierarchy.

Cost Element Reports

The cost element report in SAP PS provides a detailed breakdown of project costs, categorized by cost element. Project controllers can analyze project cost and revenue categorized by cost elements to identify cost drivers and manage budget more effectively.

Value Category

In SAP PS reports, *value categories* categorize costs and revenues into groups that are independent of an organization's financial reporting structure. These categories are specifically created to group cost elements pertinent for project management and reporting. SAP PS users can easily filter project data based on these value categories.

Value categories enable project managers to differentiate between various cost elements, such as types of labor, materials, and overhead costs, and to compare planned and actual cost and revenue.

Report Profiles

Multiple profiles can be saved to tailor the scope of performance evaluation. Important reporting groups that can be accessed using different transactions or selection parameters are as follows:

1. Project structures

2. Planned/actual cost and revenue

3. Budget and variance

4. Material, capacity, and purchasing

5. Earned value analysis reports

For example, an EVA profile has predefined fields and graphs to show KPI values calculated during the earned value analysis, as discussed in Chapter 13.

Reporting Scope

To access a report in SAP S/4HANA, users define the scope and structure of the data through profiles and selection criteria. The scope of these reports can be expanded to group projects or e limited to a project, a specific project version, or an individual WBS element to enhance focus on relevant data only.

In these reports, cut-off dates, version comparison, and exceptional reporting can be set for evaluating projects from a point-in-time perspective. This is useful for tracking changes in behavior of expenditures, schedule, and scope.

These parameters help prevent needing to define complex logic coding systems for master data objects, such as employees, customers, and project networks. Instead of manually coding the master data logic, users can use predefined SAP parameters to filter and analyze the data in reporting.

15.1.2. **SAP Fiori Applications**

SAP Fiori provides a user-friendly interface for real-time reports and dashboards. SAP Fiori apps (as well as classic GUI reports) are generally categorized under Structural reports and Financial reports in the SAP PS project information system.

Structural Apps

Structural apps help project managers stay organized, prioritize tasks, and make informed decisions to ensure project success. Some of the important reports are as follows:

1. *Manage Project Structure* **app:** It provides tools to dynamically manage and modify project hierarchies.

2. *My Projects* **and** *Multiproject Overview* **apps:** These apps provide an overview of multiple projects in the system to filter high-priority projects and drill down into specific project details for a quick health check.

3. *Single Project Overview* **and** *Network Overview* **apps:** These apps provide a comprehensive overview of a single project, with detailed monitoring capabilities for key performance indicators related to project structures and finance, such as project status and upcoming milestones.

Financial Apps

Financial controllers gain insights into cost variances and identify budget overruns or underruns using financial apps, as follows.

1. ***Project Financial Controller Overview* app:** This app provides a centralized view of key financial information for multiple projects. It displays critical metrics, like project status, budget consumption, and cost variances to project controllers for monitoring cost commitments, actualization, and budget utilization.

2. ***Project Cost Line Items* app:** This app provides a detailed breakdown of cost and revenue for a project and its associated elements. These reports pinpoint specific line items where revenue, expense, budget, or commitments need to be analyzed.

15.2. Core Data Services (CDS) Views

Core data services (CDS) views are a semantic layer in the SAP S/4HANA reporting structure that allows users to create virtual data models in real-time without duplicating data or using large data warehouses. It simplifies the way users interact with complex data structures and databases and provides a more user-friendly interface for accessing and manipulating data without the need to understand the data technically.

Project team members define their data selection criteria, apply complex joins, and aggregate data across different modules to create flexible structures tailored to specific reporting requirements.

15.2.1. Project Performance Views

The CDS views for project performance provide detailed analysis of overall project progress with real-time access to essential cost, schedule, and resource metrics. These CDS views can be integrated with SAP CPM solutions to support detailed project analytics. Custom CDS views may be created to meet unique project requirements and reporting needs, as follows:

1. **Financial Views:** Common CDC views for financial analysis may include I_ProjectCost, I_ProjectRevenue, and I_CostPlan, which can offer better insights into cost and revenue metrics and facilitate comparisons between planned and actual values across projects. CDS views such as I_ProjectActuals and I_ProjectForecast may be included to provide insight into the actuals and forecasting project performance metrics.

2. **Progress Views:** These views support project milestone reporting and schedule variance tracking for calculating the schedule performance index (SPI) to assess project schedule health. These views include I_ProjectMilestone, I_SchedulePlan, and I_ProjectStatus. Together, these CDS views offer an integrated approach to tracking and monitoring project performance in real-time.

15.2.2. CDS Views for EC&O

SAP S/4HANA provides a comprehensive suite of reporting solutions tailored specifically for the EC&O industry. It combines extensive project management capabilities to address the unique demands of the EC&O industry.

SAP has provided the following additional CDS views for the EC&O industry:

1. **Project and Portfolio Management (PPM):**
   These CDS views provide portfolio-level insights through the integrated SAP S/4HANA Enterprise Solution. CDS views such as I_ProjectPortfolio and I_ProjectPortfolioStatus oversee multiple projects, prioritize portfolio resources, and aggregate performance data from both portfolios and projects in a single view.

2. **Engineering Change Management (ECM):**
   These CDS views support tracking of design or specification changes, which can significantly impact project cost and timeline. CDS views such as I_EngineeringChange and I_EngineeringChangeObject provide visibility for effective change control during design adjustments.

3. **Document Management System (DMS):** These CDS views provide real-time tracking of project documents and update users across engineering and other teams on document changes to ensure compliance. The key CDS views include I_DocumentInfoRecord and I_DocumentVersion.

15.3. SAC Business Contents for EC&O

SAP Analytics Cloud (SAC) integrates seamlessly with S/4HANA to deliver real-time project data visualization to support quick, data-driven decisions. For the EC&O industry, SAP has designed business content packages to address complex EPC projects by offering pre-built templates, industry-standard KPIs, and dashboards specific to EC&O industry needs without requiring extensive setup. However, users have the flexibility to customize dashboards and reports according to their specific needs.

15.3.1. Project Performance

The SAP_ECO_PROJECT PERFORMANCE content package offers comprehensive insights into project performance to track key performance indicators across project portfolios and regions.

Figure 15-1. *SAC dashboard for project performance indicators*

The KPIs in this package, as shown in Figure 15-1, are organized around groups of relevant sections, such as the following:

1. **Stage Progress:** These KPIs deliver insights into project stages and completion levels to help portfolio and project managers monitor overall portfolio progress and project profitability.

2. **Resource Utilization:** These KPIs extract data from SAP HCM resource planning to show headcount allocation by region.

3. **Financial Performance:** These KPIs focus on month-by-month fluctuations in revenue, costs, and margins, while monitoring shifts in the actual margin percentage, providing a clear view of financial health over time.

4. **Project-specific Performance:** These KPIs provide detailed analysis of individual projects and show planned and actual costs, revenues, and margins. Planned versus actual values for each phase provide targeted analysis over time.

SAP Project Management extensions and third-party tools can also be integrated directly with SAC for visibility into detailed project execution, schedules, and resource utilization in real-time.

15.3.2. Bid Analysis

The Bid Analysis section of the SAC dashboard, as shown in Figure 15-2, is designed to facilitate comprehensive evaluations of bids related to projects within the engineering, construction, and operations (EC&O) industry. Integrating SAC EC&O business contents with SAP Hybrid Cloud for Customer Analytics helps organizations analyze customer data and sales performance, providing insights into profitability and revenue growth across customer segments. This functionality helps organizations assess competitive bids, optimize pricing strategies, and improve win rates.

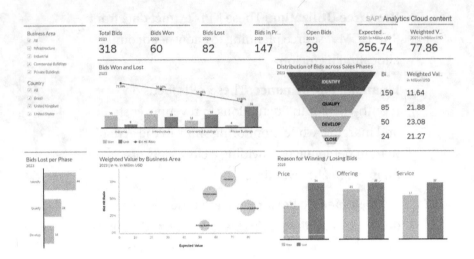

Figure 15-2. *SAC dashboard for bid analysis*

The section of SAC dashboard, as shown in Figure 15-2, provides tools to analyze various aspects of bids, including the following:

1. **Bid Comparison:** Users can compare multiple bids against established criteria to allow for detailed assessments of pricing, terms, and conditions.

2. **Win/Loss Analysis:** Insight into the success rate of bids to help organizations understand which factors contribute to winning or losing bids.

3. **Cost Analysis:** Detailed examination of bid costs to ensure competitive pricing while maintaining profitability.

15.3.3. Sales Order Forecast

The Sales Order Forecast section aims to provide insights into future sales orders to help organizations in the EC&O industry make informed business decisions regarding inventory, production, and resource allocation.

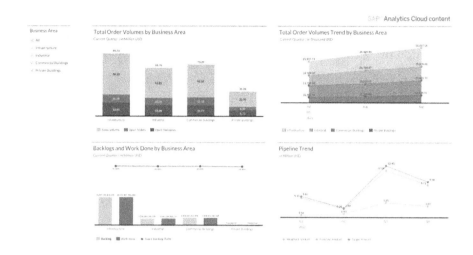

Figure 15-3. *SAC dashboard for sales order forecast*

This section of the SAC dashboard, as shown in Figure 15-3, offers a range of functionalities to enhance sales forecasting, including the following:

1. **Forecasting Models:** Use of various statistical models to predict future sales orders based on historical data and trends.

2. **Scenario Planning:** Capability to create multiple forecasting scenarios to allow organizations to prepare for different market conditions and demands.

3. **Trend Analysis:** Identification of trends and patterns in sales data that inform strategic decision-making.

15.3.4. Financial Analytics

In addition to EC&O, SAP Analytics Cloud separately provides business contents for project financials reporting and analysis. The Financial Analytics section of SAP Analytics Cloud provides comprehensive tools and insights for financial planning, analysis, and reporting. It is designed to help organizations assess their financial health and support strategic decision-making through data-driven insights. SAP SuccessFactors integrates with EC&O and financial contents to allow project organizations to incorporate financial and human resources data into a single view.

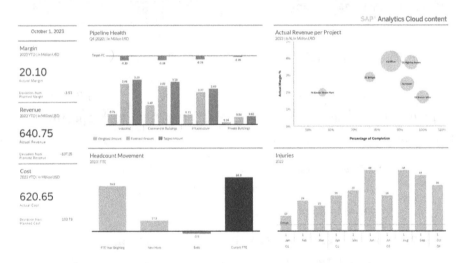

Figure 15-4. *SAC dashboard for project financial health*

This section of SAC dashboard, as shown in Figure 15-4, includes several essential functionalities that enhance financial analysis, as follows:

1. **Financial Reporting:** Users can create detailed financial reports that monitor key metrics, such as revenue, expenses, and profit margins, to facilitate better visibility into financial performance.

2. **Profitability Analysis:** Tools within this section allow users to analyze profitability across various dimensions, such as product lines, customer segments, and geographical regions, to aid in identifying the most profitable areas of the business.

3. **Variance Analysis:** This feature enables organizations to compare planned versus actual financial performance to help uncover discrepancies and understand their underlying causes. This insight is crucial for adjusting future financial plans.

4. **Workforce Analytics:** This content package provides insights into workforce performance, enabling organizations to analyze labor costs, employee productivity, and workforce planning. It integrates HR metrics that are crucial for project-based environments in EC&O.

15.3.5. Cross-Modular Analytics

SAC provides integration of EC&O business contents with other business contents provided for different lines of business within SAP S/4HANA and other SAP applications. Some of the key areas are the following.

Enterprise Asset Management

Asset Performance Analytics content provides dashboards and reports that deliver insights into asset utilization, equipment performance metrics, and maintenance schedules. It is further integrated with Financial Analytics and provides maintenance cost analysis to help identify costs associated with maintenance activities. Maintenance Planning and Scheduling supports efficient planning and scheduling of maintenance tasks, while Work Order Management Analytics allow for monitoring work order status, completion rates, and resource allocation.

Quality Management

Quality Control Analytics in SAC tracks quality metrics, inspection results, and compliance data to ensure that projects meet necessary standards. Non-Conformance Management content enables organizations to analyze non-conformance reports and implement corrective actions effectively.

Procurement and Inventory

SAC provides valuable insights into procurement activities through Procurement Analytics, which focuses on procurement activities, supplier performance, and inventory turnover. This is further supported by inventory management dashboards that offer visibility into stock levels, material availability, and order fulfillment rates, ensuring that materials are procured and managed efficiently to meet project demands.

SAP Portfolio and Project Management

SAC integrates with SAP Portfolio and Project Management for portfolio financial planning and budget control. This integration enhances the visibility of portfolio budgets and financial health to empower managers to track resource allocation and project costs effectively.

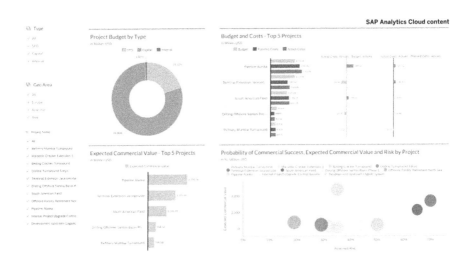

Figure 15-5. *SAC dashboard for portfolio and project management*

This section of the SAC dashboard, as shown in Figure 15-5, includes several essential functionalities, such as:

1. **Portfolio Financial Planning:** This analytics content allows for comprehensive financial planning and budgeting across projects, enabling portfolio managers to assess and manage financial risks effectively.

2. **Resource Management Analytics:** This package focuses on the allocation and utilization of resources across projects to provide insights that help in optimizing resource deployment and project scheduling.

3. **Project Performance Analytics:** This content package is useful for using Project Management features of SAP PPM dashboards and reports that track standalone projects' performance metrics. Project budget utilization and adherence to

369

schedules for projects created within SAP PPM or
projects created in third-party project management
tools can be monitored in SAC using this content.

15.3.6. SAC Planning Models

In addition to simulation projects, discussed in Chapter 13, SAC Planning
is another powerful tool for scenario-based planning and what-if analysis
using data structured as models.

SAC planning models use data visualization and live connections with
S/4HANA for a more dynamic analysis, which is particularly helpful for
resource allocation and financial forecasting. SAC planning models create
a framework for budgeting, forecasting, and resource allocation.

Projects often experience fluctuations in scope and timelines. Through
planning models, project managers can adjust resource allocations,
budget distribution, or project schedules and immediately see simulated
impacts across multiple KPIs and timelines. For example, increasing the
KPI for labor utilization can show how project duration or costs may shift
in response to higher resource usage.

SAC modeling capabilities also help financial managers. They can
simulate budget reallocations, assess the impact of delayed receivables
on cash flow, perform what-if analysis, and quickly determine actions to
reduce the impact on the company's financial health.

15.4. Conclusion

While SAP's classic Project Information System (in the SAP GUI) provides foundational project structure and cost reports, SAP Fiori apps and SAC introduce modern, real-time reporting tools for project monitoring, forecasting, and decision-making. Leveraging both of these classic and modern interfaces helps SAP S/4HANA users maintain a holistic view of project performance and manage resources more effectively across the project lifecycle.

Index

© Sohail Ahmed 2025
S. Ahmed, *The SAP S/4HANA Handbook for EPC Projects*,
https://doi.org/10.1007/979-8-8688-1466-2

Q